DIVINATION

Sacred Tools for
Reading the Mind of God

Paul O'Brien

First published by
Visionary Networks Press, June 2007
2641 SW Huber St. Suite A
Portland, OR 97219

ISBN-13: 978-0-9795425-0-3

Printed and bound in the United States of America
Portland, Oregon

TABLE OF CONTENTS

Author's Preface

Albert Einstein reportedly said "I want to know the mind of God; the rest are details." This book is about tool that can help anyone know the mind of God, which is a desire that has been inside me for as long as I can remember. My discovery of divination as a way of tuning into the divine happened in 1969, when as a teenager I was introduced to the world's oldest divination system, the *I Ching*, or *Book of Changes*. An ancient Taoist ritual that involves the casting of sticks or coins and an ancient book of wisdom, this Chinese oracle blew my mind.

I quickly found that using the I Ching helped me see life from a wider perspective, make better decisions, manage changes in my life, let go and relax into greater peace of mind. Beyond the I Ching's helpfulness to me, the discovery that humanity had developed ancient divination systems based on sound psychological principles was to change my entire life, including my livelihood.

As a young man building a career in the new field of computer software, I also studied everything I could find about the I Ching, as well as other classical divination systems. Being spiritually motivated, I also went to night school for three years to become an ordained minister and spiritual counselor. At the age of thirty, I took a leave of absence from my software career to spend two years abroad in monasteries and ashrams, and became trained as a meditation teacher. Although my professional career was in software, I had a parallel life that was preoccupied with the discovery and use of transformational spiritual techniques.

In 1988, almost twenty years after I had been introduced to it, a profound I Ching reading about a turning point in my life ironically stimulated the idea that I should develop a software version of the I Ching itself! Even though my career was in software marketing, not programming, the potential development of a computer-assisted I Ching program that could work in a mathematically and energetically authentic way was an inspiring idea that would not let go of me.

As much as anything, it was the gratitude I felt for the

support I had received from the I Ching that inspired me to risk my career and savings to develop and publish an I Ching program for the Mac that included meditative sounds and art. I called it *Synchronicity*, after the famous principle that depth psychologist Carl Jung defined to explain how the I Ching and divination systems work. I didn't realize it at the time, but *Synchronicity* turned out to be the first published divination software. It became part of my destiny to be known ten years later as "the father of interactive divination."

Tarot.com pioneers self-service divination.

Fifteen years in the software industry may have prepared me to produce a software product, but there was no rational marketing argument for publishing divination software. I could not explain how it was that I felt so strangely compelled to develop a program for which there was almost no market at the time. It was as if I were being pulled forward to spend all my savings on a project that made no sense.

My friends could not understand, and I could not explain. Of necessity, my motto became "Wherever God drags me, I will follow." I never even imagined that this labor of love would lead to my eventually becoming an expert on the subject of divination and the publisher of Tarot.com, one of the largest web sites devoted to Astrology and divination. In a real sense, making these sacred resources available via the worldwide web is the story of divination using me to reinvent itself.

Although *Synchronicity* was ahead of its time, millions of visits per day on Tarot.com now testify to the growing usefulness of divination in daily life. Ranging from the ubiquitous daily horoscope and bookstore sales of Tarot decks, to sophisticated forms of spiritual counseling, the learning about and use of divination systems has become a popular trend and a widespread phenomenon.

Along with Astrology and divination's growing popularity, there is age-old confusion, superstition and some amount of fraud associated with divination. Many of the services being promoted as psychic or divinatory are not authentic, and it is difficult for the average person to tell the difference between what is real and what is fake.

The purpose of this book is to inform you about the best divination systems—the ones that have stood the

Author's Preface

> *It is the creative potential itself in human beings that is the image of God.*
> —Mary Daly

test of time, and the ones you can do for yourself.

This is a day and age when we need self-knowledge and enlightened decision-making more than ever. The survival of our fragile planet depends on making different and better decisions about things. And we all need to start with our personal lives. Spiritual decision-making.

It is this author's hope that the use of the word "God" will not confuse or offend anyone. I could have avoided using it, but I like the word, which for me connotes the ultimate level of consciousness, the creative power of the universe and all-inclusive unconditional love. It is neither personal nor impersonal, but can be perceived as either. It is referred to herein as Higher Power, Creative Power, and the Source of Unconditional Love. I hope you can visualize how God can be conceived as an infinite resource—a source of creativity, power and love that is always available to you on an unconditional basis.

I think of God as infinite intelligence and this book's subtitle *Sacred Tools for Reading the Mind of God* refers to the way that divination can stimulate our highest faculty of wisdom—intuition. When I was a child in religion class, I was taught to listen for the "still small voice." Hearing that voice, seeing visions, and so on are the domains of intuition, not the ego or rational intellect. This book is all about intuition as a divine faculty in that it can tap into the mind of God, or divine intelligence. In a nutshell, this is the real purpose of divination.

In the following chapters, I will share thirty-five years of experience and research, greatly benefitted by extensive study of the profound work of others, including Carl Jung. We also tap experiences that led me to establish Tarot.com as well as the stories of modern day users, which I have been given permission to share.

It is my hope that you will let this book show you how authentic divination can help you, as it has helped me, to move more confidently and fulfill your highest destiny, in a chaotic and confusing world. We need all the wisdom we can get, and we need each other.

Paul O'Brien, Portland, Oregon, USA,
New Years Day 2007

My deepest gratitude goes out to the ancient Chinese sages who created the I Ching over two thousand years ago. Discovering this revered classical oracle as a teenager introduced me to divination systems, changed my life and my livelihood, and led via many byways to the writing of this book.

If I had realized how much work it was going to be, I would not have added writing a book to my duties as founder and former president of Tarot.com for five years. I could have never completed the task without a lot of help, most especially from my talented editor and research assistant, Nayana Jennings. Nayana's organizational and editing skills, as well as her consistently sunny disposition, have been key to this book's completion, after many years of our combined efforts.

First of all, I want to thank my double-Virgo mother, Rita Gomes, for supporting my core belief in myself, a work ethic that includes a willingness to sacrifice, and a more than healthy respect for details.

A number of Visionary's employees since 1989 have made it possible for me to focus on the interactive dynamic of divination, which can be captured in the form of software. In this category, there are many, but I would like to especially call out Jeremy Wells, Tyler Morrison, Eric Rogers, Carol Ward and John Petisch, my steadily supportive son Shane O'Brien, my niece Jewel Mlnarik who saved my bacon in 2000 when other programmers did not believe that Tarot.com could work, and Tarot.com's Creative Director and GM, Jessica Abel, who has been saving it ever since.

Special thanks goes out to Charles Jennings for first drafting our modern I Ching text in 1988—the background text for the original *Synchronicity* I Ching program. Thanks to Tarot scholar Christine Payne Towler, who came along a few years later to provide inspired interpretations for the world's first complete encyclopedia of Tarot meanings, which provided the interpretations within the *Tarot Magic* CD-ROM, and later Tarot.com. We are also grateful that Christine brought

iv

Acknowledgements

renowned Tarot author Mary Greer to Tarot.com and our Tarot Advisory Board.

Tremendous gratitude goes out to all of the authors and friends in the Astrology community, most notably Rick Levine and Jeff Jawer, who write the horoscopes for Tarot.com. Some of the other astrologers whose writings for Tarot.com have helped and inspired us have been Tad Mann, Monte Farber (whose turns of phrase I love to plagiarize), Stephanie Dempsey and Judi Vitale.

How fortunate Tarot.com was to have Numerologist Hans Decoz approach us in 2001 with an offer to supply his superior numerology software and reports! And Marie Diamond only made Tarot.com's divination content that much better with the addition of her Feng Shui and Chinese astrology.

Nobody can accomplish anything that is very worthwhile without being receptive to great advice. In this regard, I want to express profound thanks for the advice and friendship of Don Helfgott, Richard Kinnaird, Robert Aughenbaugh, Haiou He and Maria Palmer for their constant support, absolute honesty and willingness to straighten me out when I needed it most.

Kudos to Nancy Van Allen who is responsible for the book's layout and design, to Shari Chapman for the jacket cover, Janice Hussein for proofreading and to Sid Brewster for all of his help in so many ways over so many years.

INTRODUCTION
Reading the Mind of God

JUDGEMENT.

Judgment
Criticism, awakening, liberation

Rider-Waite Tarot
© US Games Systems, Inc.

Go confidently in the direction of your dreams. Live the life you have imagined.

—Henry David Thoreau

Divination is controversial. It provides systems for stimulating insights into the way of divine intelligence. In fact, it goes further than that. It actually facilitates a two-way conversation with God. Divination is condemned by fundamentalist religions because they do not allow direct access to the divine, except mainly to beg.

This was not always so. In fact, divination was held in the highest esteem by virtually all the ancient religions, including Judaism (as evidenced in the Bible, see Chapter 6), even if only the rabbis and shamans knew how to actually do it. The practice of using a divination system to read the mind of God, and make important decisions, has been widespread throughout human history. Only relatively recently did it fall into disfavor with the most political and powerful religious organization ever, the Roman church, which itself was not organized until three hundred years after the death of Jesus.

The Divine communicates in many ways.

The Church's penalties (including death by torture) for divinatory practices, as well as the medicinal use of traditional herbs, midwifery and other non-sanctioned spiritual or healing arts took hold during the Middle Ages. As a result of the Church's violent intolerance, divination's true nature has been cloaked in mystery and surrounded by fear in the west for most of the past 2000 years. (This was not the case in China or India with regard to their more liberal spiritual traditions, which included the I Ching, Vedic Astrology, etc.)

In the West since the Renaissance, divination has finally come out of the closet and is more popular now than ever. Gaining momentum in the 19th century with the use of Tarot cards and the translation of the *I Ching*, the proliferation of divination books and systems—including Astrology, Numerology, Tarot and Runes—has exploded since the 1970s.

Nowadays, you can perform divination anytime you want to clarify your desires or tap into your intuition.

These days, divination has become something of a mainstream phenomenon. Unfortunately, its popularity has also spawned exploitation by mass marketers via psychic phone networks, most of which misrepresent divination as a tool for fortune-telling.

Authentic divination is more like a form of meditation and prayer than predicting the future. It is more informative and fulfilling than the simple prayer taught by churches. Divination is a two-way conversation, whereby we get feedback on the divine order behind appearances. The word 'divination' derives from *divinatus*, past participle of the Latin verb *divinare*, meaning "to be inspired by the divine." For those who practice the art, divination is an effective way to access divine wisdom, for more spiritual decision-making and peace of mind.

Until the invention of printing, divination systems were only the domain of specialists employed by emperors, kings and military leaders. Thanks to literacy, printing and the internet, the ability to use these time-honored, sacred tools has become available to virtually everyone. Unfortunately, not all systems that claim to be divination are authentic.

Along with its increase in popularity, there has been a rise in confusion about what divination is, how it works, what it is good for, how to use it effectively, and how to tell the real from the fake. Some misunderstandings are the result of old superstitions, based on negative propaganda by a church obsessed with controlling people's relationship to the divine. In addition, there are thousands of phony psychic networks that claim to use Tarot and other systems for the sake of greater credibility, while they actually rely on manipulative psychology to cash in on people's insecurities.

This book aims to set the record straight about this gift from the gods (or God, if you prefer). The first two chapters of this book explain the importance of our higher level desires, the limiting power of beliefs, and the monumental challenge we face in having to cope with rapidly accelerating change and chaotic appearances. Chapter 3 describes how divination systems work, referring to the extensive research of the great depth psychologist, Carl Jung, who studied divination for over thirty years.

Chapters 4 and 5 examine divination's origins and history, including its treatment during the Christian era. Chapter 6 explores what the Bible actually says about divination and the psychic arts. The last few chapters provide examples of how divination is currently being used by people like you, and points to how it may be used in the future to shape a better world.

> *Education sows not seeds in you, but makes your seeds grow.*
> —Kahlil Gibran

THE NEW AGE

Today, divination systems are looked at as artifacts of what is referred to as the *New Age* movement. A target of ridicule by the mainstream media since it came into the vernacular in the 1960s, the term "New Age" has virtually lost all meaning. Many don't realize that the expression originally referred to the beginning of a new astrological era, the Age of Aquarius.

This kind of age is a phenomenon well known to astronomers and astrologers to last approximately 2,100 years. Such an age represents one-twelfth of the circular rotation of Earth's rotational axis with respect to the "fixed" stars. As far as we know, it was first observed circa 150 B.C. by Hipparchus, who was also the first known person to calculate the exact length of our solar year.

The entire cycle of twelve ages known in astronomy as the Precession of the Equinoxes, in which the Sun's position at the Vernal Equinox shifts backwards through the Zodiac. This creates a kind of astrological year known as the 'Great Year,' consisting of approximately 25,786 actual years. Each Great Year consists of twelve 'great months,' named after signs of the Zodiac and lasting about 2,100 years. The shift between such incredibly long ages doesn't happen in an instant; astronomers and astrologers generally allow for a transition period of a number of years for this to occur.

The Age of Pisces began around the birth of Jesus, and we are supposed to be entering the New Age sometime in the 21st century. Some claim that the Age of Aquarius has dawned already, and others predict that it won't come for another twenty years.

Age of Pisces

The Age of Pisces is characterized by the rise of monotheism, hierarchical organization and devotion.

From an astrological point of view, the energy and personality of the intellectual and idealistic sign of Aquarius differs radically from the pious and devotional sign of Pisces, the age we are leaving. In the West, the Age of Pisces was marked by the establishment of hierarchically organized religions that based their political authority on a uniform codification of their founder's mystical experiences, plus strict discipline.

In the case of Christianity and Islam, religious laws governed more than behavior—they asserted sovereignty over the realm of a person's inner experience and claimed a right of judgment over individual souls. This form of totalitarianism did not permit freedom of thought, and used fear of God's righteous wrath to ensure obedience. Those who fail to comply are condemned as "fallen" and to an eternity of torture. Concepts like hell and the devil have supported the dominance of religious fears over people's lives socially, politically and psychologically. And God's representatives, the leaders of the religion, were empowered to exact divine retributions here on earth. In terms of political powers, such as the Holy Roman Empire, this system of propaganda and brainwashing worked very well.

As a result, a social climate of fear has been the norm in the West for almost all of the past two thousand years. Fearful for both their physical and eternal well-being, people accepted what they were told they should think and do by those in power. They were taught to fear God, and certainly had reason to fear His representatives. Since church and state only came to be separated in recent times, those in power have served as spiritual middlemen, as well as political strongmen. The bishops and clergy laid claim to the secrets of the divine mysteries, to the power to grant salvation to devoted followers and to provide an early ticket-to-hell for free thinkers.

In contrast to the devotional character of Pisces, the energy of Aquarius is individualistic and free-spirited. Aquarian culture is characterized by the sharing of information and the dissemination of the healing waters of knowledge. Its approach is never hierarchical. Aquarian organizations tend to be organized as flat and wide—

dispensing with the middle manager whenever possible. It is egalitarian, humanitarian, and idealistic.

The wisdom of an Aquarian Age is the opposite of righteous, secretive and exclusive; it brings people together in cooperation, and flattens hierarchical structures by allowing individuals the freedom to separate from collective ideology and hierarchical control. For instance, in the past twenty years we have noticed the flattening of organization structures in the business sector. This equalizing effect can be attributed, in part, to the Internet, a markedly Aquarian invention. The New Age movement is a function of the same Aquarian dynamic in the area of spirituality.

Despite its name, the "New Age movement" is producing little that is new, nor is it an abandonment of traditional spirituality. On the contrary, it represents the resurrection of revered spiritual traditions after centuries of repression by religious powers of the Piscean Age. In alignment with the spirit of Aquarius, the New Age movement represents traditional folk spirituality being reclaimed by the people with the help of education, higher literacy, and social networks like the Internet.

Age of Aquarius

The Age of Aquarius is characterized by a love of freedom, fairness, rational thought, cooperation and technology.

Not everyone welcomes an age of personal and spiritual empowerment. Powerful, ultra-conservative organizations—including political parties, fundamentalist religious sects and the Catholic Church—cannot adapt. Nevertheless, spiritual consciousness and personal empowerment have been expanding since the 1960s and will continue to do so. Polarization between secretive, authoritarian structures trying to impose rigid ideologies and a cultural movement that supports freedom of thought and individual experience of the divine is to be expected.

The resulting two cultural poles are described in James Davison Hunter's book, *The Culture Wars: The Struggle to Define America*. On one hand, Hunter defines *Progressivism* as an approach to life and change based on a belief that morality should be experienced-based and subjective (reflecting the energy of Aquarius). On the other hand is *Orthodoxy*, or the belief that morality is objective and fixed, having been psychically channelled from God into scriptures (a more Piscean perspective).

The culture wars are heating up today as the fears of ideologues (people prone to fanciful ideas and theories based on enshrined belief systems) are also exacerbated by the accelerating rate of change in general. To those who are invested in the power that comes from fixed dogma, change always feels like a threat. Of course, it is blamed on the free-thinking Progressives, who are condemned as the enemies of church, state, and God himself. Chapter 2 examines how religions almost always turn originally useful beliefs into frozen ideologies that suppress spiritual and cultural evolution.

Although the ideologues in power always get most of the press, a counter-movement of spiritually and politically progressive thought is gaining momentum. The cultural shift away from authoritarian ideology has been brewing since the Renaissance and its "Age of Reason," shifted into a higher gear in the sixties. This movement now encompasses a broad spectrum of people.

> *The thought manifests as the word;*
>
> *The word manifests as the deed;*
>
> *The deed develops into habit;*
>
> *And habit hardens into character;*
>
> *So watch the thought and its ways with care,*
>
> *And let it spring from love*
>
> *Born out of concern for all beings....*
>
> *As the shadow follows the body,*
>
> *As we think, so we become.*
>
> —The Buddha

The estimated 40 million adults in this subculture, in the U.S.A. alone, were dubbed *cultural creatives* by sociologist Paul Ray. According to Ray, cultural creatives are innovators who are actively creating a new culture based on values that were not relevant in the autocratic societies of the past 2000 years. They care about poverty, the environment, civil rights, alternative health care, social justice, peace, and spiritual exploration. The cultural creatives are resurrecting more effective ways to connect with the divine. As a traditional spiritual technique that allows us to have a direct conversation with the divine, and participate in discovering our own spiritual meaning, divination is one example of this.

Freedom to trust your intuition and access divine wisdom without needing an authoritarian middleman is highly desirable in this new age, and people are seeking it out in increasing numbers. "The interest in Astrology and Tarot and I Ching books is evidence of a deeper sea [of] change in American spirituality over the last several years," said Chris Faatz of Powell's Books, the world's largest independent bookstore in Portland, Oregon. "It's evidence of the loosening of religious structures in our lives. People are finding meaning, which is good." The market for knowledge about alternative spiritual practices is growing rapidly too.

In 2005 the national Board on Population Health and Public Health Practice published a study called "Complementary and Alternative Medicine in the United States." The study found that 62 percent of adults had tried some form of alternative or unconventional treatment. Types of therapies included prayer, deep-breathing exercises and meditation. Spirituality is becoming increasingly integrated into all aspects of life, and interest is steadily growing.

The supply of materials and services available to cultural creative types will continue to increase. The Aquarian spirit will not be denied. As we enter this new age of knowledge sharing and access, the mysterious realm of the divine will become more directly available to all. Already, there are thousands of books promoting various spiritual teachers, shamans, practitioners, and New Age oracles. My purpose in writing this book is to do my part to help put the power of time-honored divination tools into the hands of awakening people, where it belongs.

Our lives are increasingly complex, fast-paced, and filled with decisions that must be made more quickly than ever; meanwhile, most people do not know how to access timeless wisdom and get answers to problems that logic can't handle. In the coming pages, we will explore how divination supports self-knowledge, and how its use improves rhythm and timing. We will see how manifesting your personal destiny requires letting go of control, and fostering a willingness to be guided to make the right moves at the right time, by the wisdom that dwells within you.

There is a universal human curiosity about the divine plan for our lives and a strong desire to know the mind of God. Thousands of commercial fortune-tellers and phone psychics actively exploit this desire. There are also many qualified spiritual counselors performing valuable services, some with the help of divination tools. This book focuses on those forms of divination that have the highest pedigree and have been proven over centuries to work best for most people. The following pages focus on five classical divination systems: Tarot, Numerology, Astrology, Runes, and the I Ching.

Five classical divinatory arts: Tarot, Numerology, Astrology, Runes, and the I Ching.

Introduction: Reading the Mind of God

> *I deserve to have what I want ... and what I want is good for me.*
> —Affirmation

This book attempts to dispel misunderstandings regarding the nature and history of these five divination systems, and to help you distinguish between sacred, time-honored tools and bogus fortune-telling services. It is my hope to encourage people who have never experienced divination to try one of its classical forms without being inhibited by superstition or fears of any kind.

We will take a look at divination's popularity through the ages, the role religious institutions have played in both supporting and fighting it, and how divination is now aligning individuals with their spiritual path in the newly emerging Aquarian Age.

In ancient times, emperors and high priests used divination to align themselves with divine providence. May the information presented here help you take advantage of these powerful, spiritual tools for the sake of your personal quest. Let these gifts of the gods guide you to manifest your heart's core desires, the dreams your soul was wired for, which are the internal signposts of your highest personal destiny.

CHAPTER 1
Your Heart's Desire is Your Destiny

You can't always get what you want.
—The Rolling Stones

od's mind can be hard to figure. We pray, we ask for something, but more often than not we receive something different. Is this some kind of detour, or is God just not listening? Could it be that we are so out of step with divine providence and our personal destiny that we make foolish or untimely requests, as in "Be careful what you wish for"? Perhaps God is protecting us against ourselves. After all, in hectic and rapidly changing world, how can we expect to be absolutely sure what is truly best for us at any given time?

> *Decide and act in sync with your personal Destiny and you will also satisfy your Heart's Desires—how perfect!*
> —Paul O'Brien

In ancient times societies had prophets, shamans or high priests who used methods of divination to help them provide wisdom and direction. Now we can do the same thing for ourselves. Some of the best divination systems are still with us, but most of us don't know how to use them or don't feel confident enough to try.

It has been taught that the best prayer is "Not my will, but Thy will be done." Surely, if we were in sync with divine will, all our prayers would be appropriate, or perhaps not necessary at all. But can we know the divine plan? How can we be sure that what we long for is in alignment with our highest destiny? How can we create lives that are full of grace—like a dance that has its regular rhythms but also room for creative improvisation?

Just as a good dancer is always experimenting and learning, the zig-zagging dance that is your personal destiny unfolding is a progressive spiritual path. Like an original opera played for the first time, your life has a unique musical score and choreography that is always new and always changing. We can think of God or Goddess as the composer. The Greeks and Romans realized the importance of this divine function and revered Fortuna, the Goddess of Destiny. But even though it is divinely ordained, the musical score of your unfolding destiny is not necessarily easy to hear, as illustrated by the story of my friend David.

Love and desire are the spirit's wings to great deeds.

—Johann Wolfgang von Goethe

DAVID'S STORY

One night as a child, David ran out into the field next to his house. The moon was full and its light glistened on the tall grass, still damp after a long, wet spring. The slim, green blades reached the tip of David's nose as his legs flew. As soon as he reached the cover of the taller reeds, his movements turned into a practice session of twirls, leaps, pirouettes, bows and stomps.

David was not supposed to be out in the night, but he secretly defied his father's conservative morals and his mother's strict code of behavior. Even at age six, David sensed that his enthusiasms were not only deeply personal but also somehow as important as the universe.

David's joy in dancing could have easily ended in that field. Over the next two decades, people who cared for him confronted his shy temperament and, with the best intentions, invalidated his most creative impulses, including his heartfelt desire to dance. Dancing was not for boys. And it certainly was not to be considered a career option for David. It was his destiny, his parents firmly insisted, to follow in his father's footsteps and become an attorney.

David was a diligent student at school, excellent lawyer material. Nevertheless, he experienced a consistent, nagging urge to keep his body moving in time to music that he—and sometimes only he—could hear. Fortunately for David, soon after he started college he met a skilled astrologer, who recognized the meaning in a conjunction of Venus, Mercury and Jupiter that occurred in the 10th house of David's birth chart. His natal horoscope made it clear that a career in the arts would be far more appropriate than law for the expression of his soul. He changed majors. Years later, thanks to the tugging of a persistent desire that was part of his nature, David experienced fulfillment as a professional dancer in a successful modern dance company. Not only did he master the art of dancing, he got in sync with the larger dance of fulfilling his personal destiny.

For David, the profound desire to dance was the kind of desire that we shall refer to in this book as a *Heart's Desire*. According to Jungian psychologist James

Hillman's groundbreaking book *The Soul's Code,* David's Heart's Desire to dance would be the calling for which David's soul was wired.

Although your ultimate calling—or true love, for that matter—may be obscured by more mundane concerns, its identity can be uncovered with honest, soul-searching work, which may include the use of some divination, as it did in David's case.

David's desire to dance is what I shall refer to in the book as a Heart's Desire. Deeper than most of our many desires, Heart's Desires are manifestations of the glory your soul was wired for. Becoming aware of this higher order of desire is the first step towards making the right choices that will take you along the path of your highest personal destiny. This chapter will explore the process of identifying your Heart's Desires, help you learn to distinguish them from counterproductive temptations, and introduce the theme of this entire book, which is how authentic divination can play a significant role in helping you understand and manifest your unique destiny.

> *Those who cannot tell what they desire or expect still sigh and struggle with indefinite thoughts and vast wishes.*
>
> —Ralph Waldo Emerson

Certainly, discovering and fulfilling your personal destiny is life's ultimate challenge and its greatest reward. When you find your path in life and are in sync with your primary missions in this lifetime, everything else just falls into place. Life feels right and good. Relationships with friends and loved ones are more grounded and satisfying. Your calling or vocation becomes crystal clear. Problems, though still challenging, are much easier to manage when you are doing what you know you are supposed to do, while being in the relationships you are supposed to have.

A stronger sense of confidence and ease arises within you after you get clear about who you are, what you want, and what roles in life you are wired for. Who doesn't want a clear picture of their true path, to achieve their deepest desires and manifest their highest destiny?

In subsequent chapters, this book will show you easy but effective ways to use time-honored divination tools to activate the power of your intuition and answer the most profound personal questions: Why am I here? What is my purpose? What is my calling? What's the best approach to manifest my heart's most special desire?

On a practical level, you may desire to find a more creative solution to an apparent impasse, or plan your next best move at work or in a relationship. Perhaps you want to know how you can most skillfully approach a particular situation, relationship, or project. These are down to earth decisions that can sometimes only be completely resolved with the help of divination tools.

> *Whatsoever that be within us that feels, thinks, desires, and animates is something celestial, divine, and, consequently, imperishable.*
>
> —Aristotle

CONFLICTED ABOUT DESIRES

If you ever feel conflicted or confused about your desires, you are far from alone. Most people are conflicted about many, if not most, of their desires. A good friend who grew up in China during the Cultural Revolution learned that it was not safe to have personal desires. My father was conditioned by the Great Depression and, like many people of that era, learned to deny his personal desires too. "If you have no great expectations, you'll never be disappointed," he would say. Unintentionally, he passed his depressing belief on to his children, as parents cannot help but do.

Whenever, for example, as a young child I shyly expressed a hope for something like a model train set for Christmas, my father would reply with his dry adult wit, "It's good to want," and turn to other things. And that was the end of it. Perhaps the family couldn't afford it—I had no idea. But I came to the mistaken conclusion—as children will often do in their innate need to make some sense of things—that whatever desires I had in life were not really important. Moreover, I learned that I was "selfish" for having them, let alone imposing them on my parents by voicing them aloud!

My confusion about desire increased even more when as a young adult I began to study the teachings of Buddhism, which are widely misconstrued as condemning desire. My curiosity about the subject of desire was stimulated about how the phenomenon of desire has been treated by all of the major religions, including my native Christianity. It seemed obvious to me that there has been a lot of confusion about desire in almost every religious tradition and culture. Denial didn't make desire go away. Maybe there was a good reason for it?

Desire is such a basic psychological experience of

every human being. We want a better job, more time to ourselves, and more or newer things. We dream of true love. We like adventure, stability, or abundance. In addition to our day-to-day desires, most of us have also experienced the strong pull of a deep sense of longing at one time or another. I call this a Heart's Desire.

While it is true that many desires that arise are not all that important—and some can even get us into trouble—Heart's Desires are in an altogether different, more significant category. Before we look at how we can tell the difference between desires that should be made priorities and those that should be ignored or turned into preferences, let's take a look at how desires come to us in the first place.

What Made Them *Your* Desires?

Our minds play host to all manner of thoughts, including desires, that arise of their own accord all the time. The unceasing flow of thought in all its various forms is an inescapable and defining aspect of the human condition. Thoughts stream into our mental inbox whether we have subscribed to them or not, like some kind of cosmic spam. Unlike junk mail, however, we have a tendency to identify with the thoughts that come to us and to make them our own. In fact, we tend to refer to them as "my thoughts" as soon as we become aware of them.

The fact that thoughts and desires come to us unbidden was driven home to me in my first ten-day silent meditation retreat some twenty-five years ago (and in every meditation practice since). I had believed that meditation was a yoga practice designed for controlling the mind in order to stop thoughts. Certainly, when I was first learning how to meditate, I had no desire for intrusive thoughts—in fact, quite the opposite! They were unwelcome, but thoughts came anyway, and in droves.

With help from my first regular meditation teacher, Ayya Khema, a Buddhist nun with whom I went around the world giving meditation retreats, I learned how the mind latches on to uninvited thoughts and then amplifies them by introducing related ideas until your brain is busily dwelling on some line of thinking or fantasy. I was

> Ayya Khema, who initiated me into the ranks of meditation teachers, was one of the most active Buddhist nuns in the world. Even at a ripe old age, she traveled from her monastery in Sri Lanka to offer the world her free ten-day silent meditation retreats. Her retreat format was so strict that some students lovingly referred to her as "Attila the Nun." Ayya knew that discipline is necessary to break through unconscious mental habits.

The lotus flower is an important symbol in Eastern religions. Because the lotus grows in murky ponds, the flower symbolizes rising above difficulty to find beauty in all situations. The sacred Lotus, *Nelumbo nucifera*, represents divine wisdom and spiritual progress. "Purity, trustworthiness, the Buddha, the virtuous man: these are what the lotus signifies," writes Huang Yung-Chuan in his book, *The Art of Traditional Chinese Flower Arranging.*

confronted by this question: how could these thoughts be mine, when they were unwelcome, not generated by me, and were actually interfering with the serenity that I was striving for?

I investigated firsthand how the mind can so easily become derailed. The importance of this discovery combined with meditation techniques of letting go of thoughts—learned from Ayya Khema—led me to become her travelling personal assistant. I helped her put on meditation retreats around the world. And I was trained by her as a meditation teacher.

I was inspired to spread the important lesson that the skill of simply noticing, naming, and letting go of thoughts that arise is the key to self-realization and peace of mind. The first step is to clear up the misunderstanding that we should be able to stop thoughts from arising.

In the meditation classes I used to teach many people have told me, "I'll never be able to meditate; I just can't stop thinking." I reassured them that anyone can learn to meditate once they understand that it's really not about preventing thoughts from arising. It is their nature to arise. Rather, we must learn to let the thoughts come and go without attaching energy and attention to them, without dwelling on them. Stopping thoughts—including the thoughts known as desires—is simply impossible. Only when we accept this fact will we be able to distinguish between the desires that serve us and those that are distractions.

The persistent thoughts with which we identify—the ones we invest in by thinking about them—can quickly turn into urges, desires, and cravings. There may be a reason for these thoughts to arise, but encouraging them by giving them the energy of our attention certainly makes them harder to let go of. Some offer nothing more than a lesson—perhaps simply serving as a reminder that we are still vulnerable to certain kinds of mental habits. Unfortunately, desire-thoughts can so quickly take over our consciousness, stimulating our emotions into reaction, that it is easy to become attached to powerful temptations that please the ego but are ultimately self-defeating.

As human beings, we are blessed with free will—the ability to choose to get involved with desires that tempt us or not. But, as Ayya Khema taught, conscious spiritual intervention requires the practice of awareness to notice what we are paying attention to and to classify it. We need to maintain an awareness of our awareness, of what we are paying attention to, in order to discriminate between the thoughts and desires we want and the ones we don't—*before* we get involved with them.

The etymology of the word *desire*—*de*, from + *sidus*, star—reveals the fact that desires come to us from above, which signifies that they have a spiritual source and purpose. Fundamentalists of all religions might insist that the real purpose of personal desires is for them to be denied or sacrificed. Denial doesn't work, but we certainly ought to ignore desires that can turn into troublesome distractions or worse.

On the other hand, there is the higher order of desires that I call Heart's Desires. These special desires have a positive, life-affirming purpose. They are meant to be honored and fulfilled, because their fulfillment is an important step on the path of our destiny.

Isn't Desire the Cause of Suffering?

Once we have identified with a desire, we will automatically focus on it and generate ideas on how to attain it, often with strong emotional attachment. This process of adopting thoughts and giving energy to them is how desires take shape and eventually consume our attention. In the case of Heart's Desires, we do want to give them energy. In fact, they need regular attention to anchor them in the subconscious, giving the creative power of manifestation something to work with as we go about our daily business. In order to do this, we need to be able to embrace our Heart's Desires without feeling conflicted or guilty about them.

Desires based on fear—fear of loss or anxiety about anything lead us into a downward spiral of emotional reaction, which gives rise to more thoughts, more reactions, more depressing thoughts, feelings of guilt, and so on—a tailspin that ends in mental and physical exhaustion. Perhaps it is because of the downward tendency of ego-based desires that most religions and social systems

> *Every conquering temptation represents a new fund of moral energy. Every trial endured and weathered in the right spirit makes a soul nobler and stronger than it was before.*
>
> **—William Butler Yeats**

The Four Noble Truths of Buddhism:

1. Suffering exists

2. Suffering arises from attachment to desired outcome

3. Suffering ceases when attachment to outcome ceases

4. Freedom from suffering is possible by practicing the Eightfold Path

advocate the repression of all desire. But black-and-white repression is too simplistic; it ignores the higher order of desire that this book and the proper use of divination are focused on. Denial and repression sound good ("Just say no."), but there is a more joyful way.

Nevertheless, let's face the fact that many desires are really not good for us, and not appropriate to dwell on, let alone act upon. By deliberately ignoring them, we gain the opportunity to strengthen our integrity, our resolve to focus on those more profound desires that point to our higher good. Practicing such discrimination is key to the successful channeling of desire. When we are relaxed and in tune with our spiritual Destiny, our Heart's Desires work to our benefit by stimulating creative and inspiring ideas. Evolution demands this.

A lot of people mistakenly think Buddhism teaches that desire is the cause of suffering. However, this is a mistranslation and an oversimplification of the Buddha's actual teaching. After all, as we have seen, it is as impossible to prevent desires from arising as it is to stop the rain, no matter how well one can meditate. Meditation, the basic spiritual practice of Buddhism, is about awareness and letting go, not repression—of desires or anything else.

The Buddha himself was motivated by desire; his Heart's Desire was for the ultimate freedom, not only for himself but also for all suffering beings. It's only when we become obsessed with or act on desires that are not in alignment with our soul's evolution that they become a source of suffering; this craving or addiction is what he taught was the cause of suffering.

Buddha's teaching on the relationship of suffering and craving—defined as a desire coupled with an emotional demand—is some of the most sophisticated psychology ever devised. The core of the Buddha's many teachings, delivered over a period of almost four decades 2600 years ago, is known as the Four Noble Truths.

The First Noble Truth is that suffering exists to the extent that the ego, which operates on a dualistic subject-object basis, is in control of our consciousness. The ego creates conflicts, defends, competes and can never be totally satisfied with anything. No matter how good

it feels right now, there can never be enough security, pleasant sensations, and control. On this basis alone, it is the lot of almost all human beings to suffer through life. Even if you are currently happy with a situation, change is constant and the feeling of happiness will not last. Even when you are getting what you want, you can experience the fear of running out, losing it, having it taken away from you, or simply becoming bored with it. This is a form of suffering. And, soon enough, you'll start craving something else or something more.

The Second Noble Truth is that the cause of suffering is not found in whether we possess or lose the objects of our desires, but whether we develop an emotional attachment to them. A desire that is accompanied by such attachment is called *craving* or *addiction*. Craving is desire loaded with expectations, emotional demands, and insecurities. It is our investment in gaining some feeling, experience, or possession we like—or getting rid of something that we don't like. In spite of the fact that cravings and attachments promise to deliver happiness, they are self-defeating mindsets that always cause disappointment and suffering. Obsessing on such desires is an obstacle to the fulfillment of your destiny.

> The hungry ghost is a Buddhist image that represents suffering, which results from cravings that can never be fulfilled.

This can be a hard pill for most people to swallow. Try convincing the average consumer that even if he gets what he wants, it's not going to make him happy. In modern times, trillions of advertising dollars have been devoted to brainwashing us with the message that status, power, exciting relationships, and material possessions are what life is all about. The psychological trap works brilliantly because the minute we get what we thought we wanted, we begin to want something newer, bigger, or different. Marketing experts know this. They are in the business of re-stimulating unquenchable craving.

Despite the illusion of satisfaction being just around the corner—if only you get the perfect body, the perfect home, the perfect job, the perfect relationship, the perfect car—the subtle but persistent sufferings of dissatisfaction and frustration never end. What we repeatedly fail to see is that our unhappy state is not being caused, as it seems, by the absence of the things we think we want. It is caused by the emotional demand itself, the

insistence that happiness will come if only we possess these objects of desires. This is the ego's false promise.

The Third Noble Truth comes to the rescue to reassure us that it is possible to become free from cravings and the suffering they cause in this lifetime. In other words, we don't have to wait until we die in order to go to heaven. Since state of mind determines the level of dis-ease, a change of attitudes and thinking processes can eliminate suffering that we would normally experience. In the Buddhist tradition, the strong tendency toward craving is called the "hungry ghost," a symbol of unconscious psychological appetites that can never be satisfied. The only way to become free of hungry ghosts and the suffering they can cause is to starve them—by letting go of our craving and neurotic attachments.

Letting go is something we can learn and this gets easier with practice. **The Fourth Noble Truth** describes techniques for letting go, which is called the Eightfold Path. As Hermann Hesse's great classic novel, *Siddhartha*, so beautifully told the story, the Buddha learned firsthand that neither asceticism nor hedonism could solve the problem of suffering. The Eightfold Path is designed to help us find and keep to "the middle way," avoiding extremes of pleasure or self-denial.

> *Suffering cheerfully endured ceases to be suffering and is transmuted into an ineffable joy.*
> —Mahatma Gandhi

The Eightfold Path offers a formula for the cultivation of wisdom, ethics, and mental development. These are the same qualities that the practice of skillful divination, which is actually a form of insight meditation, helps us develop, as we shall see later in this book. Buddha's Eightfold Path enumerates specific spiritual factors, mostly related to the practice of meditation and ethical conduct. According to Buddhist teachings, if you approach the cultivation of these factors with love, compassion, and joy, you will be able to experience an end to suffering in this lifetime.

Along the way, the magic of what we call grace happens, producing episodes of sudden enlightenment, which is not really so sudden at all—if you consider all the effort it took to let go of craving along the way. An interesting analogy is that of a prisoner who is filing away at the bars of his cell every day. He is no freer from one day to the next, but he is making progress! Such is the path of letting go.

Great Temptations

All of us deal with cravings and addictions, because they are the natural fruits of an egocentric point of view. As a spiritual counselor, I've heard people remark that they have an "addictive personality." My reply is, "Of course you do, otherwise you wouldn't be here!" According to Buddhism, the ultimate reason we are reincarnated and must return to this realm of temptation, free will, and spiritual education is because we still need the opportunity to become free from lingering addictions. One of the last things an enlightened being lets go of is the ego's need to feel special, and to forcefully fulfill its desires, including the craving for spiritual attainment itself. The Tibetan lama, Chogyum Trungpa, wrote a great book about this entitled *Cutting Through Spiritual Materialism.*

The quest for enlightenment illustrates the paradox of desire—the fact that you must have desire to be motivated to transcend being ruled by desire. Enlightenment ultimately requires the trick of letting go of the desire that drew us toward it in the first place. In order to enter the enlightened state, we need to get over the craving to be someone special—which, in the latter stages of our soul's evolution, takes the form of the ego's need to see oneself as spiritually superior. The desire to be special is at the heart of egocentricity and lies behind all of our cravings and attachments. In contrast to a Heart's Desires, the attention and power we crave are obstacles to realizing our destiny.

Sometimes I like to refer to strong cravings as great temptations because they feel so strong that they can be mistaken for Heart's Desires. One way to tell the difference between great temptations and the profound desires of a lifetime is to ask yourself, "Could manifestation of the desire possibly bring harm to anyone, including myself?" If so, it is definitely not a Heart's Desire.

The realm of intimate relationships is one of the most difficult areas for telling the difference between a Heart's Desire and a great temptation, because sexual chemistry can be so powerful. For example, let's say you fall in love with someone who is faithfully married. The attraction is compelling, your fantasies run wild, and your ego

Mataji Indra Devi was a movie star in Bombay silent films in 1927. Famous and married to a diplomat, she knew Gandhi, Krishnamurti, and Nehru as well as several maharajas.

She gave up all the glamour of her acting career to become the first woman ever commissioned as a yoga teacher by the greatest yoga master of 20th-century India, T. Krishnamacharya.

During the years I knew Mataji, she always seemed to give the same talk (before standing on her head, which she did well into her 80s). The message was "love and nonattachment"—how those two qualities go together and support each other.

Ego as Con Artist

The ego operates like a company that's creating computer viruses in order to sell virus-protection software. The ego subtly inculcates shame and fear so that you will give up your power to save yourself from shame and guilt and fear. It's a con. I have seen no better explanation of this subtle dynamic than in the book *Forgiveness and Jesus* by Kenneth Wapnick.

convinces you that the two of you would make a better combination—maybe even a match made in heaven. You feel a strong desire to seduce this person because the vision feels so right. You tell yourself that the other person would be better off, too. But in this case, harm would at least come to the other's family—as well as to yourself in the form of eventual disillusionment and weakened will power—if you were to succeed.

No matter how *right* it feels, if a passionate urge does not pass the harmlessness test, it falls into the category of great temptation, not Heart's Desire. The urge may feel as intense as any desire can—but the only true value of these kinds of temptations is educational. This is an opportunity for practicing self-control instead of self-indulgence.

In his 1975 best seller, *Handbook to Higher Consciousness,* spiritual teacher Ken Keyes does an elegant job of clarifying the subtleties of Buddha's teachings about desire, substituting the word addiction for craving. Keyes defines addictions as desire-thoughts backed by emotional demands. To make the distinction between addiction and desires in general, he refers to desires that are not so emotionally loaded as preferences.

Keyes has a technique for telling the difference between an addiction and a preference: if suffering results from a desire, it is an addiction—because psychological suffering is the symptom and the price that will be paid for any addiction. If a desire produces no suffering, it was not a craving, it was a preference. You may want it, but you also have a "win some, lose some" attitude about whether that desire is fulfilled or not.

In Keyes' system, all forms of feeling bad—from guilt to depression to jealousy—are the result of some kind of addiction, and the suffering itself serves as the indicator, the canary in the coalmine as it were. It's interesting to note that it is possible to be addicted to subtle, illusory projections such as the approval of others, the feeling that you are right, and so on. This leads to the suffering of feeling separated from loved ones or even rejected. If there is any form of personal suffering, addiction is present.

Keyes points out that we can succeed in transcending an addiction by up-leveling it to a preference, by just letting go of emotion-backed demands. It is possible, and spiritually incumbent upon us, to transform attitudes of attachment and associated negative thoughts. The irony is that the more unattached we are, the easier it becomes to receive whatever it is that we desire!

Mataji Indra Devi was a famous yoga teacher for whom I served as personal assistant and biographer in India as a young man, just before I met Ayya Khema. She knew the attractive power of nonattachment as well as anyone. After she returned from the United States to live once again in her beloved India at the age of eighty-one, she was visited by princes and celebrities. As is customary when going to see a holy person, her visitors would bring a gift, often something quite nice. What struck me was how Mataji would, without thought, give these gifts to the next person who visited her, no matter who it was. Mataji clearly understood the connection between abundance and letting go.

Ken Keyes' system of higher consciousness divides desires into two categories: addictions and preferences. In this book we add a third category of desire—Heart's Desires, which are more compelling than a simple preference, and they embody faith, hope, and love, rather than the anxiety or worries of an addiction. If there is any suffering associated with a Heart's Desire, it is like a fine gold chain—a chain of longing for the inevitable—in contrast to the burden of disappointment that results from security, sensation or power addictions.

Pinpointing and identifying your Heart's Desires can be difficult in a busy life loaded with professional and family responsibilities. Add distractions caused by craving and addictions, and the inner game can feel overwhelming. Nevertheless, learning to clearly differentiate between addictions and Heart's Desires is vitally important skill to master. Now that you understand the challenge, you can do it!

> The ancient Greeks believed the soul, or *psyche*, had three parts: the *desiring*, the *spirited*, and the *reasoning* parts.

THE OBSTACLE OF EGO

Meaning is a universal human need, but discovering the meaning of one's life is always a personal experience.

Oracle at Delphi "Know Thyself"

This is why the ancient Temple to the Oracle at Delphi was inscribed with the words "Know thyself." You are unique. Your journey of self-discovery begins with a commitment to learning who you are.

Most of us confuse our identity with that layer of consciousness which I have been referring to as ego. Indeed, in a society where individuality is celebrated and celebrity is glorified, it is difficult to transcend attachments that stem from an egocentric point of view. It's promoted constantly.

In psychology the ego is defined as the part of the self that forms the bridge between the self and the not-self, the individual and the outer world, mediating between the id (unconscious) and the superego (conscience).

The ego, as I use the term, can be compared to the Taoist view of the human dimension as that which is between and connects heaven and earth. In psychological terms, the ego is our self-image and the sense of identity we derive from that notion. While a strong ego is necessary for functioning in the world, when allowed to operate too freely, unregulated by the spiritual self, its dominance will disrupt our psychic and social balance. This is comparable to an environment polluted by self-centered corporations (ego) that are not being regulated by a conscientious government (spiritual self).

Without surrendering to inspiration and guidance from above, the ego will take itself very seriously, even imposing its will on others. Ego is the influence that seeks to pursue great temptations for short-term gratification, and messianic illusions in the long-term. "Just let me take care of it for you," the ego insists. "I am special and I can do anything. Just give me your power and I will keep you safe, fulfill your fantasies." But the ego is not a good director, unless there is a true emergency and survival is the priority. Otherwise, it can operate like a security agency that issues emergency alerts too often to effectively manage priorities.

Most of our desires are ego-driven. I might crave to have the figure of a model, desire attention or fame, or want to win the lottery. It makes no difference—it's all about me. The ego's agenda is often competitive and usually a bit frantic, since ego is a protective mechanism that tends to view situations in black-and-white survival terms, as us versus them. The ego tries to stay in control of our thinking, so the domination of our thoughts by ego-based desires is not surprising. Such desires tend to have a fantastic quality that makes them easy to spot when you are paying attention. But once they have taken over consciousness, blind spots of denial make our addictions hard to notice, until they have produced damage that cannot be ignored.

The ego is clever. Its powers of self-deception should never be underestimated—and this tendency is handily exploited by con artists and politicians. Even without outside influence, if left unchecked, the ego will sow seeds of fear and guilt in order to fortify a dominant position in your psyche. Ego's pitch goes something like this: "Life is scary, and you can never be too careful, but don't worry, just give me control and I will protect you from fear and guilt." Its inner war on terror provides every excuse for increasing domination of your mind.

The ego also sabotages the enjoyment of whatever desires are achieved. That's why when we get the raise, the perfect house, or whatever, we will still soon feel renewed discontent. We can quickly begin to worry about losing it, become fixated on a bigger or better version, or simply become bored as the ego starts looking for something new to crave. Even though most of us have had the experience of always wanting more, we have a hard time learning the lesson and continue chasing fantasies, as if the next time they will finally be real and permanently satisfying.

It's simple to be happy, I heard an Indian poet say on Delhi television, *but it's difficult to be simple!*

We are conditioned to believe that getting more of this or that will bring happiness, when we really need to look to Heart's Desires for meaning and satisfaction in our lives. Without spiritual guidance it's easy to invest our energy in tempting but ultimately downward spirals.

This is the place where divination, if used sincerely, can provide a soul-saving intervention. The skillful use of divination can help us turn things around by putting the ego in its place, directing it to follow the guidance of Higher Power instead of running the show.

SELFISHNESS AND SCARCITY CONSCIOUSNESS

Ego has a subject-object orientation by definition, for the egocentric point of view is that of a self opposed to everything that is not-self. Ego-based desires generally operate on the basis of zero-sum thinking—the concept that there is not enough (love, success, money, and so on) to go around, that life is a competitive struggle for limited resources. In spiritual circles, this is called scarcity consciousness, and it can show up in two ways.

The first is a guilt-ridden "if I get it, then someone else must go without" philosophy of self-denial. Feeling guilty over one's personal desires is a widespread phenomenon. Learning about limitations is, after all, a natural stage of human growth. But most of us who grew up in a religious culture have been heavily conditioned—by parents, church, and teachers—to put the needs of others before our own, together with an assumption that our dreams may be too big for us, too unrealistic. For instance, we may think that a potential partner is too good for us, that we don't deserve something that is truly exquisite, or that the time or effort spent on our own desires takes away from attention we should be giving to others.

> "Maybe the human task is to bring our behavior into line with its intentions, to do right by it, for its sake. What you do in life affects your heart, [and] alters your soul.... We make soul with our behavior, for soul doesn't come already made in heaven. It is only imagined there, an unfulfilled project trying to grow."
>
> —*The Soul's Code* by James Hillman

The mental habit of thinking small and automatically sacrificing personal desires—ignoring oneself for the sake of others—is a form of codependence. We make ourselves smaller, even if we pretend that we are martyrs, whenever we enable another person to take advantage of us. Knowing your Self, with a capital 'S', is key to unlocking your destiny, and denying your Heart's Desires only causes suffering.

Scarcity consciousness manifests in a second common form, the "I better get it while I can" attitude. This mindset leads to the pursuit of immediate gratification for security or pleasure with little or no concern for others. Remember, if a pursuit involves ignoring pos-

sible harm to other people, a desire cannot qualify as a Heart's Desire, or even as a good thing. People living this paradigm are called self-centered or selfish.

Unfortunately, the label *selfish*, which is used widely in a negative moralistic world, is too quickly applied in the raising of children, because making them feel guilty for their desires, makes them easier to control. "Stop being selfish" is an admonishment used by parents, often because they are overwhelmed by too many demands at once. But the guilt produced by judgmental techniques confuses a child, while conveying a self-negating lesson.

Once we become adults we are able to more objectively see that, in a broad sense, everything a person does is selfish. Ultimately, none of us choose anything that we don't want, for some reason or another. Even martyrs are choosing what they perceive to be their higher good. This understanding should in no way excuse lack of compassion or egomania. Rather, we can refer to this awareness as enlightened Selfishness, with a capital 'S'.

Enlightened selfishness depends upon understanding and accepting that life is an open system imbued with creative intelligence, as opposed to a closed system where resources are limited and we have to protect our turf. A person who exhibits an enlightened selfishness is able to root for everyone and takes pleasure in doing so. There is plenty to go around, thanks to the creativity and abundance of the universe. There is never any reason to begrudge your own success or the success of another. In fact, they go hand in hand!

This enlightened selfishness is a form of abundance consciousness, a wish for happiness that includes oneself, in the knowledge that we are interconnected with all beings. All sentient beings are in this together. All living beings are connected. As Deepak Chopra has pointed out, with every breath you take, you breathe in some cells of every person who ever lived. We are all one.

The cornucopia, or horn of plenty, is a symbol of unlimited abundance.

If we are going to trust in our heartfelt desires that don't harm anyone—the ones that contain directions from Destiny—we need to stop worrying so much about being selfish. Sai Baba, a hugely popular Indian guru, teaches "It is your duty to be happy." Indeed, it is our spiritual responsibility to uncover and follow our Heart's

Chief Listener

In order to make decisions, an executive needs good information. Once in the early days of Visionary Networks, I made a sales call at Apple Computers to persuade them to bundle a free sample copy of my I Ching program "Synchronicity" with every Mac. A bold Aries friend, who was an Apple employee, sneaked me in to see CEO John Sculley's office, since he was out of town. Although the office was huge and elegant, the thing that impressed me was the stack of business cards on his desk that listed his title as Chief Listener.

Desires, and to care about others without being affected by their opinions about what is good for us.

The bottom line is that what your heart truly wants is in alignment with what is good for you, and you deserve to have it. Allegiance to your Heart's Desires is a noble path that takes courage. Having compassion and helping others is a sublime path of spiritual service, and even if such "karma yoga" is not your primary yoga, good acts are natural offshoots of fulfilling your own highest destiny. Real Heart's Desires always reinforce the greater good, while providing your life with meaning and direction.

Once you realize that the fulfillment of your Heart's Desires is a divine directive, guiding you toward a destiny that will unfold sooner or later, no matter how many lifetimes it may take, your mind will become less conflicted and your life more simple. You will let go of trying to force things to happen in the limited ways that can be directed by your ego. When you look beyond egocentric fantasies to the greater good, you will be inspired to place your ego out of the way. When you let go of pursuing great temptations, you are dancing the dance of your life, following in harmony as Destiny leads the way.

DESIRE'S HEALTHY ROLE

Heart's Desires are the good seeds that take root in the depths of your soul, which is their true home. Compared to ego-based desires, they are rare. But they are possible to catch with a bit of careful attention.

For starters, Heart's Desires just feel right. Thinking about them is accompanied by joy more than anxiety. The primary discomfort that can accompany a clear awareness of a Heart's Desire is a bittersweet tinge of longing. Unlike appetites demanding immediate gratification, Heart's Desires are divine signals that point to your lifetime path of fulfillment. They may not feel as urgent as strong temptations or addictive urges in pursuit of fantasy, but they have more depth and endurance, and they feel like they belong to us. Heart's Desires ring true because they are an important part of who we are.

Heart's Desires are never casual or trivial. They only show up in the most important areas of life: your vocation or path of service, intimate relationships, creative freedom, family life, spiritual development, and healing. Later chapters of this book focus on how to develop your own divination practice to receive ongoing "dancing instructions" in these areas.

Parental and societal conditioning, peer group pressure, and low self-esteem can cause you to neglect or suppress your Heart's Desires. It is important to make a conscious intention to uncover and become aware of them. The reason these desires exist in the first place is to motivate you toward the greater good, to provide you with the inspiration and direction you need to fully play your part. Once you have established their authenticity, trust your Heart's Desires and develop ways of divining the best times and ways to cooperate with them, to support them, to help them give birth to a higher love.

We've all heard the expression, "Be careful what you wish for, because you just might get it." Before one starts the process of manifesting anything, it is critical to know that it's real and worth the effort. We need to use our left brain faculty of discrimination to discern our true Heart's Desires—as opposed to strong ego-based temptations, which can be a harmful waste of time. The former Polarity Institute on Orcas Island, Washington, where I received some training, taught that discrimination was one of the two primary qualities of the mature feminine (along with receptivity). In the face of such a highly tempting world, discrimination often shows up by saying 'no thanks,' an important skill.

As our friend David eventually learned from the innate love he had for dancing, our deepest desires persist for an important reason. In David's case, it was about his vocation. It took him a long time to see this, because his desire to dance was in conflict with his attempts to please his parents and become successful on their terms. Even though he instinctively loved to dance, he didn't realize how important this passion was, or how intrinsically it was linked to his Destiny, his true identity. David's story shows that it's not easy to pursue your Heart's Desires, or even identify them, after years of suppression.

> *Acceptance of one's life has nothing to do with resignation; it does not mean running away from the struggle. On the contrary, it means accepting it as it comes, with all the handicaps of heredity, of suffering, of psychological complexes and injustices.*
>
> —Dr. Paul Tournier

DIVINING YOUR HEART'S DESIRES

The way children are brought up in our global society discourages both visionary thinking and passionate expression. If children are taught that it is best behavior, or more 'grown up,' to keep their dreams and aspirations to themselves, then they forget about them, or disregard them as daydreams when they arise. As we get older the chores, bills, and responsibilities pile up, and heartfelt desires easily fall to the wayside, neglected and forgotten. But rest assured—your Heart's Desire is never completely extinguished. The longing for its fulfillment continues to live within you, and can do so for lifetimes. Perhaps it's barely apparent as just a tiny spark of passion, perhaps as the memory of a dream, but unless you are dead inside (which does not include anyone who reads this book), the pilot light stays on, however faintly. So, even if you can't see your inner pilot light right this minute, don't give up.

A suppressed desire can reappear as a quiet hint or a barely audible whisper. It could arise as a sudden flashback of a past feeling. Later in life, an unrealized Heart's Desire might show up as a nagging feeling of regret for paths not taken or dreams unfulfilled. No one wants to look back on life and say, "If only I had explored the one thing I really cared about." To avoid such a fate, you need to sort through the longings, needs, cravings, expectations, addictions, ego, guilt, and temptations in order to uncover and be true to your Heart's Desires. Only then can you begin the process of manifesting them as you are designed to do.

Sonia Choquette, psychic and author, teaches an exercise to help people become aware of a Heart's Desire, which begins with making a list of ten things that you desire. When people do this exercise, their initial answers usually involve wealth, beautiful children, new cars or houses, and so on. There's nothing wrong with any of that, but we need to go deeper.

The next step is to write down what you feel passionate about—what's most interesting or important to you. These answers get closer to the heart of the matter and may recall lifelong dreams, personal relationships, and untapped creativity. There often isn't much overlap

> Getting what you want has everything to do with love. Some years ago, I discovered a functional definition of love that has stood the test of time. If I love you, it is to the extent that I support you getting what you want (as long as what you want is not harmful). The easiest and most fun way to get what you want in the long run is to help others get what they want.

between the two lists. The point of such an exercise is that we often think we know what we want, and imagine that it involves getting more or better things. But if we waste energy pursuing security, pleasure, or power over others, that will distract us from manifesting our most meaningful and satisfying desires. We need to constantly review our desires and where they are coming from. Let your left brain help you to discriminate wisely!

You must be totally open and honest with yourself about all desires, without judging any of them as wrong or bad. If you are serious about being happy and giving, there is no room for denial and projection. Many of your desires may be ego-based and perhaps wildly unrealistic, but even in this they serve a purpose, they have educational value for you. Accomplishing a clear awareness of our desires can be challenging, because secret temptations can be embarrassing to admit, even to ourselves.

At one time or another we've probably all thought about dropping everything and running away. Few of us would admit to our fantasies of winning the lottery or being a ruler. When doing the soul searching to identify Heart's Desires, it's important to be thoroughly honest. If you need help going through the rigorous process of objective self-examination, find a counselor or a wise mentor to help you understand yourself more clearly.

Self-knowledge is the first step toward identifying your most profound desires. Sonia Choquette's writing and thinking exercises can help. Authentic divination provides an excellent set of tools for self-knowledge. Astrology and Numerology can reveal your innate potentials and possible liabilities, your strong tendencies, and what types of desires will be most natural for you. Any authentic divination reading or report will provide a deep inward look, while providing valuable clues about the best approach to take—in alignment with your most natural style. Divination stimulates your intuition whether your focus is on a relationship, a meaningful career, health, family, creativity, or peace of mind.

Divination can unlock the doors to "applied synchronicity."

The story of my friend Barbara illustrates how useful divination can be—in her case, to help her take a deep look at her compatibility with a romantic partner. Barbara had been seeing a wonderful man—let's call him

Bill—for a few years. They enjoyed the time they spent together, they had a lot of affection for one another, and she began to think that Bill might be the man she had been looking for to fulfill her Heart's Desire for a life partner—a desire many of us can relate to.

One challenge they had was the geographical distance between their homes. He lived an hour and a half away from the city where Barbara lived and worked. They would see each other every weekend when she would drive to Bill's ranch. It was a stunningly beautiful location; there was plenty of room for Barbara, and eventually she and Bill began to make plans for her to move in. She put her house on the market, arranged her schedule so she would only have to work in town three days a week, and got ready to move to the country.

But as the time drew nearer for Barbara to move in with Bill, he became more and more emotionally distant. He resisted any conversation that involved imagining a future with Barbara. The closer the day came, the more he withdrew. To make matters worse, Barbara's sun sign is Libra, so she is a natural communicator at heart. She loves to share her feelings and dreams and visions with people close to her. However, Bill remained as recalcitrant as ever. While he never said anything specific, Barbara's intuition was raising a red flag, and she began to doubt his commitment to being with her.

Fortuna, the ancient Goddess of Destiny, is often pictured with a nautical wheel. Divination provides both the steering wheel and the map to help you navigate the ever changing currents of your life.

In order to make better sense of what was happening, Barbara ordered one of Tarot.com's Numerology compatibility reports. It revealed that the couple would be highly compatible, but as business partners. And truly, in this area, they complemented each other very well. She thrived on change, risk, and adventure. He was more conservative, especially with money, and required stability above all. They were able to have fine intellectual exchanges, but emotions were off-limits according to his profile, and this was indeed Barbara's disconcerting experience. The reading affirmed what Barbara suspected, and she knew that this did not bode well for their relationship.

It took some time after digesting this report for Barbara to muster the courage to let go of the romantic relationship. Numerology helped Barbara face their

breakup with acceptance, not blame, and enabled her to remain true and open to what will fulfill her Heart's Desire in the relationship area. The transition was less difficult, and they are still friends.

Although Barbara found a numerology compatibility report useful, there are other forms of divination that could have helped. For instance, Heart's Desires will show up in your astrological and numerological birth charts. A divination ritual, using the I Ching, Runes, or Tarot cards, can also help to identify Heart's Desires, as well as provide timely advice. It's good to get an authentic short reading based on a query such as "What is the best approach to take vis-à-vis this [strong desire or person of interest]?"

If a Tarot card or I Ching hexagram keeps appearing, it's pointing to something important, perhaps even a Heart's Desire. On the other hand, if it repeats a message of a cautionary nature, you can interpret that as advice to stay away from what might be a downward path. When we are under the influence of strong temptations, the feeling can be intense, and a timely divination intervention can do wonders to provide clarity and fortify our resolve to raise our sights and focus on a destiny-related desire instead.

Divination can be used as a sort of litmus test—along with harmlessness—to determine if a desire is worth pursuing. If it passes both the divination and harmlessness tests, you can assume that a desire's realization would be to the good—and not just to your good, but the good of all beings. It may even be a Heart's Desire serving as a sign from above and a pilot light within, with its unfolding fulfillment as part of your Destiny. If so, go for it!

Timing is Everything

Not only does authentic divination support Self-knowledge and help us get clear about our Heart's Desires, it can help us manifest them, too. Interactive forms of divination like Tarot and the I Ching are most often used to help one make better choices. Skillful decision-making requires good information and good timing, which is supported by these divination systems.

> *The world is a series of changes, sometimes in your favor and sometimes against you. When you are in charge, do good; when you are overruled, bear it.*
>
> —Pythagoras

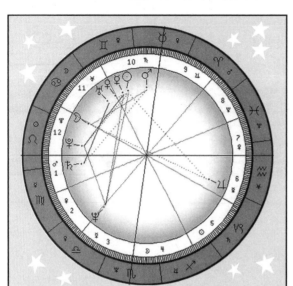

Author's Astrological Chart.

Looking back, I wish that I had been more of an Astrology buff, because my natal chart tells the whole story. I have four planets in Gemini in the 10th and 11th houses—the domains of career and humanitarianism—that form one base of a funnel pointing to Jupiter in Aquarius in the 6th house, the domain of service. What this pattern in my chart signifies is expansion through service to humanity via mass media, which is a good description of my current work!

Good timing depends on knowing when to say 'yes', and when to say 'no', when to sleep on it, when to go for it, and when to delay gratification. I know from my own experience starting and running a business that making the right decisions at the right time is the primary skill needed by a CEO. Sometimes it's best to wait a little while, to decide not to decide just yet. In the modern fast-paced world, we have trouble with timing because we think we have to fix everything and make it happen as quickly as possible. Assertiveness training is all the rage. In the martial arts, on the other hand, based as they are on the same wisdom as the I Ching, we are taught that there are times when it's best to assert oneself, but there are also times when it is advisable to do nothing, and even other times when it is advisable to retreat or run like hell.

Although it shows up most visibly in the public lives of prominent leaders and successful executives, skill in decision-making applies to every one of us, for we are the chief executive officers of our own lives.

Fortuna, the ancient Roman Goddess of Destiny, is often pictured with a nautical steering wheel (although these days she would probably be pictured with a deck of Tarot cards). As Her sacred tools, divination systems, can provide a steering device as well as a map, so that you not only know the territory, but can safely and successfully navigate the shifting currents of your life. The direction and timing of the turns you make and the attitudes you choose are what will be the primary determinant of your level of success and happiness.

Fortunately (notice how this word relates to Fortuna), we experience all kinds of coincidences in life, which are not meaningless coincidences at all. Carl Jung called these meaningful coincidences "synchronicity." They are Fortuna's subtle way of steering our attention in the right direction. The occurrence of synchronicities is part of Destiny's gyroscope. Spin a gyroscope and you have a dynamic top that never goes in a straight line, but always keeps its balance. Destiny can surprise us with unexpected twists and turns that provide synchronistic signs and clues. We have to learn to see them. This was certainly true for me.

> *You are not living by human laws but by divine laws. Expect miracles and see them take place. Hold ever before you the thought of prosperity and abundance, and know that doing so sets in motion forces that will bring it into being..*
>
> —Eileen Caddy

I was attracted to the software business in 1973, long before most people knew what the word "software" meant. My initial attraction had nothing to do with my later vision of creating software for divination. In those early years, I was fascinated by the phenomenon of software itself, the insubstantiality of it, the wizardry of its creativity in being able to turn ideas and code into experiences. And, at the time, if you could just explain it, selling software was a good way to make money.

I was so attracted to the idea of software, that I set out to learn everything about it—how it was developed, how it could be distributed and marketed. I took extra courses on programming as well as marketing. And I jumped into the field.

After seven years of this work, I began to feel bored with the business side of it, even though I had risen through the ranks to become a marketing director. I told myself that the digital world and the corporate world both felt too cold and mechanical, and few of my spiritual friends could relate to the software business. I wanted to find a new career away from computers, so that I took off on what was supposed to be a one-year sabbatical to do social work in India, to learn about myself and to explore my interest in yoga and meditation.

That sabbatical stretched for nearly three years. After working as a personal assistant to one of the world's greatest yoga teachers, followed by a stint assisting a well-known Buddhist nun on an international meditation tour, I came back to America in need of a job. After years of living a life of voluntary simplicity, my

needs were minimal, and I saw many professional possibilities. I took some vocational tests, used Richard Nelson Bolles' workbook *What Color Is Your Parachute?* and went through a lengthy process of self-appraisal. Guess what? At the end of all that soul searching, I found myself drawn back to the software business! In a moment of egoless clarity, I realized that it was actually a good fit for me and that I missed many things about it. I didn't know it then, but my affinity for software was to play a major role in the discovery of my true calling.

The expertise I gained from the software business served as the perfect platform for the unfolding of my vocational destiny, which was to invent interactive divination systems and make them available worldwide via the Internet. Even though this Heart's Desire took the form of becoming an extreme financial risk-taker and starting a business, the essence of it was a path of service that involved creative freedom in a medium that I had always been fascinated with.

> Getting clear on our Heart's Desires does not mean being attached to the form they will take.

It's not easy, or even necessary, to envision the form that our Heart's Desires will take, and we can be overly limited by looking for familiar patterns. We must learn to be open to the possibility that our dreams can take shape in unexpected ways.

Even though they usually appear as mere coincidences, synchronistic events offer us helpful signs all the time. I could have never predicted, or even visualized, the way my vocation was about to turn. In his recent book, *Synchrodestiny: Harnessing the Infinite Power of Coincidence to Create Miracles*, Deepak Chopra coined a term to describe the relationship between synchronicity and one's destiny. He calls the phenomenon "synchrodestiny"—great word for it.

As we shall see in more depth in Chapter 3, synchronicity is one of the key principles that defines how divination works. When we cast a reading from the I Ching or pick Tarot cards, we are intentionally creating a coincidence. Ultimately, there are no accidents, and the coincidence of the cards we picked or the way the coins we tossed landed has meaning that the divination system can interpret for us. I sometimes refer to divination as "applied synchronicity," which helps us keep dancing in step with our beloved unfolding Destiny.

CHAPTER 2
Troubled Times Call for Wisdom

The Hierophant
Inspiration, morality, education

The Winged Spirit Tarot
© US Games Systems, Inc.

Chaos and uncertainty are opportunities for the wise.
—Tom Peters, *Thriving on Chaos*

ancing in harmony with one's destiny is more challenging than ever. The ancient Chinese curse, "May you live in interesting times," has come true with a vengeance. Even if most who get to read this book feel relatively secure on a survival level, we live and work in an age of conflicting beliefs and mounting anxiety. Time seems to move faster and this accelerating rate of change is increasing stress to levels that threaten health and sanity.

Environmental devastation, war, global warming, weapons of mass destruction, corrupt political leaders and the rise of terrorism are examples of anxiety-producing realities we hear about in the media every day. All the while, our minds are also being bombarded by insecurity-provoking advertising and fear-mongering propaganda, making it difficult for people to remember what's meaningful and important. No wonder high levels of anxiety and self-doubt have become epidemic. No wonder cynicism is such a popular defense reaction.

> *These are times of unwitting and involuntary sacrifice. Our fantasies of infinite expansion are being called to account.*
> —Christine Payne-Towler, Tarot scholar

In addition to stirred up fears and doubt, we get countless interruptions and daily distractions that reduce our attention span, making it even more difficult for us to stay clear about what matters most to us. It is too easy to become disconnected from one's intuition and natural creativity, and extremely difficult to reconnect to these divine resources, even when it is truly necessary.

Recent studies show that several million adults in the United States suffer from Generalized Anxiety Disorder, where the ability to cope with change has broken down. The predictions of Alvin Toffler's prophetic book, *Future Shock* (published in 1970), appear to be coming true. As Toffler predicted, the pace of change has accelerated beyond the ability of normal people to manage it well.

Information overload is part of the problem. As life gets more complicated, we do need more information,

PRIESTESS

Master of two kinds of knowledge—information and intuition—the High Priestess archetype in Tarot embodies wisdom, serenity, objectivity, and intuition.

but there's often too much information to sort through. And it's often impossible to tell the reliable from the bogus. Even information we currently accept as true has a shorter lifespan, as rapid change and new discoveries make old theories and philosophies obsolete.

At the same time, if we put off decision-making while waiting for more information (as we often do), we are liable to miss valuable windows of opportunity. So, how can we determine which portions of available information are true or meaningful so that we can make good decisions in a timely manner? After all, better decision-making is what we need most if we are to successfully navigate the rapids of an information-saturated world.

Of course, there is a positive side to all this change. While changing conditions challenge us to learn and adapt, they also bring new opportunities for growth and evolution. One example of positive change is the subject matter of this book—how classical divination systems have resurfaced in new forms, including the Internet, to become available to people worldwide.

Authentic sources of esoteric wisdom support the intuitive side of our brain to help the overburdened logical side make better decisions more quickly. Divination systems make it possible for individuals to channel natural wisdom when they need it. As we shall see, the real purpose of authentic divination is not to predict the future, but rather to help us develop self-knowledge and to make better decisions in a timely manner.

Decision-Making—The Royal Skill

These days we are required to make more decisions, more quickly and accurately—before rapidly moving windows of opportunity pass us by. This is stressful, but knowing you made a good decision is the best stress relief there is. Nothing facilitates peace of mind better than knowing that you are paying attention, making the right moves at the right time, and staying in alignment with your highest good. It's all in the quality of the choices you make and your timing in making them.

Making the best decisions requires letting go of attachment to the details of imagined outcomes. Once you have made a clear decision, it's easier to have faith

in your own judgment, make a commitment and confidently take action toward the manifestation of your desire or objective.

When it comes to success and happiness, making good decisions is indeed the single most important priority. A president negotiates treaties; an investor decides to sell short; an executive changes careers to satisfy her soul or to make more money. Making timely choices is the highest-leverage activity human beings can do to benefit themselves and others. That is why good leaders and executives are rewarded so highly—it is their primary job to make good decisions that will affect lots of people.

The importance of making skillful decisions is not confined to public or corporate leaders. The lives of every one of us are filled with challenges for which there are often no easy or logical answers. Personal relationships, sensitive negotiations, conflicts of interest, timing issues and responding to traumatic events are a few examples that everyone can relate to. Even if we are not personally dealing with problems of survival, staying balanced and effective in an age of accelerating change and compounding anxiety is a daily challenge for all of us. Living without confidence in our creative ability to influence change can lead to depression, or even violent reactions, to the helpless feeling of not knowing whom to trust or what to do.

If we care about the happiness and success of everyone including ourselves, we need to get serious about improving our decision-making. Cope we must; prosper we can. So how do we learn to make life's crucial choices more creatively, rapidly and effectively? How do we come to trust ourselves more and make better choices? The answer is to cultivate wisdom.

> *God made Truth with many doors to welcome every believer who knocks on them.*
>
> —Kahlil Gibran

DEVELOPING WISDOM

Wisdom is not an easy quality to develop because it requires continuous learning and experimentation. It requires courageous questioning of what you thought you knew. It involves taking risks. Wisdom involves an interplay between two types of learning capacities—left-brain and right-brain. Logic, reason, business, policy,

and utility reside in the left brain. Creativity, intuition, inspiration, and emotion are the domain of the right brain. Wisdom originates when intuitive insights, which arise from a deeper connection to the present moment, converge with knowledge earned by the learning and logical analysis of the left brain.

Wisdom is not something you can memorize or study to learn, at least not in the conventional sense. It is not something that can be transmitted by a spiritual teacher or gleaned from the pages of a book. Wisdom arises from within the crucible of your own direct experience. It is the karmic fruit of what you learn from the choices you make and the actions you take. Wisdom is a quality of mind and soul that springs from the synergy of right-brain and left-brain processes coming together. Its development can be supported by teachers, counselors and divination systems, but ultimately wisdom arises within oneself from conscious experience that is carefully digested.

> *[Intuition] does not denote something contrary to reason, but something outside the province of reason.*
>
> —Carl Jung

Left-brain reasoning is necessary in order to operate in the world. This kind of knowledge consists of factual information based on proven observations. We are blessed by a huge body of this kind of practical information resulting from scientific discovery—knowledge that is extremely useful, and now, universally available.

We can add to our practical knowledge through reading and study—as well as our own trial and error—but we should closely examine whatever we deem as true. A belief we have accepted on faith—without question or intellectual testing—cannot be considered trustworthy. As the old proverb goes, if it seems too good to be true, it probably is. If we want to fulfill our destiny, it is our responsibility to give everything we consider believing a dose of critical reflection, and do it over again every so often even after we have adopted a belief.

Right-brain learning happens through the mysterious faculty of intuition. It is non-linear, and able to venture beyond the scope of logical analysis. This is what is referred to as the intuitive or "psychic" realm. We become conscious of our intuition the more we learn to notice and interpret synchronicities and other hidden connections. Intuition draws its insights from direct

experience in the present. It is an ability to read between the lines, a spontaneous connecting of the dots.

The cultivation of wisdom depends on the right and left brains working in harmony together. For instance, since scientific discoveries can be faithfully reproduced and science-based beliefs proven, our intuition can accept them as true without us feeling that we have to prove them for ourselves. In situations like this—in which a mundane form of intuition known as common sense is called upon—the right brain is supporting the left.

Amidha Buddha:
The Boundless Light

Wisdom also requires that left brain logic support right brain knowing. Good intuition should always make sense upon reflection. If an intuition fails the common sense test in light of things your left brain knows, then your right brain may have been hijacked by fantasy rather than intuition. It's vital to be guided by what you know to be true. No matter how spontaneously or magically an insight may arise, if it doesn't pass the common sense test, it should be considered suspect. This happens all the time. Creative types and inventors will testify to this. For every creative breakthrough there are hundreds of fanciful ideas that appeared brilliant.

Be careful to differentiate between intuitive insights and wishful thinking. Ultimately, you cannot afford to delegate your common sense testing to anyone else—counselors, psychics or ministers. They work for you!

In his book, *Practicing Wisdom*, even the Dalai Lama makes a strong point of not letting faith override intelligence.

> It is important not to be blinded by faith alone—taking everything on board on the basis of faith ... If you do, there is the danger of losing your critical faculty. Rather, the object of your faith or devotion must be discovered through a personal understanding derived through critical reflection ... Both faith and intelligence are crucial factors for our spiritual development ... For faith to have sufficient power to drive our spiritual progress, we need intelligence, a faculty that can enable us to recognize the right path and to cultivate deep insight.

The Dalai Lama goes on to point out that it's even important to reject the literal truth of a scripture,

"When it contradicts your valid experience, even if it is the word of the Buddha himself." What he points to is the critical importance of reasoning and understanding to real spiritual development. Even the Buddha stated in a sutra that people should not accept his words simply out of reverence for him. Rather, they should test them against their critical understanding and personal experience, just as a seasoned goldsmith would test the quality of the gold by subjecting it to a rigorous process of cutting, burning and rubbing.

An intuitive experience often includes what is called an *aha* moment. An 'aha' moment not only feels right, but it will usually also make sense—once you have had a chance to digest it and look at things from the new point of view. Every true 'aha' moment is enlightening. As one of my teachers, the Buddhist nun Ayya Khema, used to say, every moment of clarity and insight purifies us and predisposes us to more of the same. Little enlightenment experiences lead to new insights. The development of wisdom is cumulative.

Inviting and allowing mystical realizations that make new sense of things is one of the skills that we need in order to more skillfully manage change. This is how wisdom develops. Like dancing, you need to stay light on your feet to grow in wisdom. Using divination as a type of meditation—enhancing one's connection to the sacred without the baggage of ego interference—is one way to do that.

> Even though organized religions have declared war on divination, there are more positive references to divination in the sacred texts than negative ones (see Appendix C).

Blind Faith is a Learning Disability

When most people consider wisdom, they think in terms of acquiring it rather than developing it, as if we could borrow it from the experience of others. (Or we believe that it is not really important that we be wise, just that we be rescued or 'saved.') People seeking wisdom have traditionally turned to religion. This means focusing on scriptures and religious dogma, since church, temple and mosque have promoted doctrine and laws as the path to wisdom. When it comes to the development of wisdom, this dependence upon the written word and the insistence upon swearing allegiance to a rigid ideology full of self-limiting beliefs is a problem.

Even if religion can be, as we will see, a block to the

cultivation of wisdom, its appeal is understandable. After all, the major organized religions were each inspired by an enlightened being. This spiritual master—one who manifests his or her divine Self to a greater degree than the rest of us—shares the essence of that experience with a group of followers and shows them how to reproduce it for themselves. The transmission of mystical experience happens via oral instruction including personal guidance in experiential mystical practices like meditation. Scripture comes later. Unfortunately, while writing can transmit inspiring stories, it can never capture the essence of transformational experience.

Some of the bloodiest wars have been waged over conflicting beliefs. In Europe in the Middle Ages, a war broke out over which shoulder should be touched first when making the sign of the cross!

On top of that, none of the scriptures of today's major religions were composed by the founders, themselves. In the case of Christianity, the oldest known writings about Jesus are the epistles of Paul, the earliest of which was written around A.D. 59, thirty years after Jesus' death. It was many more years before the first of the four gospels were composed. Although he was alive at the time, Paul never met Jesus. Although his epistles contribute half of the books of the New Testament, Paul writes almost nothing about Jesus' words or life, focusing on his visions of Jesus as having risen from the dead, as the Jewish messiah prophesied by the ancient prophets.

Paul's description of Jesus—who he was and the meaning of his life and death—is based primarily upon his dreams and visions, which were not shared by Peter or James the brother of Jesus.

Paul was history's greatest missionary and his interpretation of who Jesus was won out three hundred years later when the Roman church was formed. Other sects, which were declared heretics believed that only the known sayings and deeds of Jesus accurately represented what his message and teachings were about. We can accept the interpretations of Paul or others, if we like, but in order for our personal wisdom to develop, whatever we believe needs to be a conscious and willing choice independently made by us.

For three centuries, the followers of Jesus had plenty of choices about what to believe. For more than three hundred years, there were a number of sizeable Christian sects organized around differing interpretations of the

life and teachings of Jesus, and each had different stories and scriptures to refer to. As Professor Bart Ehrman points out in his book, The *Lost Christianities: The Battles for Scripture and the Faiths We Never Knew,* prominent Christian groups in the first three centuries of the common era, included not only the followers of Paul, but the followers of James the brother of Jesus, the Ebionites, the Marcionites, the Gnostics and others.

During this period, Christian beliefs ran the gamut—from viewing Jesus as an enlightened Jewish prophet, to seeing him as a purely spiritual being, to the concept that he was both God and man. This last idea, which was promoted by the Paulists, was voted on and won out at the Council of Nicea in A.D. 325, and the other groups were officially declared "heretics." (Professor Ehrman notes that during the first three hundred years, each of these groups saw the Paulists as the heretics!)

No matter how enlightened a religion's founder was, religious groups invariably organize themselves around a political hierarchy's chosen doctrine, supported by edited scriptures. As I have noted, the problem with regard to wisdom development is that wisdom can only be cultivated through personal experience. Because of the nonverbal nature of mystical experience, instructions for following a master's example and thereby attaining wisdom are impossible to put into words. Writing is better for conveying laws, opinions and stories. Self-redemption is so personal it requires customized spiritual instruction and practices for each individual.

The personalization of spiritual practice is a central aspect of the yogic traditions of Hinduism and Buddhism, whereas direct instruction from a personal teacher, or guru, and personalized practice have always been considered necessary for serious spiritual development. During the year-and-a-half that I lived in various Indian ashrams, I learned the concept of *sadhana,* the term for the particular set of spiritual practices a seeker of wisdom adopts for her or himself, according to the type of yoga that was deemed most suitable for that individual's temperament and personality. There is no "one size fits all" mentality when it comes to Eastern religious practice.

> For anyone interested in historical details, I would recommend the works of the University of North Carolina's Professor of Religious History, Bart Ehrman. He has compiled an extensive body of research on early Christianity and the formulation of the Bible. His books on the disputes and political battles around the formation of the orthodox Christian belief system, supported by many recovered documents (some dating back 1900 years) make for fascinating reading, even for non historians.

48

Whenever I visited a new ashram in India, I would be asked why I wanted to be there. My response was, "I would like a good environment to practice my sadhana, and hope to have an audience with the guru, if possible." Although I stayed at many ashrams, never once was I asked what my sadhana was, nor was I required to participate in any particular rituals or activities, although welcome to do so. I was completely free to do my own thing, no questions asked, as well as participate in ashram services (or chores) to any extent I chose. The yogic tradition acknowledges that the development of wisdom cannot be systematized for mass consumption and provides the personal freedom necessary to develop it.

The major western religions, with their zeal for conformity of doctrine and law, do not encourage enough personal freedom to support the cultivation of wisdom, which is an inside job. Although enlightened individuals can and do arise from within a dogmatic religious society, the mystical experiences that produce sainthood or enlightenment often happen *in spite of* the rules and priorities of the religious establishment.

> **New Thought Religion**
>
> Unity, Religious Science, and Science of Mind churches—primarily Christian—also respect founders of other religions. Here the emphasis is on following Jesus' example, rather than being 'saved' by him. It focuses on love and forgiveness and union with God through 'scientific prayer' and meditation. Accessing "the Kingdom of Heaven within you" holds practical meaning for New Thought Christians.
> —Paul O'Brien, New Thought minister

Thou Shalt Believe (or Else)

Most Christian groups have organized around orthodox righteousness rather than spiritual practices designed to help people have mystical experiences of their own. In societies governed by this kind of religion, religious education consists primarily of indoctrination, supported by official interpretations of selected scriptures. In fact, according to Professor Ehrman, Christianity was the first major religion to make the importance of correct belief its central feature. As a result of this, one's relationship with the divine was supposed to be based more on beliefs than spiritual practices or experiences.

The impetus to compile a body of Christian scripture that supported an official doctrine came out of the Council of Nicea, convened in A.D. 325 by Constantine, the first Roman emperor to make Christianity a state-sanctioned religion. (As far as we can tell, Constantine continued to promote the Roman sun god and only became a Christian on his deathbed.) The formulation of orthodox doctrine was finalized later in the fourth century, as the Paulist interpretation of Jesus' life and

> *It is a characteristic of wisdom not to do desperate things.*
>
> —Henry David Thoreau

message was crystallized into the doctrine of what was to become the Roman Catholic Church.

Professor Ehrman's fascinating book and DVD series, *Lost Christianities*, points to the conversion of Constantine as one of the most significant events in all of Western history because it led to Christianity soon becoming the exclusive state religion of the Roman Empire (which stretched from Ireland to Egypt). The Christian population grew from approximately 5 percent in 300 AD to 50 percent in 400 AD, quickly growing to 90 percent, with help from the persecution of those who still followed the less organized pagan religions.

We know that at the Council of Nicea there were many Christian scriptures that were rejected as part of the official canon. Much to our historical and spiritual impoverishment, many of these were burned or have been lost. At the time, there were serious disagreements about the nature and mission of Jesus that needed to be decided upon if the Church was going to become the political force that Constantine envisioned. As we have noted, such debates had been a feature of Christian discourse during its first three hundred years. At Nicea, it is recorded by the Roman historian that competing doctrines that were represented were simply voted on. The Paulist interpretation won the most votes and the rest is history.

When one considers that defining Jesus as the prophesied Jewish messiah depends on believing that he defeated death via a physical resurrection—the central article of Paul's visionary faith—it is easy to understand why organized Christianity would require beliefs to be centrally important. For most people, including many of the early Christian groups, a dead man resurrecting himself was a difficult thing to imagine, let alone believe.

In order to support the belief in Jesus' conquest of death, it became necessary for Paul and others to come up with other paradoxical beliefs—the concept of Jesus as a sacrificial lamb who died for the world's sins, and the need for salvation from this world required the acceptance of other premises, such as the idea that Jesus is both God and man, that God is a trinity of

three persons, that Jesus fulfilled the prophecies of the older Jewish prophets, and that simply *believing* in his conquest of death was the primary requirement for salvation. These were not premises that were taught by Jesus, or even held by a majority of Christian groups. Nevertheless, these ideas became official doctrine—with disbelief in them punishable by torture and death—of what was to become the largest religion on earth for the next two thousand years.

The practice of canonizing scriptures by declaring certain writings to be the absolute unchanging truth—the "word of God"—was subsequently adopted by Judaism and Islam. (Before, the Jews had treated their scriptures as being about laws and histories.) Naturally, the process of deciding what was to be orthodox doctrine produced political struggles over the selection and editing of scriptures. Perhaps nobody foresaw how particular beliefs would come to be enforced to the extreme, often with the threat of torture and death.

Let's acknowledge that not all organized religions are close-minded, and that even those that are can make positive contributions to society. I chose to become an ordained New Thought minister because New Thought is a form of Christianity that is practice-oriented and open-minded about beliefs. As a single father I valued spiritual community for myself and my son and saw that organized religion can provide some peace and comfort in a confusing world, a reinforcement of ethics and positive values, and opportunities for charitable works and giving. It is not my intention to bash religion.

The important point is that when allegiance to doctrine is enforced in a totalitarian way, beliefs are no longer freely adopted, but instruments of control. It's no accident that the Torah, or Old Testament, with its severe rules and stories of a jealous, demanding and punitive God, is one of the oldest alphabetic texts known to man. Thus, one of the first things the early Jewish patriarchs did with writing was compile long lists of laws, which they then enforced to the letter, and we have been doing it ever since. The long-term result is that we now define faith as holding to and defending, and not questioning, certain doctrines, rather than having confidence in our own spiritual experience.

> "The Bible came to occupy a prominent place, since it was the only book many people had. But because of the lack of educated clergy, people often read the Bible with little awareness of its historical (or spiritual) context. The Bible existed, not as a mere book—however sacred—but as the only book. This situation still prevails today in many parts of the country. Several years ago, when I was house-hunting in Tennessee, I was struck by the large number of homes I saw that had a Bible but no other books."
>
> —Richard Smoley, in "The Religion of No Religion."

51

Blind adherence to "articles of faith" restricts the ability to accept the world as it is, and severely limits possibilities for creative change, including conflict resolution.

A forced allegiance to our indoctrination stunts our ability to develop our intuitive abilities in general, but most specifically in terms of connecting with the divine.

Most people never become responsible for their own beliefs about the meaning of their life or the possibility of divine experience. The masses of people believe in, and never question, the beliefs they are taught as children. As long as our beliefs are not freely chosen by us, one could say that we are limited by a spiritual learning disability. Our path to wisdom is blocked by a closed mind, a mind that is not free to experiment in its relationship with the divine, an immature mind that is not able to find out which beliefs actually work in terms of becoming wise and free from suffering.

Faith becomes defined as conforming to doctrine, rather than as confidence in one's ability to connect directly with divine wisdom—perhaps with the help of a personal guru, yoga and meditation, or a divination practice. It is interesting to note that the word 'confidence' in Latin means to have faith in oneself.

One clear historical example of how practice-based spirituality can devolve into book-based religion is the history of the Sikh religion. Sikhism's enlightened founder, Guru Nanak, began a lineage of gurus that only lasted for nine generations, according to the surviving Sikh establishment, although others did not agree that the direct transmission by a living guru tradition ever really ended. Nevertheless, the leaders of Sikh society reorganized the religion around devotion to their holy scripture, the Guru Granth Sahib, which is housed in the ornate Golden Temple in Amritsar, India. Also known as Adi Granth, the name of this book means "the greatest guru of all."

The Granth Sahib came to be thought of as the guru, but as we have seen a book can never substitute for a living master. The emphasis of spiritual development shifted from personal instruction and practice to the following of laws, including a set of rules called *the five Ks* that all orthodox Sikhs must conform to. These rules govern the cutting of hair and certain symbolic trappings of dress that must be worn at all times.

In contrast, many members of the Sikh religion split off after the death of the last official living guru. They claimed that the mantle of living spiritual leadership was passed on to the eleventh guru, with an unbroken line of living gurus persisting to this day. These sects, which include the Radha Soami and the Namdharis, have preserved the practice of initiation through oral transmission. Nevertheless, they also respect the Adi Granth—much like New Thought Christians respect the Bible or Buddhists respect the Pali Canon—but they do not require following all the rules that were set up by the prevailing religious establishment.

> *It's the repetition of affirmations that leads to belief. And once that belief becomes a deep conviction, things begin to happen.*
>
> —Muhammad Ali

Take Responsibility for Your Beliefs

From the point of view of fundamentalist religions, a person must have faith in the official words and interpretation of scriptures. To stop questioning and to hold to ancient rules and beliefs is to be trapped in a state of spiritual immaturity. Beliefs are important tools that help us make choices, but unless they are evolving in coordination with all of our learning and knowledge, they are outdated and become worse than useless. They can hold us back from the realization of our divine destiny. We have to take ownership of our beliefs and be responsible for updating them, as we learn and achieve wisdom through hard-earned experience.

Older religions like Hinduism and Buddhism have scriptures and common beliefs too, but do not depend on them for spiritual redemption. It is understood in yogic culture that no written record, "sacred" or not, can ever transmit the vibrant, magical quality of the enlightenment experience. That is unique and personal for every individual. Even today, the eastern religions acknowledge this truth, as do mystical enclaves of esoteric Christianity, the whirling dervish Sufis of Islam, and other devotion or practice-oriented paths.

To the extent that we are focused on staying true to doctrine, we will not be able to fully develop our intuition. The magic of profound spiritual experience will be less available to us as a result.

Historically, we know that Judeo-Christian-Islamic religions have enforced a strict orthodoxy demanding absolute allegiance. Differences of opinion have been

punishable by excommunication, even death. To this day some Christian and Islamic fundamentalists advocate returning to the ancient Biblical punishment of stoning people for a wide variety of sins, including loss of virginity outside of marriage, and hundreds of other moral infractions (including the use of divination).

Fundamentalism is defined by extreme allegiance to dogmatic righteousness. Extremism is characterized by the belief that the end justifies the means. This has resulted in the moral justification of violence. Witness the countless "holy wars" (the ultimate oxymoron) throughout history, including the Inquisition. Sometimes, it would seem, God wants you to kill—in spite of the fact that this is forbidden by the Ten Commandments and runs counter to the peaceful teachings of Jesus and the founders of all religions. Religious extremism leads to the worst sorts of intolerant behavior—including atrocities, torture and slaughter. Obviously, the life-and-death enforcement of official interpretations of culturally biased laws makes it more difficult for humanity to experience the qualities of peace, love and harmony that the religions' founders originally advocated.

> *I have no objections to churches so long as they do not interfere with God's work.*
>
> —Brooks Atkinson, Pulitzer Prize-winning journalist and critic

With no trust in or support for a direct experience of the divine, the cultivation of wisdom is retarded. This is more of a problem today because of the accelerating rate of change and accompanying increase in stress. We need a more flexible and adaptable approach to living that only wisdom, based on personal surrender to direct experience, can provide. This requires a well-developed intuitive faculty, not blind adherence to a set of rules designed to control people. With false promises of easy salvation backed up by horrific threats if you don't believe in scriptural interpretations, fundamentalist cults make it virtually impossible for their followers to learn how to trust their god-given intuition.

Religions that Support Wisdom Cultivation

As we have seen, there are still some religions that support the intuitive experience of the inquiring mind through training, rather than pinning one's hopes for liberation on blindly following doctrine and prayer. Buddhism, Hinduism and Taoism are more experiential than the Western religions that dominate the world

today. The emphasis in these Eastern paths has been much more on practice rather than on belief—specifically, meditation or other yoga, for the sake of direct experiences leading to personal transformation. This requires a different, more living kind of faith—a growing confidence in one's own ability to directly experience the divine.

Taoism is fascinating because it seems to produce good results and is the least dogmatic of all the major spiritual paths. I deeply appreciate the image of the eccentric wandering Taoist who shares his company with Nature. At the very least, he is a metaphor for the meandering parts of all our lives—the unexpected turns and magical surprises. When I was composing our original I Ching text for I-Ching.com, I spent a lot of time with the 56th hexagram, Lu, which I entitled the Wanderer. A couple of the lines are: "Any journey is ruled by the twin houses of mystery and discovery. Each new day is launched on a fresh landscape, which reaches out to grab our full attention." Such is the journey of life from a Taoist point of view.

Buddhism is more structured than Taoism, but it also supports freedom of belief. Anyone who has spent time in Buddhist cultures quickly notices that its practical philosophy improves people's ability to manage change with grace. Once, I practiced in a monastery in the poorest part of Burma, one of the poorest countries of the world. For all its problems, it is a place where Buddhist meditation is still widely supported and encouraged. The cheerfulness and generosity of the materially impoverished population was nothing short of remarkable.

Insofar as it is focused on the present moment, divination is a form of meditation. This book is based on the idea that divination can add value for people who are looking for a mature spiritual practice that cultivates wisdom. Most followers of Wicca, the fastest growing spiritual movement in the United States, include Astrology, Tarot and other forms of divination among their attunement practices.

Wicca is based on direct personal experience and connection to the divine, through a nurturing attunement with nature. In her book *Witch Crafting,* Phyllis Curott

Buddhism has the characteristics of what would be expected in a cosmic religion of the future: It transcends a personal God, avoids dogmas and theology; it covers both the natural and spiritual, and it is based on a religious sense aspiring from the experience of all things, natural and spiritual, as a meaningful unity.

—Albert Einstein

Wiccan Beliefs

1. *Wiccan Rede* states, "As long as it harms none, do as you Will"—the Wicca equivalent of the Golden Rule.

2. The Law of Return is known as the Threefold Law. Any energy you put out will come back to you times three—good or bad.

3. A Wiccan takes responsibility to prevent what can be prevented, and accepts the outcome of the decision not to do so.

4. The Ethic of Constant Improvement encourages Wiccans to always pursue growth and development of the body, mind, and spirit.

5. The Ethic of Attunement is the foundation of the Wiccan's connection to nature, as well as spirit.

writes about a single belief that describes all neo-pagan, Wiccan, and magic-based religions as *immanent divinity*. Immanent (not to be confused with imminent, which means inherent) divinity, means "the Divine is everywhere present in the world. Everything that exists in the natural world—you, other people, plants, animals, earth, sky, air, water, weather, moon, sun, stars, galaxies, everything—is a form, an embodiment, of divine energy. And everything is interconnected by that sacred energy." One of the forms of the divine intelligence that operates within and through us is intuition, an idea that fits nicely into the Wiccan point of view.

This kind of religion is highly personal, and most Wiccans do their spiritual practices on an entirely individual basis. There is no church, power hierarchy, authority, or scripture. While Wiccans will sometimes gather to collaborate in working with divine energy, or to share experiences, the most important work is done alone. One's personal relationship with Divine energy—arrived at through intuition, practice, direct experience and sometimes divination—is the religion.

Because divination is a meditation that increases intuitive understanding and wisdom, it only makes sense that divination was an integral part of spiritual practices like Hinduism, Buddhism, Taoism and Wicca—religions which date from the earliest times. Used properly, it can produce the same experience of divine guidance that was cultivated and taught by the founders of all the major religions.

BELIEF SYSTEMS NEED TO EVOLVE

Our beliefs are powerful operating assumptions that we rely on to make choices. They are useful, even essential. They can also become obsolete or restrictive, but are not required to be permanent and unchanging. After all, we are learning beings who never get anything completely right. In the Zen Buddhist tradition, there is an admonition, "Cease to cherish opinions." From a Zen point of view, all beliefs are opinions—operating assumptions subject to change. Even though they cannot be proven objectively, we accept them as true because they can be useful. But we have to be careful

because the power of believing is strong. Proof of the power of beliefs is the fact that placebos are 30 percent effective—better than many drugs on the market!

Our beliefs condition every attitude we have, and every decision we make. An important question, which is hardly ever asked, is to what extent are we consciously choosing our beliefs? How well do we learn, thereby allowing our beliefs to evolve for the sake of developing greater wisdom? Let's take a look at the nature of beliefs, how we acquire them, what they are useful for, and what their limiting effects can be if we are not careful.

Many people believe what they are taught to believe, including the strange notion that having a stubborn unchanging belief system is a sign of character. The most powerful religions glorify their scripture as "the word of the one true God," or in the case of secular religions like communism, the one correct utopian vision. For most people, believing in doctrines is what the word "faith" has come to mean. However, as Edith Hamilton (author of *Mythology*) put it, "Faith is not belief. Belief is passive. Faith is active." In other words, we must become responsible for our own beliefs.

An unwavering scripture-based faith is considered by fundamentalists to be important enough to defend violently. But blind adherence to "articles of faith" restricts the ability to accept the world as it is, and severely limits possibilities for creative change, including conflict resolution. In the context of fear-based programming, where survival is the priority, fiercely defending one's limited beliefs as if they were sacred boundaries can seem to make sense, however.

Like absolute power, black-and-white righteousness corrupts. Despite the utterances of self-proclaimed prophets, no one can be absolutely certain about the objective truth of any belief. It is a tragic use of energy to try to convince others or ourselves that we are absolutely right, much less pummel others into pledging their allegiance. Humility is a much better spiritual investment.

Most humans are so heavily programmed in a belief system that they are afraid to look outside the box of what they've been taught, even if it doesn't make any sense to them. They are trapped because they have been

> **"Do you really believe in this stuff?"**
>
> As one who develops divination software, this is a question I am asked. Here's how I respond: "It's not about believing in anything. To benefit from a divination experience, the only thing you need to believe in is your own common sense. Divination is a good way to stimulate your intuition to think outside the box about problems that logic can't handle. If your beliefs prevent you from approaching divination with an open mind, it won't work for you. Either divination stimulates your intuition and creativity, or it doesn't. Give it a sincere try. If it works for you, terrific—but you are not required to adopt any beliefs for it to do so."
> —Paul O'Brien

taught that anything counter to their religion's official doctrine is the devil testing their faith! The development of intuitive powers is always stunted by a closed mind. In truth, there are many paths to God and they can be as personal—or even impersonal—as an individual's unique temperament might require. For the best spiritual results, we need to approach the Divine in ways that feel right to us, without guilt or fear entering in.

Intuition development and wisdom depend on having faith in yourself and your divine heritage as a being made in the image of the divine. Fortunately, there are people who are able to achieve enough psychological and spiritual maturity to break through the trance-like limitations of their indoctrination. They are able to transcend their childhood programming, and become free to choose and live by beliefs that ring true for them. This doesn't mean that they reject everything they have ever been taught. Far from it. But these people have met the challenge of learning how to trust in the divine intelligence that lives deep inside of themselves and every living thing. They know how to access the kingdom of heaven within themselves through their own intuition.

Make no mistake, beliefs and opinions are necessary in order to operate in this world. This is why it behooves us to choose wisely. In terms of happiness and success, mature beliefs simply work better. The key to developing them lies in consciously choosing our beliefs, staying flexible in our ability to learn and adapt, and exercising the freedom to shed old ones that we discover are no longer valid. Trust yourself! To the extent that you are interested in true freedom and wisdom, you will let your beliefs evolve.

Ego-inspired efforts to be "right" give rise to biases that impair our ability to perceive clearly, learn new things, navigate change, and get along with other people. Nobody likes a self-righteous person, even when we agree with them! How often do humans alienate or reject others because their opinions are different? Some of the bloodiest wars in history were fought over simple differences of opinion. In the Middle Ages, a war was once fought over which shoulder should be touched first when making the sign of the cross!

> *The power of intuitive understanding will protect you from harm until the end of your days.*
> —Lao Tzu

If we are going to manage our way through difficult times of accelerating change, it is vital that each of us take responsibility for what we believe, and develop our own intuitive abilities. We must be willing to exchange the illusory pursuit of absolute righteousness for the freedom to learn and grow, even as we occasionally stumble.

Core Beliefs

As naive children, we naturally imitate and adopt the beliefs of parents and other early childhood role models. These operating assumptions worked for us then—if only to make us feel more secure. Unfortunately, many of our infantile interpretations about the nature of the world become lodged in our subconscious. Counselors call these our core beliefs. They no longer make sense for us as adults, even if they did serve a purpose to protect us as children. Since they still reside in our subconscious mind, they cause us to unwittingly make the same immature choices over and over. And there's nothing we can do about except to become highly self-aware, because until then we don't even know what our core beliefs are!

One example of a core belief I adopted early in life was the idea that I had to be perfect to be loved. As a child, believing this helped me make sense of a family life that was not emotionally nurturing. But when I became an adult, this assumption made it difficult for me to succeed in my relationships and career. Everything in my life was limited or negatively impacted by this core belief, which was basically a fear that there was something wrong with me, that I was not good enough.

Eventually, through deep emotional work, I was able to recognize and name my core belief. Once understood, I was able to take the necessary personal risks to move beyond it. After I became aware of the limiting effects of this core belief, I noticed it more often. This allowed me to chip away at it and eventually replace it with more realistic and flexible beliefs about myself that have attracted much happier results.

Awareness is more than half the battle, and without it we will certainly stay stuck. Our beliefs must be subject

---

Divination can help you:

- Make decisions that logic can't handle
- Reduce stress around life's changes
- Better manage sensitive relationships and social situations
- Develop superior timing
- Access creative insight and intuitive power
- Achieve well-rounded personal success

to change, or personal development stops, because life is a gradual awakening and a continuous educational process. Spiritual maturity has far more to do with the shedding of childish beliefs than the self-righteous defense of any beliefs. Arrogant narrow-mindedness is a major enemy of spirituality. Limiting one's freedom to explore stunts the development of intuition and wisdom. Spiritual maturity requires a growing trust in our ability to intuitively tune into divine order, and get in sync with our destiny.

BEYOND THE LIMITATIONS OF REASON

Reason is a very useful faculty, but when we try by means of the left brain alone to figure out the workings of the universe—or even to conduct a relationship with another human being—we fall short. Logic plays a significant role in penetrating some of nature's secrets by taking things apart and seeing what they are made of. This is good, but intuition helps us make discoveries beyond the domain of rational processes, not by taking things apart, but by creating new combinations. And wisdom, as we have seen, requires the synergy of both sides of the brain.

An intuitive awakening lies at the root of not only every religion, but also every major scientific discovery. Why should religions exist if not to cooperate with such an experience? Otherwise, it's just a stealthy form of totalitarianism. And why does the scientific establishment seem to lack respect for intuition, by not giving it the credit it deserves for most of science's greatest discoveries?

Part of the problem is that intuition is mysterious and impossible to measure in a scientific way. Its messages are rarely obvious, and never quantifiable, because it operates on a frequency that is higher and finer than the ordinary consciousness that would measure it. Intuition communicates by means of a vague hunch, a meditation insight, a dream, or some compelling desire. It may take the form of a symbol, a creative inspiration, or a feeling of certainty about the best solution. It can happen via seemingly random coincidences or as the deliberate result of stopping and looking at things from

> "I'm convinced that we can write and live our own scripts more than most people will acknowledge. I also know the price that must be paid. It's a real struggle to do it. It requires visualization and affirmation. It involves living a life of integrity, starting with making and keeping promises, until the whole human personality the senses, the thinking, the feeling, and the intuition are ultimately integrated and harmonized."
>
> —Steven Covey, Author of *The 7 Habits of Highly Effective People.*

a wider point of view, which is one of the functions of divination.

Divination also operates on a higher frequency, one that allows the intuitive faculties of heart and soul to lead your life's direction. You need to have an open mind, to think outside the box of your current beliefs, in order to hear the nonintrusive voice of wise counsel. Through the active stimulation of your intuition you have your own personal channel for guidance from above.

> Truth is the daughter of Inspiration; analysis and debate keep the people away from Truth.
> —Kahlil Gibran

A general challenge with intuition is that it is difficult to conjure up on demand. With the possible exception of an authentic divination experience, intuitive insights tend to spontaneously pop into the stream of normal consciousness when we least expect them. An intuitive insight, or epiphany, can manifest in many ways—from a spontaneous hunch to a fully developed idea. It is usually a bit surprising, and sometimes so subtle we don't notice it for what it is. It may arrive as a brilliant idea, a sudden feeling of certainty about the best path to take, or as a seemingly outrageous coincidence.

Like an improvisational dance, the movements of intuition are not bound by strict rules or black-and-white ideas of what is right. Anyone with a healthy body and a willingness to try can be moved by music to kick up her heels, and every such dance will be unique. Those who are experienced dancers feel confident enough to flow with the music. Letting yourself be guided by your intuition in the dance of life can become just as fluid and uplifting.

A divination practice will help you go with the flow by stimulating and supporting the following wisdom-development factors: self-knowledge, mental clarity, skillful detachment, focused relaxation, more dependable intuition and better timing.

- **Self-Knowledge:** The big picture reports of Astrology and Numerology reveal innate tendencies, potentialities and challenges in an objective way.

- **Mental Clarity:** When a divination ritual is used to address a perplexing issue or situation, the first step is to write it down. Articulating exactly what you are dealing with makes it easier to get clear about what it means, and what kind of results you want.

> *I could not say I believe. I know! I have had the experience of being gripped by something that is stronger than myself, something that people call God.*
>
> —Carl Jung

- **Skillful Detachment:** The process of consulting an oracle separates the inquiring mind from the issue at hand; it creates a healthy distance between you and your subject. The more detached you are, the less threatening your dilemma appears, and the less that fear is able to impact your interpretation. Your mind is able to see things from a wider perspective, taking advantage of creative new ideas that arise.

- **Focused Relaxation:** It's easy to worry that any decision we make will turn out to be a mistake. This anxious feeling works against you, making it more difficult to achieve clarity or objectivity. A state of focused relaxation, supported by a divination ritual, is ideal for intuition and creativity. Divination aligns the conscious, subconscious and super-conscious parts of your mind to coordinate gracefully with divine intelligence.

- **More Dependable Intuition:** Divination invites intuitive insights to arise from within you. A reading provides a structured outlet for the universe to express itself through timeless principles. No matter how the message is delivered—in writing or the spoken word—it's not the words themselves but your interpretation of them that activates your intuition. Although readings are often uncannily accurate, the deeper value comes from your use of intuition to read between the lines, to learn what rings true for you.

- **Better Timing:** In this age of accelerating change, we can easily feel bewildered. Managing change depends upon a good sense of timing. Divination makes it easier for us to notice and take advantage of the synchronicities in our lives, enhancing our ability to stay in sync and make the right moves at the right time for greater success and fulfillment.

The benefits of spiritual development through the use of divination systems are available to everyone. But if divination can offer so much, how does it work? How do these tools stimulate and support our intuition? The next chapter explains how divination works its magic in psychological detail. May greater wisdom be the result of our understanding!

CHAPTER 3
How Divination Systems Work

THE STAR

The Star
Hope, idealism, grace

Palladini Tarot
© US Games Systems, Inc.

Human beings must be known to be loved; but Divine beings must be loved to be known.

—Pascal

The word *coincidence* describes the situation in which two or more events come together in time. In common usage the term carries the connotation that although things may seem and feel like they were arranged, their concurrence was basically a meaningless accident, as in "just a coincidence."

> *Coincidences are God's way of remaining anonymous.*
>
> —Bill Moyers

People who use divination, on the other hand, know that ultimately there are no accidents, and that coincidences are not meaningless. They also understand that coincidences can be useful as signs from above, if one knows how to interpret the signs.

In reality, every moment is a confluence of coincidences. Your very existence is the result of a multitude of coincidences — your mother and father getting together, the particular set of sperm and egg, supported by ovulation and fertility, that produced you! Your existence is the result of many coincidental elements, but that does not mean that you are not meaningful or important.

The human ability to notice and decipher the meaning of coincidental events and natural occurrences—the proverbial "signs and omens" of scriptures—is well documented across cultures throughout human history. It is a universal folk practice that has survived even in modern parts of the world. If, for example, you're debating whether or not to take a trip to Italy, and you win an Italian phrase book in a raffle, you might interpret that event as a sign to go.

The Bible contains countless examples of the reading of signs and omens to interpret God's will—one is the story of Gideon who asks God to give him a specific sign of an unusual nature, which he receives, to confirm what he thought was God's decision for him (Judges 6:36-40). Some excellent books have been written about the interpretation of signs and omens, and a few are listed in our bibliography.

Divination systems, some of which are almost as ancient as reading signs and omens, take a more deliberate approach. They were invented to generate coincidences that do not depend upon external events, which can then be reliably interpreted. A system like Tarot, or its more ancient cousin, the I-Ching, involves the deliberate production of a coincidental pattern—the cards you happen to pick at that time, or the coins you toss. The pattern consist of symbols—the images on the cards, the mix of yin and yang lines in I Ching—which have been interpreted by sages to help you further your depth of understanding in order to know yourself and/ or make a decision.

Unlike the interpretation of signs and omens, the use of a divination system does not rely on psychic ability. Throughout history society's leaders turned to divining specialists—shamans, seers and oracles such as the famous oracle of Delphi—who used some type of divination system to create a pattern that could be interpreted to give advice regarding important challenges, opportunities and trends. For hundreds of years, the power of divination rituals was reserved for the limited few who had power and money, and everyone worshipped at the altar of Destiny.

Tyche: Goddess of Fortune. Tyche was highly regarded by the residents of ancient Greece. They honored, worshiped and celebrated her as their link to fortune, good luck, and success.

In classical times humans personified Destiny as a powerful goddess, and made great efforts to stay in her good graces. The Greeks called her Tyche. To the Romans she was Fortuna, the Goddess of Fortune, good and bad. Her symbols were a nautical steering wheel and a horn of plenty. To stay in sync with this original Lady Luck, it was necessary to let her steer the course and to follow her signals. For the most part, this required paying attention to signs and omens, the meaningful coincidences or synchronicities of daily life. By learning to notice and interpret patterns, one would develop one's intuition and improve one's fortunes.

Systems of divination provided humanity with a more reliable way to decipher the will of the gods, because they include a body of knowledge to guide our interpretation. The inspired knowledge of astrological signs, I-Ching hexagrams and Tarot archetypes was codified by ancient sages in order to satisfy our natural desire to make sense of human situations and relationships, to help us develop better timing that is in sync with nature, and as a result make better decisions in the most important areas of our lives.

> We are Divine enough to ask and we are important enough to receive.
>
> —Wayne Dyer

Through divination systems, humanity has been gifted with symbolic languages to interpret divine will. The symbols and archetypes that form the heart of all divination systems represent the dynamics of human life, including social and political interaction. Because it employs the language of archetypes and symbols, a divination ritual is more than a meditation technique. It can stimulate insights, provide timely advice and direction from the divine.

In my experience as a meditation teacher, I have heard prayer described as talking to God, with meditation as listening. Since divination is a process of not only communing with the divine but also interpreting divine will, it is a form of meditation that also delivers insights and advice. This type of meditative listening has a distinct advantage, because it is possible to receive information from the Divine when there is an organized language of symbols that we can interpret coming back to us, via the magic of a coincidental pattern we are generating for that purpose.

The academic question of how divination works has been taken up by a wide array of people, from philosophers to educators, psychologists to skeptics. Opinions have come from a broad spectrum of self-appointed experts—from New Age gurus to religious fundamentalists. Some fundamentalists purport the "fallen angel" theory—that the devil possesses diviners in order to lead people away from God.

Then there's the order-out-of-chaos theory promulgated by skeptics: We have such an urgent need to find order for ourselves in this chaotic world, that we are naively susceptible to inventing meaning in an oracle's random patterns. Humanity's greatest psychologist, however, was able to reconcile the scientific and the mystical, while advancing the sophistication of psychology in the process. His name was Carl Gustav Jung.

Carl Gustav Jung

Carl Jung was an avid user of astrology, as evidenced by this excerpt of a letter to B.V. Raman, a world-renowned Hindu astrologer, about Astrology and Jung's Synchronicity principle.

"Since you want to know my opinion about astrology I can tell you that I've been interested in this particular activity of the human mind for more than 30 years.

"As I am a psychologist, I am chiefly interested in the particular light the horoscope sheds on certain complications in the character. In cases of difficult psychological diagnosis I usually get a horoscope in order to have a further point of view from an entirely different angle.

"I must say that I very often found that the astrological data elucidated certain points which I otherwise would have been unable to understand. From such experiences I formed the opinion that astrology is of particular interest to the psychologist, since it contains a sort of psychological experience which we call "projected"—this means that we find the psychological facts as it were in the constellations.

"This originally gave rise to the idea that these factors derive from the stars, whereas they are merely in a relation of synchronicity with them."

JUNG'S INSIGHT

Despite the skepticism of the religious and scientific establishment, the perceived gap between the empirical and the mystical has been closing now for over a century. Major credit for bringing these two camps within hailing distance must go to the founder of depth psychology, Carl Jung. Jung has done more for the understanding and promotion of divination than any other scientist. As part of his psychology, Jung made it a point to study the world's religions, mythologies, and divination systems, rather than to focus on pathologies, and simply dismiss the spiritual as irrational or irrelevant.

Sigmund Freud (who also used the Tarot) took an early interest in Jung's ideas. The men compared and debated ideas for years through correspondence. Freud described to Jung his theory of the unconscious mind—the reservoir of forgotten or repressed energies and experiences, often of a sexual nature, that reappear in adulthood as the various kinds of neuroses. But Jung's psychology would not only focus on psychological forces emanating from an individual subconscious, but also from what he termed our *collective unconscious.*

Jung explained how this collective unconscious included mythologies and belief systems inherited from the culture. This collective unconscious was a sort of psychic reservoir of accumulated knowledge, cultural conditioning that informs all of us, and in fact defines who we

are as a species. The following is a bit of Jung's explanation of his ideas from *The Archetypes and the Collective Unconscious:*

> While the personal unconscious is made up essentially of contents which have at one time been conscious, but which have disappeared from consciousness through having been forgotten or repressed, the contents of the collective unconscious have never been in consciousness, and therefore have never been individually acquired but owe their existence exclusively to heredity. Whereas the personal unconscious consists for the most part of complexes, the content of the collective unconscious is made up essentially of archetypes.

Jung's theory of the collective unconscious made the entire unconscious realm much larger—and considerably more positive—than Freud's vision of a dark, foreboding nether land of demons and insatiable sexual hunger, ever eager to overcome our will and devour us.

ARCHETYPES

Jung's collective unconscious is populated by what he called *archetypes*. His fascination with divination systems like the I Ching, Tarot and Astrology stemmed from his perception that each of them comprised a balanced set of universal archetypes, and that they actually worked!

The way Jung saw archetypes was similar to Plato's concept of Forms—the ideal forms that provide the templates for all of nature, including human beings. Jung took this concept, refined it, and applied it to his formulation of depth psychology. Jungian archetypes are the common landscape of attributes and psychological forces that human consciousness is shaped by.

Individuals manifest different archetypal qualities in different proportions, but to some degree the energy or attitude of every archetype is contained within everyone of us. There is something reassuring in knowing that we all contain different combinations of the same stuff— the same instincts, desires, needs, impulses and fears. Viewed positively, this means we all share the same great potentials; only the proportions of factors are distributed

Being conscious of how you express energetic archetypes allows you to guide them in a positive direction.

Zeus

The gods of ancient Greece and Rome—mythological personalities manifesting some powerful quality or characteristic—were personifications of archetypes, often appearing in dreams. Their power over the human psyche was enormous.

differently. We also have all the same problematic tendencies too—again in different proportions.

Astrology, when properly understood, illustrates the universal nature of archetypes. Because of the tabloid "what's your sign" treatment by popular media, most people don't realize that according to real Astrology, everyone has each of the twelve signs active in their chart—in different placements and proportions for different individuals.

Archetypes represent qualities of consciousness or energy that inform human experiences, situations and roles. For instance, when we think of a Queen as an archetype, we are thinking not of an actual queen, but of feminine energy in a position of great influence. According to a Jungian understanding of archetypes, such queen energy is one element within every individual's psyche, as is every other archetype. One of the Queen cards in Tarot, for instance, could be referring to a personal realm or social context—like a nurturing mother.

Throughout the world there are many different sets of archetypal images which are modified by culture, and no single representational system is the correct one for everybody. Also, the use of archetypes to understand personal dynamics is more art than science. In fact, Jung believed that archetypes, by definition, cannot be pinned down. Due to the fact that they reside in the collective unconscious, they can only be expressed. If a behavior or action is consistently present across cultures and throughout history, it is a manifestation of a universal archetype.

Jung explained that archetypes have a dark side as well as a positive side, and he called this dark element the shadow. The shadow is a fitting image for all that humanity represses, fears or denies in itself. Shadow energy can emerge most powerfully when an individual is ignorant of her or his own psychology, and it usually manifests as a projection of evil onto others. As Laurens van der Post, a friend to Jung for sixteen years, writes in *Jung and the Story of Our Time:*

> [Jung] called... the "shadow" a pattern that had at its disposal all the energies of what man

had consciously despised, rejected, or ignored in himself. One sees immediately how aptly the term was chosen, because it is an image of what happens when the human being stands between himself and his own light. ...The trouble started only when the part of the human personality which was conscious behaved as if it were the whole of the man. There was nothing this unconscious world abhorred more than one-sidedness. ...Coming to terms with the shadow, the problem of reconciling the opposites in a whole greater than their parts, was an ultimate goal of his seeking.

Self-integration is one way of stating an overall goal of psychological healing. Jung's psychology used the conscious mind to mediate the mysterious contents of the unconscious, and bring more of the shadow into the light. Archetypes in and of themselves are neither positive nor negative. Like electricity, they are awesome sources of power that cannot be fully understood, and which must be carefully applied, in order to be healing rather than destructive. If the human ego identifies too much with an archetype—is "overshadowed" by it—rather than consciously tapping its energy, serious problems can result.

No matter how conscious we are, difficulty and pain will occur in life. Sometimes the only power we have is in the way we choose to respond. People are referring to archetypes when they say, "I don't know what came over me... I was not myself." Jung acknowledged the destructive power of archetypal energies when they operate outside of awareness, and take over to the point that an individual becomes out of control. He realized that if archetypal forces within the psyche are not recognized, respected, and channeled carefully, an individual's sanity, if not his life, could be in danger. Hitler, Stalin and all the other tyrants throughout history have personified the destructive power of archetypal energy when it overpowers and destroys the individual, in extreme cases taking with it millions of other innocent beings.

Awareness and respect are required for the skillful channeling of archetypal energies. Only when we recognize an archetype operating within or through us, are we

"No matter how much of a mess we may have made of our lives, it is always possible to tap into the part of the soul that is universal, the infinite field of pure potential, and change the course of our destiny. This is synchro-destiny—taking advantage of this connection between the personal soul and the universal soul to shape your life."
—Deepak Chopra, *The Spontaneous Fulfillment of Desire*.

Jung and the Suits of Tarot

Significant work has been done correlating Jungian archetypes and psychological conditions to the Tarot deck. In his last book *Man and His Symbols*, Jung wrote, "Four functional types correspond to the obvious means by which consciousness obtains its orientation to experience. Sensation (i.e. sense perception) tells us that something exists; thinking tells you what it is; feeling tells you whether it is agreeable or not; and intuition tells you whence it comes and where it is going." These four states have been correlated to the suits of the Tarot as follows:

TYPE	SUIT	ELEMENT
Intuition	Wands	Fire
Feeling	Cups	Water
Thinking	Swords	Air
Sensation	Coins	Earth

able to channel the energy carefully. The art of powerful living is to be able to connect our unconscious power centers—the archetypes—with conscious choices, commitments and actions. This is how we become more of all we can be, and develop greater self-knowledge and integrity, the springboards for wisdom and success in life. Awareness plus effort was central to Jung's psychotherapeutic style. They are also a result and requirement of successful divination, an ancient self-therapeutic approach which Jung was the first psychologist to explain.

For deeper information on the Jungian theory of archetypes or the Shadow, see Carl Jung's collected works, edited by Joseph Campbell in *The Portable Jung*.

A Balanced Set of Archetypes

Our need for greater spiritual awareness and better intuitive decision-making has spawned the invention of brand new divination systems, available for sale in toy stores as well as New Age book stores. By definition, a divination system—whether it is called angel cards, soul cards, stichomancy or whatever—contains a set of archetypes. In most cases of newly invented divination systems, this is represented by a deck of cards. Some sets are more inspired than others.

For a divination system to be a useful tool for reflection, its set of archetypes needs to be balanced between light and shadow, as is the case with the classical systems we focus on in this book. Numerology, Astrology, Tarot, I Ching and Runes predate the age of marketing and they pass the test, instinctively reflecting a balanced range of human experience, including the darker tendencies of human experience. A collection of warm-fuzzy archetypes might make people feel good—and therefore sell better—but it will not serve as an accurate

reflector of human conditions, or a good tool for decision-making.

A system of archetypes needs to be a complete and balanced set of universal forms or ideas. For instance, the I Ching offers sixty-four primary archetypes—in the form of calligraphic images and associated text (our website, I-Ching.com, also has original paintings for each hexagram)—each representing a unique situation or attitude related to personal relations, business dealings, social situations and the like. For example, the twelfth hexagram P'i or Standstill is described as follows: "Heaven is above, drawing farther and farther away, while the earth below sinks farther into its depths. It is a time of standstill and decline" (Wilhelm/ Baynes version). One would never find the expression of such dire straits in the cards of most newly invented divination decks, even though this represents a common human experience that we have to deal with from time to time.

Like the I Ching, the other four classical divination systems reflect a realistic proportion of life's shadow elements, and as a result can offer useful advice on how to deal with challenging situations. Runes represent the range of human experiences in a set of twenty-four inscribed stones. The rune hieroglyphic named Hagalaz, or hail, for instance, describes sudden dramatic change, disaster, loss and destruction.

Tarot decks contain seventy-eight cards, each representing an archetype or universal human condition. Each card has a shadowy aspect along with a forward-moving message. This is easy to see, starting with the first card of the Tarot deck, the Fool. While this image is now usually interpreted as signifying innocence and openness, the character in older Tarot decks is portrayed as inept, uneducated and ridiculous—in short, as foolish. Tarot offers a particularly rich matrix of archetypes. Every card has a numerological component as well as an astrological component. Tarot's twenty-two trump cards also reflect the twenty-two highly symbolic characters of the Hebrew alphabet.

Probably the best-known set of archetypes is Astrology's collection of the twelve signs, houses and the planets, which represent elements of human nature,

Wands

Fire

Cups

Water

Swords

Air

Coins

Earth

with both positive and shadow qualities. For instance the Leo character, which can be seen as a generous benefactor, can also express egocentricity and arrogance. Another classical system, Numerology, assigns meanings to numbers. Based on an understanding that the entire universe displays numerical properties, Numerology's meanings can be described by a base set of numbers. For instance, the number 11 represents intuition, idealism, invention, insensitivity, and fanaticism—a list of characteristics that includes darker manifestations.

It cannot be overemphasized that archetypes are metaphorical, not literal. One does not expect to become Queen of a monarchy because a queen card is drawn. Likewise, physical death is not the meaning of the Death card, as those who fear death could imagine.

The Beltway Snipers of 2002 were a prime example of literally interpreting a Tarot archetype. The Death card was found at the scene of one of their random shootings, with the words "Policeman, I am God" written on the back of the card. Occult groups around the country responded appropriately, pointing out that, despite the killer's use of it, the Death card actually means transformation, and is often seen as indicative of a positive event. *ABC News* even published a special report called "Tarot Novice?" by Michael James. The author wrote, "If a serial sniper sought by police left the 'death' tarot card found near a shooting scene in Maryland, he or she likely doesn't have much of an understanding of tarot...." Indeed, when I was asked by the press to comment, based on my position as founder of Tarot.com, I stated my suspicion that the sniper might be subconsciously using the Death card to project his own death wish (a wish that is coming true at the time of this writing by means of a death sentence).

The Synchronicity Principle

Jung not only articulated the role of archetypes in the subconscious, dreams, and divination, he defined a second factor to explain the "meaningful coincidence" of divination systems, which he named *synchronicity*. Jung first used this term publicly in 1930 at Richard Wilhelm's funeral in his description of how the I Ching works. Synchronicity relies on a subtle relationship that

> "Synchronicity gives us a sense of hope, a sense that something bigger is happening out there than what we can see, which is especially important in times like this when there's so many reasons for despair. If your belief system is such that intuition and synchronicity are real and significant, you will notice them. If your belief system is that they're hogwash, you won't."
>
> —Carolyn North in *Synchronicity: The Anatomy of Coincidence.*

74

exists in time—between two or more different events, which could include inner events of insight or creative inspiration synchronizing with the outer events of one's life. Jung gave credit to Albert Einstein as his inspiration for the theory of synchronicity. Like no scientist before or since, Carl Jung explored the territory connecting objective behavior with a person's inner experience, including the spiritual dimension.

In Jung's essay entitled "Synchronicity, An Acausal Connecting Principle," he contrasted the Western mind-set—influenced by early Greek philosophy with its focus on cause and effect—with the Eastern perspective, which views details only as part of a whole.

> This ... involves a certain curious principle that I have termed 'synchronicity,' a concept that formulates a point of view diametrically opposed to that of causality. Since the latter is merely statistical truth and not absolute, it is a sort of working hypothesis of how events evolve one out of another, whereas synchronicity takes the coincidence of events in space and time as meaning something more than mere chance, namely, a peculiar interdependence of objective events among themselves as well as with the subjective (psychic) states of the observer or observers.

To Jung, the Eastern approach provides a more holistic viewpoint, reaching beyond the linear approaches and tunnel vision of the unassisted intellect. Jung pointed to a power of discernment that can take advantage of "the irrational functions of consciousness…sensation and intuition."

This was obvious to the sages of ancient cultures. In modern times, we have excelled at applying a logical, objective line of inquiry toward discovering and inventing many useful mechanical tools. We have been obsessed with the question, "What are things made of?" As my friend the late Terence McKenna pointed out, the ancients were interested in a different question than this materialistic one. They wanted the answer to the question, "What kinds of things go together in time?" In other words, what is the relationship between subjective experience and objective reality at any given moment?

> *I can say that being prepared for an opportunity is only part of the synchronicity. Besides being qualified and experienced, uncontrollable elements such as timing and luck often play heavily.*
>
> —Randy West

The consideration of time, and the value of having good timing, is more useful than logical analysis when it comes to politics, social rituals and affairs of the human heart. Even though the Chinese made momentous technological inventions like moveable type and gunpowder hundreds of years before Europe, the Eastern cultures have been just as interested in the practical challenges of human happiness.

Everyone has experienced amazing coincidences that turned out to have carried great meaning in their lives—synchronicity in action. Let's look at three kinds of synchronicity.

The first occurs when an individual has a thought, and then some related external event occurs at the same time, and within their field of perception. We immediately sense the meaning in these occurrences. In her article "A wink from the Cosmos," Meg Lundstrom wrote about the phenomenon. "Art was sitting at his computer typing an e-mail missive when his cat Coal jumped from his lap onto the keyboard. Before Art's startled eyes, as the cat shifted from key to key, its paws tapped out the word 'emerson' on the screen. 'To make it even weirder, I've been studying Ralph Waldo Emerson intently for the past year, and the study has taken on a very symbolic meaning to me,' he says, still in shock."

The second type of synchronicity occurs when an internal mental process corresponds to an event that happens concurrently, but at a distance. For example, Sarah was just finalizing her divorce, and went to Asia for a little soul searching. While visiting a Buddhist temple, she had her fortune read. "Your second love is your true soulmate," was the message she got. Upon returning home a week later, she received an

> "I was walking down the street thinking about a friend I hadn't seen for some time, and when I looked up, there was my friend standing at the corner with his wife and he was looking at me in some surprise, for as it turned out they had been speaking of me in the same moment that I had been thinking of him, and so we congratulated ourselves on having arrived there at the corner at just the right moment for these facts to be revealed to us. We talked for a while... and when we parted I had the happy sense that the substance of my day had been revealed. Only later did I recall that none of us had referred to our fortunate meeting as a coincidence, which is what it was, of course. But coincidence is a word that we have learned to distrust, a term of mild derogation employed by parents, teachers and other grown-ups to dismiss the marvellous: 'only a coincidence' was the way they usually put it, and in that word only we understood meaning and significance to lie not in the world of the coincidental, but elsewhere, in a more real world of non-coincidence, in which events could be held accountable according to an iron law of cause and effect."
>
> —Stephen Osborne, "The Coincidence Problem," *Geist*, Winter 2002

e-mail from an old friend describing a powerful dream he'd had the previous week about searching for her, and had to locate her just to put his mind at ease. He had been Sarah's boyfriend in college and her second lover.

The last type happens when an internal thought relates to an external event that hasn't happened yet, but where no causal relationship seems possible. For instance, a friend of mine was telling me about a series of dreams she had been having in which the ocean suddenly rises, flooding above the windows. In her dreams, she was safe, but she couldn't figure out what made the water rise so fast. A few days after she told me of her dreams, the 2004 "Boxing Day" tsunami devastated Asia.

The last two types of synchronicity cannot be known immediately, they can only be verified later. In Jung's eyes, the occurrence of such meaningful coincidences points to an interconnected union of the material and conscious worlds.

We in the west have also had the idea that events tend to cluster around a moment in time, as evidenced by folk sayings like, "good things (or accidents) happen in threes." In today's world, we tend to dismiss such notions as merely superstitious. However, Jung pointed out that events in our lives, especially emotionally charged ones, could stimulate archetypes within us, which can attract similar events, in turn providing meaningful synchronicities.

How does synchronicity apply to the divination process? Art Rosengarten, in his book *Tarot and Psychology: Spectrums of Possibility*, describes how divination is a technique of "applied synchronicity." He writes, "In effect, Tarot, like I Ching and other such oracular methods, intentionally manufactures the probability of meaningful connection to occur via (seemingly) random selection."

When you formulate a query for an oracle system, you are deliberately entering a mental state of receptivity for a synchronistic response to the inquiry. Then, by picking particular cards, throwing coins, and so on, you are injecting a seemingly random element into the equation, but a personal one that is activated by your energy—your choice of cards, tossing of the coins, tim-

> *Any attempt to determine the nature of the unconscious state runs up against the same difficulties as atomic physics: the very act of observation alters the object observed. Consequently, there is at present no way of objectively determining the real nature of the unconscious.*
>
> —Carl Jung

ing or rolling of the dice.

My introduction to divination as a UC Berkeley undergraduate is a prime example of how important one's attitude and approach to divination can be. A spiritually oriented female classmate, with whom I was flirting, offered to show me how to cast an I Ching reading. Skeptical, but using the opportunity to spend more time with her, I went along. She asked me to write down a subject of personal concern. I scribbled something that didn't mean much to me, in a lame attempt to be humorous. I certainly was not taking my first encounter with an oracle very seriously.

After I tossed the three coins six times, she showed me how to look up the pattern in the large Wilhelm/Baynes version of the I Ching which she had. The I Ching's response to my frivolous inquiry was to return its fourth hexagram, entitled "Youthful Folly." It was immediately obvious that the I Ching was ignoring my question. It seemed to reflect my flippant energy instead. Chastised, but still unconvinced, I consulted the oracle again—this time to test it. Once again it ignored my frivolous query and returned a reading "questioning the sincerity of the seeker." Once again it reflected my energy—I had tried to test it and it tested me right back. Through its oracle, Higher Power was displaying that divine quality known as a sense of humor!

The sudden realization that divination reflects and clarifies one's intent as much as it dispenses practical wisdom was a great lesson for me—one that changed my life. Since that day over thirty-five years ago, I've used the I Ching and other divination systems like Tarot as intuitive decision-making aids that help me see beyond my ego and exercise better timing in my life.

> Serving as a guide without an interfering ego, divination systems can provide immediate access to profound resources.

A form of what I call *applied synchronicity*, divination offers a systematic way to produce a meaningful insight experience. It is a spiritual practice that can be used deliberately for expanding awareness and personal transformation. As Jung put it, the I Ching oracle interprets an "inner unconscious knowledge that corresponds to the state of consciousness at the moment." What a gift; what an opportunity!

Jung was fascinated by how the I Ching provided a

systematic methodology for understanding any human situation—not by analyzing its components, but by viewing individual elements in context, as part of a seamless cosmic whole. As he put it, "There is no need," he wrote, "of any criteria which imposes conditions and restricts the wholeness of the natural process.... In the I Ching, the coins fall just as happens to suit them."

This is key to understanding Jung's worldview. The world is an interconnected web of the subjective and objective, with synchronicity providing a link between the two. Jung overlapped with the new quantum physics of the 20th century in his explanations of synchronicity and consciousness. He showed how quantum physics, which empirically demonstrates behaviors that can only be described as "paradoxical synchronicities," contributes to understanding how divination systems work too.

> *As far as the laws of mathematics refer to reality, they are not certain; and as far as they are certain, they do not refer to reality.*
>
> —Albert Einstein

THE SCIENCE OF MYSTICAL EXPERIENCE

Science relies on reason and logic, valuable tools to be sure, but when we depend on logic alone to divine the workings of the universe—or even to manage a relationship—we fall far short. Intuition is something other than reason, so it is no surprise that the role of intuition is grudgingly accepted in scientific circles. While logical analysis has contributed to unraveling nature's secrets, intuition has helped us make discoveries beyond the domain of rational processes. Fortunately, a number of people—including prominent scientists and business leaders—have rediscovered ancient technologies for intuitive decision-making and creative problem-solving known as divination systems.

The discoveries of modern physics seem to validate the synchronicity principle, as they overthrow assumptions about the universe being strictly mechanical. Thomas McFarlane discusses this in *Quantum Physics, Depth Psychology, and Beyond.*

> **Although scientific materialism provided the dominant worldview of modern Western culture, it did not exist to the total exclusion of other alternatives. Nevertheless, these alternatives did not succeed in fundamentally challenging the dominance of materialism. Instead, this**

Quantum Physics converges with Jung's synchronicity theory—everything that happens in a given situation at a given time participates with, and affects, everything else at that time.

challenge largely came from within empirical science (i.e. the new physics) itself.

When a person consults the I Ching, he or she generally tosses sticks or coins and records the way they land as a six-line pattern called a hexagram. Naturally, we ask, how can any sort of truth be divined from such happenstance? Such moments are not entirely random, however. An event in the external world triggers inner knowledge, and the two realities merge within our working consciousness. L.T. More wrote of one such incident in his book *Isaac Newton*:

> On one memorable day, an apple falls with a slight thud at his feet. It was a trifling incident which has been idly noticed thousands of times; but now like the click of some small switch which starts a great machine in operation, it proved to be the jog which awoke his mind to action. As in a vision, he saw that if the mysterious pull of the earth can act through space as far as the top of a tree ... so it might even reach so far as the moon.

The dynamics of synchronicity might seem to fly in the face of scientific method—based on the ability to objectively measure and predict cause and effect—yet the synchronicity principle was validated by the basic discoveries of quantum physics. In the proof of their Uncertainty Principle in 1927, which still stands, Werner Heisenberg and Erwin Schrödinger demonstrated that, in the realm of sub-atomic particles, the act of perception influences what is being perceived, and objective measurement is impossible. Some things just happen together in time!

Thomas McFarlane, in another book, which was entitled *Einstein and Buddha,* further describes the contrast between Newtonian physics and the new findings:

> Electrons—which were previously thought to be particles—were found to exhibit the properties of waves. Conversely, light—which was previously thought to be waves—was found to exhibit some of the properties of particles. This confusion of classical distinctions between particles and waves was resolved by Niels Bohr's principle of complementarity, according to which the

wave and particle concepts are understood to be mutually exclusive but both necessary for a complete description of quantum phenomena.

The discoveries of the new physics can be interpreted to describe the essence of synchronicity. Substitute the terminology of physics with Jungian terms and you get, "the collective unconscious and the material world are understood to be mutually exclusive but both necessary for a complete description of reality." Everything that happens in a given situation at a given time participates with, and has an effect, however subtle, on everything else. Bohr, Heisenberg, Schrödinger, and many others who have dedicated their professional lives to exploring quantum physics have done much to emphasize the connections between matter and mind. In fact, Heisenberg incorporated into his family coat of arms the ancient Taoist yin-yang symbol, which signifies the interconnectedness of all things in time and space.

Ultimately, when one extends Heisenberg's mathematical proof of the Uncertainty Principle beyond subatomic physics, it becomes clear that ultimately scientific objectivity does not exist, only statistical probabilities. As Jung put it in his foreword to Wilhelm's *I Ching*, "every process is partially or totally interfered with by chance, so much so that under natural circumstances a course of events absolutely conforming to specific laws is almost an exception."

In his book, *New Directions in the I Ching*, mathematician Larry Schoenholtz points out several scientific theories that also validate the synchronicity theory:

> The spontaneous disintegration of certain atoms through radioactive emission is an event for which modern physics cannot provide an answer. But it is quite in keeping with a synchronistic view of things. No less a figure than the physicist Sir James Jeans says of this mystery, 'Radioactive break-up appeared to be an effect without a cause, and suggested that the ultimate laws of nature were not even causal.'

If we add the radioactivity puzzle to those of quantum theory—such as the Bohr's complementarity principle, and Heisenberg's Uncertainty Principle, as well as much of Einstein's general theory of relativity—the

"When it comes to scientific evaluations of astrology, the pickings are slim. There is only one figure to my knowledge who has tried to evaluate astrology in anything like a scientific way: the French researcher Michel Gauquelin (1928-91). After scrutinizing thousands of birth charts, Gauquelin came to conclusions that discomfited both conventional scientists and astrologers. He discovered that prominent members of various professions did indeed tend to have certain planets in certain places in their charts. Doctors often had Mars in a particular position, while politicians had Jupiter, and writers, the moon. Control groups taken from the general population had no such correlations."

—Richard Smoley in "The Stars We Are," *Gnosis*, Winter 1996.

We can never fully know the collective unconscious because it exists outside of our consciousness.

—Carl Jung

argument for a nonlinear worldview becomes unassailable. So it happens that the answer to a long-unsolved quandary can just pop into our heads. So it happens that events oozing with connective portent appear to have no causal relationship. But meaning does arise, and it is no accident.

This mutual interplay between matter and mind is key to future pursuits of knowledge and understanding. When the unified field theory is finally worked through—and the evidence is mounting—the clockworks of the cosmos will reveal a set of unifying equations, and the synchronicity principle will come into full recognition among all scientists. We look forward to that day.

In terms of managing the practical affairs of everyday life, looking for the meaning in synchronistic events works better than striving to predict things according to strict notions of causality or statistical probabilities. Perhaps ancient observers, who lacked our computational and record-keeping technologies, realized this and devised the I Ching, Astrology, Tarot, Runes and Numerology to put their understanding to work. Using the magic of applied synchronicity within a rich set of traditional archetypes, they strove to predict and cooperate with the way events are destined to happen, with the way things tend to go together in time.

Carl Jung did more than anyone to help us understand how divination systems work, and how they combine ancient wisdom with modern psychology. By defining and explaining the concepts of archetypes and synchronicity, he gave us criteria by which to better manage our lives, and he showed how divination systems can truly be helpful.

Jung realized that the nature of the principles he described was paradoxical. In *Psychological Reflections*, he wrote:

> **Microphysics is feeling its way into the unknown side of matter, just as complex psychology is pushing forward into the unknown side of the psyche. Both lines of investigation have yielded findings which can be conceived only by means of antinomies, and both have developed con-**

cepts which display remarkable analogies. If this trend should become more pronounced in the future, the hypothesis of the unity of their subject-matters would gain in probability. Of course there is little or no hope that the unitary Being can ever be conceived, since our powers of thought and language permit only of antinomian statements. But this much we do know beyond all doubt, that empirical reality has a transcendental background.

So, while it is possible to investigate and explore the realms of the mysterious—even to use them in our personal quests for wisdom—it is likely that they will never be "proven" in the scientific sense. But isn't the best proof how well something actually works?

Once you learn how to use divination systems to their best advantage, you will appreciate the supportive role they can play in the cosmic dance that is your life. When you dance with a skilled partner, the one who is leading has ways of signaling the next steps. Similarly, if you want to develop a sense of rhythm in your life, you need to stay in tune with signs and omens from above, including the synchronicities produced for your guidance by divination. In his recent book, *The Spontaneous Fulfillment of Desire*, Deepak Chopra refers to this skill as "synchrodestiny." Dr. Chopra shows how meditation can help us become more sensitively attuned to synchronistic signals as they arise in our lives. Divination is a form of meditation specifically designed for this.

> *The universal order and the personal order are nothing but different expressions and manifestations of a common underlying principle.*
>
> —Marcus Aurelius

Traditionally, meditation was called *raja yoga*, the royal yoga. Meditation makes everything better, including the twin benefits of divination—self-knowledge and skillful decision-making. When you learn how to systematically tune into what Dr. Chopra calls the universal soul to divine your destiny—and then make the right choices on your highest path—the fulfillment of your Heart's Desires will emerge almost effortlessly.

CHAPTER 4
Origins of Divination

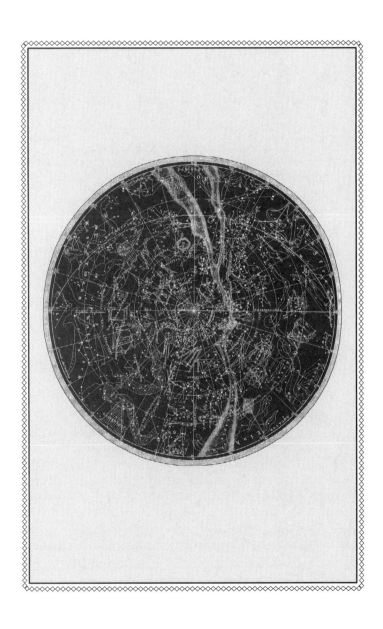

Believe nothing, no matter where you read it, or who said it—even if I have said it—unless it rings true for you.

–Guatama Buddha

Human beings have always looked for the answers to life's great mysteries. Why are we here? Who or what controls our destiny? How does life work? What does the future hold? There is archeological evidence that a need to know and deep spiritual seeking are universal human traits, and that some form of divination has been used since the earliest times, to support this quest.

Many cultures, including Chinese, Mayan, Mesopotamian and Indian, looked upwards to heavenly bodies—stars, planets, constellations, eclipses, and comets—not only to tell time and understand the seasons, but also for signs of portent or to decipher divine will. Others paid special attention to terrestrial omens such as animal migrations, weather patterns, and forms of tossed sticks, bones, amulets, or rocks. African tribes have used bones in divination rituals for many thousands of years.

> *Now! Now You Provider, who make the Stones alive, I have just come to question You.*
>
> —Cherokee shamanic prayer

Chinese Taoists read patterns on tortoise shells, which evolved into the hexagrams of the I Ching. Vikings consulted the runestones. Ancient Roman shamans observed the entrails of slaughtered animals and grains that hens pecked at and formed messages (alectryomancy).

Other cultures have looked to inner space (such as the Australian aborigines with their dreamtime), or have used hallucinogenic plants for vision quests (such as the Mazatec Indians of Mexico who use *Salvia divinorum* for spiritual rituals and divination). There are also numerous passages in the Old Testament documenting Jahweh's instructions for using a sacred set of dice called Urim and Thummim to make decisions in His name. (See Chapter 6, *The Gift of Prophecy—Divination in the Bible.*)

Even though various forms of divination have been used in all societies, the widespread use of sophisticated

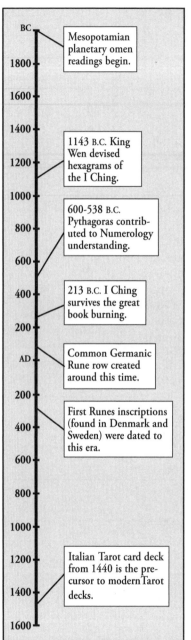

BC
Mesopotamian planetary omen readings begin.

1800
1600
1400

1143 B.C. King Wen devised hexagrams of the I Ching.

1200
1000

600-538 B.C. Pythagoras contributed to Numerology understanding.

800
600

213 B.C. I Ching survives the great book burning.

400
200

Common Germanic Rune row created around this time.

AD

200

First Runes inscriptions (found in Denmark and Sweden) were dated to this era.

400
600
800
1000

1200

Italian Tarot card deck from 1440 is the precursor to modern Tarot decks.

1400
1600

divination systems across all classes of people is a very recent development. The spread of divination systems had depended on oral transmission, which in preliterate times was largely the exclusive domain of the rulers, chieftains, official soothsayers, priests, sages, prophets and shamans. Although belief in magic was practically universal up to and through the Middle Ages, including primitive divinatory practices of folk magic, knowledge of divination systems and what Tarot scholar Bob O'Neill calls *learned magic,* could not spread until the invention of printing.

The Chinese invented paper more than two thousand years ago, and by 1045 a printer named Bi Sheng had created the first primitive moveable type, which served to increase the production of reading material. His method was used to reproduce the oldest book of wisdom—the *I Ching,* which is also the world's oldest and most venerated divination system. Johann Gutenberg's invention of the Western printing press in the 1450s gave rise to printing of books in Europe, and the reproduction of card decks, including Tarot cards.

As literacy increased, more translations of ancient texts were made and knowledge of divination systems was able to spread over time. Today people around the world can experiment with all kinds of divination systems, including those from other cultures. There are five systems in particular that are rooted in history and are widely used throughout the world today: Astrology, Numerology, I Ching, Tarot and Runes. Because they have stood the test of time and each of them incorporates a sufficiently complex and balanced set of archetypes, I refer to these five as the world's classical divination systems.

Because all the forms of classical divination have roots extending back hundreds or thousands of years and deal with much material that is mythical to

us, there is some uncertainty regarding the story of their origins. In addition to the legends, we have learned much from archeology, history and empirical evidence. The bits of this research provided here will serve more as a point of reference than a summary of what is known. (Please refer to the bibliography at the end of this book to locate more resources on subjects of interest to you.) The different divination systems and their histories are presented here in chronological order.

ASTROLOGY

Early Astrology was a marriage of astronomy and mythology. Several ancient cultures—including Mayan, Indian and Chinese—mastered astronomy to determine celestial events like solstices, equinoxes, moon cycles, seasons, and eclipses. They also used it to help interpret events or determine auspicious times for various activities. Astrological traditions from cultures other than our own have remained in continuous use since ancient times, including Vedic Astrology and the Mayan Calendar. Western Astrology as we know it is a descendent of Mesopotamian celestial observation and omen-reading that began around 2000 B.C.

The Mayan Calendar is one of the earliest astrological systems.

According to archeological evidence, it is likely that there was a religious, as well as astronomical, significance to megalithic constructions such as Stonehenge and Easter Island built in various parts of the world from 4000 to 2000 B.C. Some historians assert that the mathematical sophistication of these early cultures was equal to that of Renaissance Europe, and that this knowledge was passed along to Mesopotamia around the same time as the development of star-based omen lore in 3000–2000 B.C.

There is little known about the practicing astrologers of these times, except that they also would have been astronomers, and that at least part of their divination practices involved interpreting patterns of events based on observable movements in the heavens.

In 538 B.C., Mesopotamia was conquered by the Persians, who contributed their greater mathematical sophistication to Mesopotamia's astronomy. Humans

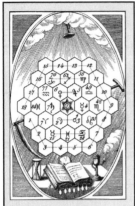

Project Hindsight, an effort by a group of scholars to translate ancient astrological writings, published the translation of the earliest natal horoscope tablet. This project is supported by subscriptions to the series of booklets that contain the text translations, as well as essays by the translator/editor and master astrologer Robert Hand to explain the philosophies and techniques of ancient practitioners.

were now able to calculate the paths of planets across the sky (or around the Earth, as was the understanding of the time), and develop horoscopes much like the ones we use today. The oldest natal horoscope ever found is dated April 29, 410 B.C.

Modern Astrology, including sun sign interpretation, was systematized by Ptolemy in his book *Tetrabiblos* during the second century A.D. Ptolemy synthesized much of the contemporary astrological thinking and arranged it into a consistent and unified body of work. Much of modern Western Astrology borrowed from Ptolemy's work.

After the fall of the Roman Empire, Astrology was condemned and suppressed by the Church. It didn't find a widespread following again until eighth century Spain during the wars with the Arabs, who had continued to use Astrology. The Emperor Charlemagne hired an astrologer and took up studies on the subject. Astrology was used by the ruling class throughout the European Reformation (fourteenth to seventeenth centuries), and then fell into disfavor until the Theosophical movement revived interest in the United States during the 1880s. Ironically, it was during this period of neglect by the ruling classes that Astrology became almost respectable among the general public, and this trend of interest in and use of Astrology is still increasing today.

I CHING

The Chinese *I Ching*, or *Book of Changes* in English, represents sixty-four archetypes that make up all the possible six-line combinations of yin and yang, called hexagrams. Yin/yang is the fundamental duality of the Universe whose dynamic tension gives shape to all phenomena and the changes they go through. Examples of the yin/yang polarity are female/male, earth/heavens, dark/light, in/out, even/odd, and so on. The interpretations of the sixty-four hexagrams describe the energy of human life divided into sixty-four types of situations, relationships or dilemmas. Each hexagram can be analyzed in a number of ways. Divide the six-line forms in half and you get trigrams (three yin or yang lines) that represent the Chinese version of the eight

fundamental elements: sky, earth, thunder, wind, water, fire, mountain, and lake. These eight trigrams, known as "Hua," also serve as the compass points in the ancient art of placement known as Feng Shui (pronounced fung-shway).

The I Ching is the oldest of all the classical divination systems. It is also one of the oldest books in the world. Its first interpretive text was composed around 1000 B.C. The I Ching's actual discovery and much of its early history are the stuff of legends.

There are a number of myths surrounding the origins of the eight trigrams and the development of the I Ching divination system. In one tale, Fu Hsi, the first emperor of China (2852–2737 B.C.), is said to have observed a turtle emerging from the Yellow River. Knowing that true wisdom came from the direct and close observation of nature, he had a sudden realization of the significance of eight symbols he saw on the turtle's back. He saw how the sets of three solid or broken lines, the trigrams, reflected the movement of energy in life on Earth.

A similar myth describes Fu Hsi's contemplation of other patterns in nature, including animals, plants, meteorological phenomena, and even his own body. These myths describe how he identified the trigrams that arose from his understanding of the connection of all things, through the interplay of yin and yang.

There is evidence of early Chinese divination where tortoise shells were heated over a flame until they cracked, with the emerging patterns (presumably trigrams) being read. In some cases the shells were marked with their interpretations and stored for reference, and I have had the privilege of seeing a few of them preserved at the National Museum in Taiwan, China.

Fu Hsi was the mythical First Emperor of China. He is reputed to be the inventor of writing, fishing and trapping, as well as the discoverer of the I Ching trigrams on the back of a turtle. He lived around 3000 B.C.

Another version also involving tortoise shells describes descendents of the "many Fu"—an ancient clan of female diviners—who read the shells of live turtles. According to the legend, they became the queens and royalty of the Shang Dynasty—which had been considered mythical until archeological evidence proving its existence was unearthed in 1899. Some say Lao Tzu, the enlightened forefather of Taoism and the author of the *Tao Te Ching*, was a descendent of this clan.

The I Ching has sixty-four hexagrams—patterns consisting of all the six-line combinations of yang and yin—using solid lines for yang and broken lines for yin.

"The I Ching does not offer itself with proofs and results; it does not vaunt itself, nor is it easy to approach. Like a part of nature, it waits until it is discovered. It offers neither facts nor power, but for lovers of self-knowledge, of wisdom—if there be such—it seems to be the right book. To one person its spirit appears as clear as day; to another, shadowy as twilight; to a third, dark as night. He who is not pleased by it does not have to use it, and he who is against it is not obliged to find it true. Let it go forth into the world for the benefit of those who can discern its meaning."

—Carl Jung, in the foreword to Richard Wilhelm's I Ching.

The Taoist/Confucian tradition posits that juxtaposing a set of the possible permutations of yin and yang with elements of Chinese creation mythology produced the foundation of the *I Ching*. Pairing up the various combinations of yin (the literal ancient meaning of which is the shady north side of the hill) and yang (meaning the sunny south side of the hill) gives you four primary symbols. With the addition of another yin or yang line, the eight trigrams emerge.

The earliest composition of *I Ching* interpretations is attributed to King Wen. Toward the end of the Shang Dynasty, when the unjust emperor Zhou Wang imprisoned Wen, he reportedly used his confinement to meditate on the trigrams, pairing them up to produce sixty-four possible hexagrams. Each pair of trigrams took on a meaning specific to their combination. In what we might assume was an enlightened state of mind, King Wen assigned each of the sixty-four hexagrams a name, adding a few sentences to explain its meaning. It is said that his son, King Wu, added additional interpretative text, bringing the *I Ching* closer to its current form.

Confucius, who came a few hundred years later, was possibly the *I Ching*'s greatest patron, taking the interpretative texts to the next level with the addition of his extensive commentaries. Confucius was primarily interested in the *I Ching* as a manual for how to live a life of the highest virtue, as opposed to its usefulness as a divination system. According to his *Analects* (VII, xvi), Confucius, who lived to be an old man, is reputed to have said, "If some years were added to my life, I would devote fifty of them to the study of the oracle, and might then avoid committing great errors."

Historical evidence substantiates the theory that the *Book of Changes* and its sixty-four hexagrams were part of an ancient oral tradition that predates recorded history in China. The basics of the *I Ching* text—the names of the hexagrams and their judgments—were likely composed in the eighth century B.C. However, the practice of using the hexagrams to refer to specific interpretations probably didn't occur until the fifth century B.C. Between 475 and 221 B.C. (known as the Warring States period), the *I Ching* texts were consolidated into a book to make it easier to consult and share with others during that time of extreme upheaval. Shortly after, the *I Ching* was spared in the Ch'in Dynasty's massive book burning because it was considered one of the five "Great Classics."

The *Book of Changes* was canonized and studied intently by scholars during the Han Dynasty of 202 B.C.– A.D. 220. Between the third century B.C. and the turn of the millennium, significant additions, known as the 'Wings', were written regarding the individual lines in the hexagrams, and the meaning of the trigrams. These commentaries are generally attributed to Confucius, who lived around 500 B.C. More work was done, and the I Ching we use today is not substantially different from the 168 B.C. version. The main difference is that the hexagrams appear in a different order. The order in use today was first proposed around 100 B.C., but was not the standard until the third century A.D.

Throughout what we know of Chinese history, the rulers of China, as well as the general public, used the I Ching as best they could before printing was available. It is woven into the fabric of this ancient culture and its influence has been fundamental to the Eastern world-view as a whole. It has only been in the last 150 years or so that Western culture was even exposed to basic Taoist concepts—such as German and English translations of the *I Ching* and *Tao Te Ching*. Carl Jung's explanation of the I Ching's psychological validity and value, and the widespread open-mindedness about all things spiritual during the 1960s, made using the I Ching a common experience in the Western world.

Nowadays, the most common method for casting the I Ching involves tossing three coins six times to create the six-line pattern, or hexagram. A traditional technique for deriving a hexagram, dating from about 500 B.C., involves a fairly complicated process of select-ing and sorting fifty sticks, usually yarrow stalks. The best yarrow stalks for this were the ones that grew on Confucius' grave, but the supply was limited! After the coins or stalks are tossed and sorted out, one looks up the interpretation in the sacred book. As we shall learn in Chapter 8, a new and more convenient way of casting the I Ching for oneself is via the Internet, including my first website, www.IChing.com.

> "When China formed the world's first civil service, the I Ching provided a philosophical framework for governmental and everyday matters.... In modern times Chiang Kai-Shek extolled the I Ching as an oracle and as a basis of the 'Ultimate Virtues'.... No such conceit afflicted Mao Tse-Tung, who consulted the book regularly during the years of planning and fighting that led up to the Long March."
> —Tom Riseman, in *Understanding the I Ching.*

93

Dr. Katya Walter, author of the *Tao of Chaos*, studied the remarkable correlation between the sixty-four hexagrams of I Ching and sixty-four codons of DNA. In an interview on Visionary Networks' *Oracle of Changes* CD-Rom, she said, "The I-Ching gives us answers that correlate to a mathematical reality at the deepest level of physical and mental activity."

NUMEROLOGY

The world is built upon the power of numbers.

—Pythagorus

The art of Numerology has existed since the ancient discovery of mathematics. To this day, most cultures attach special meaning to certain numbers and their position in a sequence. As we have just seen, the Chinese I Ching describes the differences between even (earthly) and odd (heavenly) numbers. Numerology has also been used to correlate the significance of numbers to an alphabet, giving each letter a numerical value. A well-known example is the Hebrew alphabet of twenty-two characters—the same as the number of trump cards in the Tarot deck. Because of the applicability of numbers to alphabets, numerologists are able to use words or names, in addition to numbers, to reveal divinatory meaning.

There are three major forms of Numerology— Kabbalic, Chaldean and the Pythagorean. They can be used in any combination to produce a reading, but whatever system you prefer, I suggest using it consistently so as not to confuse yourself. The one you find that you are drawn to is good enough.

Kabbalic Numerology—which is often used to interpret names—originally derived from Hebrew mysticism, is an outgrowth of the Hebrew alphabet with its twenty-two vibrations. Later it was adapted for the Greek alphabet, then the Roman alphabet. Thirteenth century Kabbalists believed that the Old Testament was written in a secret code inspired by God. They used Numerology as a tool to decipher this code. It also happens that twenty-two-base Numerology adds a significant dimension to the interpretation of the twenty-two Trump cards of the Tarot deck.

Chaldean Numerology has closer ties to Astrology, having originated in Mesopotamia, which was also the birthplace of Western Astrology. It is also related to the Vedic system of India, as well as the Kabbalah. The basis of Chaldean Numerology is that each letter has a unique vibration and is assigned a number from 1 to 8 based on its energetic quality. The number 9 is kept separate from the other numbers—*except* when it appears as a sum of vibrations—because it is considered the most sacred number. In Chaldean Numerology, single digits reveal the *outer* nature of a person, while double digits describe *inner* qualities.

The third and most popular form of Numerology is the method developed by Pythagoras, the Greek mathematician and metaphysician of the 6th century B.C. Pythagoras is famous for his formulation of the Pythagorean theorem, which calculates the hypotenuse of a right triangle, a basic construct of modern geometry. According to legend, Pythagoras was the founder of Numerology and practiced it to divine the fates of individuals, predict the events of certain locations, and use name changing as a means to alter destiny. In the Pythagorean system, numbers were assigned to letters in the Greek alphabet based on their position in the sequence. Pythagorean Numerology generally uses both the name and the date of birth, and then examines the relationships between them, much like the Chaldean method. The basic vibrations are 1 through 9, and the master vibrations are 11 and 22, which are never reduced to a single digit.

In the 1800s, when scientific discoveries regarding magnetism, light, and electricity were progressing rapidly, the idea that energy patterns of vibrations corresponded to numbers became popular. Overall, the use of Numerology for self-knowledge and divination has continued to blossom with undying popularity.

> "Numerology is a language that allows you to expand the horizons of your spiritual awareness. Numbers can open doors in your psyche that you may not have known existed."
> —Hans Decoz, in *Numerology: The Key to Your Inner Self.*

RUNES

Runes are letters of an ancient Germanic alphabet with each conveying a unique symbolic meaning. The word *rune* means "mystery" in Celtic and Germanic languages. Though sometimes associated with fortune-telling, most Runes practitioners realistically point out that the Runes were not designed to predict the future. By accessing ancient wisdom, Runes were designed to produce a greater awareness of the connection of all things, the nature of cause and effect, and the interactions between our personal lives and the rest of the world. Like any balanced archetype system, Runes represents

Runic calendar

"The motto for the Runes could be the same as was carved above the gate of the Oracle at Delphi: 'Know thyself'... The Runes are a teacher. They put you in touch with your own inner guidance, with the part of you that knows everything you need to know right now."
—Ralph Blum, in *The Book of Runes*.

an overview of human psychology, the physical world, and the universe.

Present day Rune casting involves asking a specific question, then interpreting the meanings of the symbols inscribed on a set of stones (sometimes sticks or cards). The techniques for selecting Rune stones are varied. A single stone can be chosen from a bag in answer to a question, or a number of stones (usually three or nine) can be laid out in a variety of patterns, similar to a Tarot spread, for interpretation. Or, a handful of stones can be drawn, then cast onto a special cloth, where unique meanings can be assigned to Runes in the face-up and face-down positions.

Choosing a method of Rune casting is largely a matter of personal taste. None of these methods, or others omitted here, should be considered more authentic than the rest, since there is no reliable record of precisely how Runes were cast for divination in ancient times. When using the Runes, listen to your own wisdom in selecting the appropriate technique.

There is historical research regarding the formation of the Runic alphabet, and the people who used it. The word 'Runes' refers to the unique symbolic mystery or idea behind each rune-stave—the inscribed shape or carving in wood, clay, or stone. Though considered by modern historians to have been savage in their excursions, the Vikings were in touch with the Earth and the cycles of nature. According to Nordic mythology, Odin, father of Thor, discovered and invented the Runes. Seeking divine knowledge, Odin hung upside down from a tree limb and was enlightened with the knowledge of the Runes.

Archeological evidence suggests that symbols found on early rock carvings throughout Northern Europe and Scandinavia during the second Bronze Age and early Iron Age led to the development of the rune-staves. The derivation of the Runes' meanings, like the origins of the rune-staves themselves, remains mysterious. In *Germania 10*, Tacitus—the Roman politician, orator, historian, and author from the first century A.D.—describes a number of forms of divination, including ways of interpreting the flights and calls of birds. It was later surmised that the shapes of the rune-staves were derived from the patterns of bird flight. Also, Tacitus writes of omens being read in the snorts, whinnies, and neighs of pure white sacred horses kept by the public in sacred forests. The obvious link to these sacred horses is the nineteenth Rune, *ehwaz*, "the horse."

There are a variety of theories about which alphabets the rune-staves were related to—including Greek, Latin, and North Italic alphabets. O.V. Friesen proposed the idea that near the Black Sea in the third century A.D., Goths invented rune-staves based on the cursive and capital letters of the Greek alphabet. Danish scholar L. F. Wimmer identified similarities between some rune-staves and Latin, and also concluded the creation of the rune-staves would have been in the third century A.D. However, these theories are questioned because the earliest inscriptions—from Norway and Denmark—can be dated to the second or third century A.D., which means their invention, distribution, and rise in popularity was already underway for quite some time by then.

Rune-stave: the inscribed shape carved in wood, clay, or stone.

The most widely held view of the rune-staves' origin is that they derived from the North Italic scripts of Italy, which, like Latin, came from the early Etruscan alphabet. Both rune-staves and North Italic alphabets were written from left to right as well as right to left, but many of the rune-staves do not resemble North Italic in form. Some claim that the Germanic tribes of the alpine regions could have learned the North Italic alphabet as early as the fourth century B.C. The Futhark alphabet, as we call it today, evolved from this encounter and by the second century B.C. it was spreading northward. It appears likely that the Common Germanic Rune was created between the fourth century B.C. and the first century A.D.

TAROT

This system of divination now known as Tarot first became popular in card form in Europe during the early fifteenth century, assisted by the invention of the printing press. Early images of twenty of the twenty-two Major Arcana cards (Arcana means "secrets") can be seen in an Italian deck of A.D. 1440. The Visconti family's decks, forebears of Tarot decks in use today, appear to

have been created as a recreational pastime for the nobility. Across five centuries, the structure of the modern deck of Tarot cards remains identical to the game decks enjoyed in the fifteenth century. The Marseilles family of decks, still in print today, is the oldest of the standard Tarot deck pattern.

Even though Tarot may have started as a card game, members of secret societies assigned mystical meanings to the cards, adding corresponding astrological, numerological and kabbalic symbols over time. There is no doubt that the images on modern Tarot cards have roots at least as old as Western civilization, going back as far as Egypt and maybe China. Because Tarot now incorporates a synthesis of Astrology, Numerology, the Jewish Kabbalah and harmonic theory, our Tarot scholar, Christine Payne-Towler, refers to Tarot as "the flash cards of the Western mysteries."

The highly symbolic Tarot deck provided a way to secretly preserve ancient teachings and divination systems during a period when the Christian church was hell-bent on repressing such knowledge. The Church's persecution of so-called heresies, which was sometimes represented in Tarot images, caused the esoteric information to be sheltered by small groups of like-minded people, by whom it was carefully preserved, and selectively shared in the guise of a card game.

Frenchman Antoine Court de Gébelin deserves much credit for the establishment of modern Tarot, including its use as a means of divination. In 1781 he announced that he had discovered the mythical teachings of Thoth, the Egyptian god who invented magic and writing, in the symbols on the Tarot deck. Jean-Baptiste Alliette, known as "Etteilla," was the first to create a deck of thirty-two cards to be used specifically for divination in 1770.

By the mid-nineteenth century, Eliphas Lévi had expanded Court de Gébelin's work by joining it with the Jewish mystical system, the Kabbalah, although he

Speculations on the origin of Tarot

- Allegories of Sufi masters
- Grail legend depictions
- Chaturanga, an Indian forerunner of chess
- Indian holy texts
- Gypsy imports
- Hebrew lore
- Greek philosophy
- Patterned after Mesopotamian copper cylinders
- Symbols handed down from pre-historic oral stories
- Symbols from ancient Central American Indian cultures
- Wisdom of prehistoric matriarchal cultures
- Teaching aids of the Waldenses, a persecuted Christian sect
- Surviving lore of the Order of Knights Templar
- 13th century alchemists

did not abandon Egyptian symbolism in his deck. Lévi's work was key in fueling a Tarot revival. Lévi does not get as much credit as he deserves, largely due to the efforts of A.E. Waite, the English Tarot scholar of the early 1900s who translated Lévi's works from French to English. Various members of England's Order of the Golden Dawn went so far as to rearrange the order of the traditional Tarot deck, assigning some different astrological correspondences, as well as making other small changes. In order to establish its own reputation and influence, it was in the Golden Dawn's interest to discount Lévi's more traditional teachings, even to deny the validity of all Tarot knowledge that had come before. Waite's translated texts included many notes encouraging the reader to dismiss Lévi's ideas.

To a large degree, these efforts were successful. Today it is not uncommon to hear claims that Tarot originated in England, when in fact the French, Italians, and Spanish were using it over 100 years earlier than the English. Most decks in popular use today are derived from Waite's 'Rider-Waite' deck—or the *Book of Thoth* Tarot, an even more creative deck designed by Aleister Crowley, who was also a member of the Golden Dawn society.

> In 1909 Arthur Edward Waite and artist Pamela Colman Smith published the first Tarot deck that included pictorial scenes on all the cards. Today you can choose from hundreds of decks.

THE SURVIVAL OF DIVINATION

We have taken a brief look at the origins of the classical divination systems that have survived into modern times. Given the distances the world's classical divination systems have had to travel—through time and space—not to mention the intense persecution their practitioners endured in Western society for hundreds of years, it is a minor miracle that they are still with us. Even though divination systems arise from the collective unconscious, totalitarian governments and fundamentalist religions seem to consider the profound insights

> God has graced every tradition with insight into the divine mystery, from the most primitive to the most sophisticated—each has a gift to bring to the world.
>
> —Bede Griffiths

that divination can stimulate as some vague threat to a social order based on wealth, status and power. In their fearfulness, proponents of the status quo fail to realize that higher aspirations never threaten lower ones.

Authentic divination systems passed down by our ancestors are our sacred heritage. From a practical point of view, their ability to provide fresh guidance through the changes of our lives and world is our collective good fortune. They help us satisfy our primordial need to better understand life and our place in the Universe. Their usefulness has allowed Astrology, Numerology, the I Ching, Runes and Tarot not only to survive, but thrive in the face of all odds. In the next chapter, we take a look at what a monumental challenge the survival of divination has been.

CHAPTER 5
Enemies of Divination

He who sees the entire world of animate and inanimate objects in himself and also sees himself in all animate and inanimate objects, because of this does not hate anyone.

—Ishavasya Upanishad

hroughout the past two thousand years in the west, divination has been exposed to serious opposition. From organized religion to establishment scientists, from totalitarian governments to cynical mass media, it has had powerful foes. They typically represent its spiritual potential as a waste of time, a hoax, or the work of the devil. These views are righteously repeated ad infinitum, and like so much of doctrine are never re-examined, as if they were objective truth, fixed once and for all.

The pharaoh requests a dream interpretation by Joseph.
—Genesis 41

Religious fundamentalists continue to insist that God forbids divination in the Bible, completely ignoring the numerous passages where God explicitly sanctions it or even directly commands its use. We will look closely at specific verses in the next chapter, and a complete list can be found in Appendix C.

In this chapter we look at the most powerful forces that are still bent on dismissing or condemning the spiritual process of divination. Our purpose is to reveal their motivations for such prejudice, and to show how authentic divination systems, as opposed to fortune-telling and superstitious folk magic, are blessings to humankind and have not earned such condemnation. This serves one goal of this book, which is to bring divination out of the occult underground and into the light, free from the darkness of fear and superstition, so that it can be used to shed more light in people's lives.

The most vigorous enemies of divination throughout the ages can be divided into three categories: ideology-oriented social institutions, the scientific establishment, and commercial exploiters.

"The Devil Made Me Do It"

A supernatural entity of pure evil—the Devil—is a relatively new concept that arose along with monotheism. Pagans believed that, like humans, gods were capable of great deeds and personal foibles. There were trickster gods, as well as gods of sexuality, wine, festivals, and just about everything interesting. Christianity based its image of the Devil on various pagan gods to discredit paganism. In order to convince people that their souls were in danger, a force of evil opposed to one all-good God was necessary.

In 1486, two monks, Heinrich Kramer and James Sprenger, wrote *The Malleus Maleficarum*, or "The Witch Hammer," which popularized the devil myth—whose look was derived from the horned gods, Pan and Puck, who were still active in the psyche of European country folk. It's tragically ironic that this book, which served as a how-to manual for hunting and torturing witches, became the world's first best seller after the invention of the printing press.

Between 1450 and 1470, a Franciscan friar in Italy proclaimed that the trump cards of the Tarot were created by the Devil. Later, in the 17th century, a religious Sicilian duchess replaced the Devil and Tower cards with images of a ship and a castle, respectively.

INSTITUTIONAL FOES

As mentioned earlier, the Western world's three major religions, and several governments, have fostered a strong prejudice against divination. Constantine, the ruthless Roman emperor who adopted Christianity as the state religion and helped organize the modern day Bible, first made divination a capital offense (circa A.D. 357). This was church and state!

It should come as no surprise that the loudest group opposed to divination today is the huge fundamentalist Christian sect, which bases its beliefs on a narrow interpretation of the same Bible that Constantine helped put together at his Council of Nicea in A.D. 325. With regard to divination, fundamentalists still stubbornly cling to the few verses in which God seems to condemn it.

Actually, in most of the verses cited, the scripture is instructing the Hebrew people to steer clear of particular superstitions, false prophets, scam artists and tricksters (as does this book, for that matter). As we shall see in the next chapter, there are even more passages in the Bible where a divination system is used by the high priests, with God's explicit blessing, if not command. The God of the Bible, it turns out, is certainly not of one mind about divination!

It's difficult to understand why religions should be hostile to divination at all. After all, the Old Testament and the Chinese *I Ching*—two of the oldest spiritual classics in the world—both prove that systems of divination have been used since before recorded history.

One can easily surmise that organized religions are hostile to divination because these institutions are not really interested in replicating the type of direct mystical experiences that inspired their founders. It is for the same motive that totalitarian governments have been hostile to divination—because they oppose greater personal power for individuals, which would lessen their influence. (Throughout history, immature leaders, consumed by power and greed, have failed to understand that Power needs to be governed by Wisdom.)

The institutions of church and state—which have been responsible for criminalizing divination—have gone too far, but critics of divination in modern times do have some basis for complaint. Throughout the ages, various interest groups have corrupted or abused these sacred tools, employing divination practices for personal gain. As a social phenomenon, con games are even older than divination!

Divination may not be about fortune-telling, but fortune-tellers and con artists misrepresent it as such to make a quick buck. A number of city, county, and state governments have responded to complaints regarding psychic fraud by passing laws to criminalize the practice of fortune-telling—and divination systems by association. Although the outrage over spiritual swindling is understandable, the failure to differentiate between honest practitioners and consultants and those who misrepresent them reflects our general ignorance about the true nature of divination, as well as a lack of consideration for spiritual practices outside the orthodox mainstream. It is safe to say that such laws have a large component of religious prejudice behind them. After all, scams involving home repair are common, yet legitimate contractors are still allowed to do their work.

This attitude of official disfavor hasn't always been the case. The gift of clairvoyance has been prized by an assortment of rulers throughout history. Court diviners were a regular occurrence everywhere from China and Japan to ancient Mayan civilization. The Oracle at Delphi was one of the most famous sites in the Western world, and operated for almost six centuries. It was believed that Apollo spoke through the Pythia, the prophetic women who verbalized the prophecies. Leaders

> **North Carolina Outlaws Divination:**
>
> "It shall be unlawful for any person to practice the arts of phrenology, palmistry, clairvoyance, fortune-telling and other crafts of a similar kind in the counties named herein."
>
> —1951 statute (repealed in August 2004)

World Leaders Use Divination

- First Lady Nancy Reagan was well known for relying on Astrology. She regularly consulted an astrologer when planning Ronald Reagan's presidential schedule.

- In 550 B.C. Croesus, King of Lydia, prepared to invade Persia. He asked the Oracle of Delphi to predict the outcome. The oracle reported that if Croesus crossed the river, a great nation would fall. In fact, Croesus was captured; subsequently he denounced the powers of the Oracle and demanded to know why it lied. The Oracle responded that a great nation did fall—his own.

- Napoleon discovered an ancient divination system, known as the Book of Fate, in Egypt, along with the Rosetta Stone in 1799. He had the oracle translated into German (for secrecy's sake), and used it for strategic decision-making throughout the rest of his life, along with Tarot.

- Queen Elizabeth I was known to consult Dr. Dee, the famous seventeenth century scryer, on affairs of the state.

- Astrology reached its highest level of political importance when Emperor Septimus Severus declared sun worship the official religion of Rome during his reign from A.D. 193–211. Astrology was a key component of this religion.

- The Dalai Lama, political and spiritual leader of the Tibetan people, uses a Tibetan form of divination using a dough ball and dice.

from around the world made pilgrimages to this site for guidance and instruction.

In recent history, mass media has also spread confusion about divination. As divination systems are used more, they find their way into popular entertainment venues, where they are often misrepresented or ridiculed. The growing interest in Tarot was documented by the *Trends Journal* in 1998:

> The resurgence of the Tarot is not a fad, but part of a widespread new-millennium trend. Once available only in several traditional designs and found only in specialty mail-order catalogs and back-alley occult emporiums, Tarot has exploded into dozens of varieties and is now found prominently displayed at the check-out counters of the major bookstore chains.

Tarot references are showing up everywhere from sitcoms to comic strips. For instance, on an episode of the TV show *Friends,* Phoebe was despondent after a visit to her reader, because the Death card had been drawn. She became convinced she was about to die. The episode revolved around her comedic attempts to wrap up her life in the company of her disbelieving friends. The resolution? The reader had made a mistake in interpreting the card, and it was the reader who died! But this is just as ridiculous, for anyone who knows Tarot knows that the Death card is not about physical death. This type of ultra-literal interpretation is not only stupid, it tarnishes all forms of divination.

Language itself has had a hand in misconceptions surrounding divination. It's often assumed that the dic-

tionary is the compendium of meaning in the English language, yet experience reminds us that words can have different meanings for different times and cultures. The word "passion" is a good example. The *American Heritage Dictionary* refers to it as "a powerful emotion, such as love, joy…," and this is probably the most common meaning today. The Latin origin, which meant, "to suffer," is tied to the Biblical era when the word signified the suffering and death of Christ. A similar difference of meaning is the case with divination.

Defined by the dictionary as "the art or act of foretelling future events or revealing occult knowledge by means of augury or an alleged supernatural agency," one would be led to believe that divination is just another word for fortune-telling. This official definition reveals a culturally biased misunderstanding of the way divination works, what it is for, and its benefits.

As we have seen, the primary value of divination is as a method for gaining a clearer awareness of what's happening in a person's life *right now*—not in the future. Based on historical research, psychological understanding, personal experience, and divination's widespread use for thousands of years, we know that the process has sound psychological legitimacy, without any need to attribute its efficacy to some external supernatural agency or special psychic powers. Divination is an art, yes, but it should never be an act. It is essential to distinguish the fortune-tellers from the tools for intuitive decision-making and wisdom development that we refer to as divination systems.

A thousand years of fundamentalist hysteria—including thousands of burnings—demonized divination as "the work of the devil." This dark period of European history was followed by the so-called Age of Enlightenment, which glorified the logic of reason and scientific laws as the only valid criteria for truth (outside of religion, of course), further denigrating divination and intuition's roles. Given this history, it is no wonder that misunderstanding about the true nature of divination is widespread to this day.

COMMERCIAL EXPLOITATION

The misunderstanding and misuse of divination has been made worse by the rapidly accelerating evolution of communications technologies, along with the extreme commercialization of all things marketable. As a result, classical systems like Tarot have been co-opted by professional fortune-tellers who use telephone networks or the Internet to mass market their services. But just because there is misrepresentation or misuse of a tool, that does not mean that the tool doesn't work when used properly. The fact that you can hit somebody on the head with

a hammer does not make the hammer bad. The tool works for the use it was designed for.

The ability to predict events is one of humanity's most universal and favorite fantasies. Since we've all experienced premonitions at one time or another, it seems reasonable that a person with a gifted intuition might be able to do it somewhat consistently. Advance or inside knowledge would confer such a powerful advantage that people are willing to pay for the possibility that they might pick up something valid. Unfortunately, while the desire to predict changes is understandable, fortune-telling services have always been and will always be a scam.

To be sure, some rare individuals do have intuitive powers beyond the average person. But generally not all that much, and no human being's envisioning power is very consistent either, especially under pressure. An additional problem with psychics is that such an ability is impossible to prove or measure. It is said that only a gifted intuitive can clearly recognize another gifted intuitive. If you are willing to be suggestible to predictions made by others, you need to place your trust in the reader's accuracy and wisdom, no matter how off she might be right now. After all, highly intuitive people have cloudy days too!

Predicting the future is not what divination is really about.

Many people have precognitive experiences on occasion, some very accurate—but such experiences do not usually happen on demand. Considering all the dreams that come to all the people, in all the world every night of the year, it is not surprising that once in a while, reality will coincide with a vision from a dream. The same is true for fortune-telling. If enough predictions are made, some are bound to come true. While there are probably a few individuals in the world who do have psychic powers, their number is extremely small. The safety net is to try to learn to trust your own intuition before you decide to rely on anybody else's.

If you do decide to use psychic services, staying in alignment with your own intuition and intelligence is still crucial. Going against what rings true for you is foolishly giving away your personal power—and your money. Test all information. Ultimately, nobody else can provide you with wisdom. That is an inside job; it must be developed. Counselors can help us learn and stimulate our process of awakening, but that's about all they can hope to do. The goal of wisdom is not only to gather information, but to learn how to learn.

I have had psychic readings in my life that were just plain wrong. In spite of the power of suggestion, I respected my own instincts and consciously chose not to believe the predictions offered. One memorable instance occurred when I was in India working as personal secretary for Mataji Indra Devi, one of the great Yoga teachers of modern times. I lived there and worked as her biographer and personal assistant for eleven months. Once a well-known psychic and old friend from Los Angeles (whom I will call Margie) visited Mataji at her residence in Southern India. Margie was quite a charming person and we became friends over the course of a few weeks. One day she offered to give me a reading, which did not involve the use of any divination system, just pure clairvoyant prophecy.

Margie warned me that I was about to have health problems involving my feet. Well, in a hot and filthy environment like India, you definitely do not want to have problems with your feet! Close to the dusty ground, they are more liable to get infected than most body parts, and such an infection would severely limit mobility and could be serious. I just crossed my fingers and silently said to myself, "Cancel, cancel … I do not want to take that in … I choose not to believe that." To this day some twenty years later, except for the occasional athlete's turned ankle or blister from new shoes, I have not had any trouble with my feet.

These days, fortune-telling is massively advertised by psychic reader networks. Their ads or infomercials can be seen on cable networks, daytime talk shows, magazines, direct mail and the Internet. In some cases, the psychics claim to use divination systems such as Tarot, Astrology, or Numerology, presumably in order to lend an aura of legitimacy to their predictions. Some readers may be gifted, but in general most psychic networks will hire anyone who is willing and able to follow a script for $10 an hour.

> *Intuition comes very close to clairvoyance; it appears to be the extrasensory perception of reality.*
> —Alexis Carrel

109

Miss Cleo Reader's Script:

OK. Are you ready for your first card? Well as I look at the set I have placed down for you, I see some interesting things arising—some of it deals with love, money, and changes. Hopefully there (sic) going to be for the better.

Now your first card represents your situation, maybe some problems your (sic) having, and maybe a little bit about yourself. (BECOME MORE SINCERE NOW)

Your first card is the card of Sorrow, this is the 3 of swords. This card is just letting us know that there is some type of disruption in your life. Something perhaps weighing on your mind?

There seems to be something confusing you. Not that it's a big deal but this card is giving off a strong vibe of anxiety. Which indicated something stressing you out. Actually this card is warm in my hand.

What seems to be disturbing you please? (REFER TO SPECIFIED BOOKLET)

The fake use of divination systems like Tarot and Astrology by fortune-telling actors has created the confusing impression for masses of people that predicting the future is what divination is all about. As we have pointed out, this myth is insidiously effective because of the universal fantasy of predicting the future. This desire is so attractive that many people are easily sold on the idea that there are others who can and will do it for them. Charlatans prey upon this fantasy, knowing as the great showman P.T. Barnum put it, "There's a sucker born every minute." It's particularly unfortunate that hucksters' claims to legitimacy often derive from their pretended use of divination systems that, when used with sincerity, could really empower people.

A well-known scandal in the late 1990s featured Tarot as a cover, and a supposed Tarot reader calling herself "Miss Cleo," who became the center of a well-publicized psychic hotline fraud case. As the TV spokesperson for the telemarketing scam, this Los Angeles actress posed as a Jamaican shaman. Miss Cleo was able to attract countless individuals with promises of free psychic readings through ubiquitous television ads and infomercials. The callers would dial the toll-free 1-800 number, and then be patched through to a 900 number with a per-minute charge. Often they were put on hold, unaware of when the billing had begun, or told they would get additional free minutes and then were charged for the time.

Amateur actors pretending to be psychics were directed to spend minutes at the start of each call telling the caller their extension number, describing membership programs, or selling services. The callers were being billed for listening to advertisements! Some people received bills for hundreds of dollars for calls they didn't even make.

This fraud translated into billions of dollars for the mother companies, Access Resource Services and Psychic Readers Network, and resulted in thousands of complaints to regulatory agencies. The FCC ultimately charged the companies with unfair telemarketing and fraud. They settled out of court, and were required to forgive $500 million in uncollected debts, and pay $5 million to the U.S. Treasury, as well as discontinue their

Psychic Phone Services "Cold-Reading" Technique:

Often, employees of psychic hotlines are not particularly intuitive, let alone psychic. They're simply working at a dishonest trade to pay the bills. In most cases, in spite of advertising and appearances, there is no divination happening at all—they learn a method called "cold-reading" as part of their employee training. The trick is to ask leading questions, observe behavioral clues, and sometimes, just guess. Recipients of these readings will tend to overlook the mistakes, and only remember the accuracies of the psychic. Reginald V. Finley took a job as a telephone psychic and describes his experience:

"... the callers had given me plenty of information about themselves. Even them not speaking gave subtle clues that any observant person would pick up on. Breathing, background noise, pauses, interjections, tone of voice. All these factors play a role. I guessed rather easily whether someone had children, were married, dying, or ill. Even the sex of their children I guessed. (Hey, you've only got a fifty-fifty chance of getting it right, so what did I have to lose?) No special powers here though. It was all done utilizing reason, probability, and luck. Is it by chance that I guessed that a man was dating a woman whose name begins with an 'M'? Not at all. He told me. Part of his reading went as follows:

Psychic: I don't know why, but I see someone in your life.

Gullible 1: Really, what do you see?

Psychic: I see someone whose name starts with an 'M' in your life.

Gullible 1: Wow, (clue #1) Uhhh, where did that come from?

Psychic: (Utilizing clue #1 to suppress doubt) I don't know, I'm certain (now I am) that someone whose name starts with an 'M' will be an important factor in your life.

Gullible 1: That's amazing! I'm dating a woman named Martha.

"At this point I could have told him anything, true or false. It doesn't matter what I say at this point because, hey, I'm psychic. Did I simply make a good guess? Darn right I did, but a very ambiguous one at that. He could have easily applied the letter 'M' to anything. He began to assist me in trying to discover what the significance of the letter 'M' was. Even if the 'M' didn't pertain to his past or present, I could have easily transferred it to his future. Either way, I win. I'm psychic, remember?"

phone-y psychic business.

Techniques used by such companies and others to bilk people were beyond scandalous. The "readers" were trained to keep callers on the line as long as possible—usually a fifteen- to twenty-minute call average—or face termination. At rates as high as $4.99 per minute, the charges added up fast. Bonuses were available to readers who could collect callers' mailing and e-mail addresses that were then used for e-mail spam and direct mail campaigns. Such so-called psychics often read from scripts, use cold-reading techniques, and make things up in an effort to keep callers on the phone.

One woman who worked for a psychic hotline quit after two days because she couldn't bring herself to swindle desperate callers. Though the company she worked for claimed that people call for entertainment purposes, this was clearly not the case. One man who was on the verge of homelessness spent the last of his money asking for career counseling from a psychic. Another woman was in a physically abusive relationship, and would have gotten much better counseling from a free domestic abuse hotline. When life's changes are too overwhelming to handle, it is easy to be lured into seeking advice in supposedly spiritual places. The psychic hotlines took advantage of people by making a business of dispensing useless advice. That would be bad enough. What makes it worse is their misappropriation of classical divination tools that actually could help people, though in a less dramatic fashion than the commentary of someone posing as a psychic miracle worker.

Some ask why people would continue to call if there wasn't some truth to the psychic predictions they received. The answer is that a desperate desire to believe a prediction—all the easier if no personal effort is required for the outcome—is an expression of hope. It is encouraged by the fact that some predictions come true and the ones that don't are forgotten. Mathematician John Allen Paulos, from Temple University, called this the "Jeane Dixon effect." Most of Dixon's predictions were either completely wrong, or so general that it would be easy to find truth somewhere. She was a popular psychic who leveraged Astrology, and became famous for advising movie stars, including former President and Mrs. Reagan. (The First Lady later determined that Dixon's powers were gone and turned to competitor Joan Quigley for astrological guidance.)

It is important to note that there is a difference between psychic readers and bona fide divination readers and counselors. For example, there are hundreds of Tarot scholars in the world who have real knowledge of the archetypes of the Tarot, as well as intuition that has been honed over years of use. Genuine Tarot readers, as opposed to psychics pretending to use Tarot, are distinguished by a couple of important factors. The first is their thorough knowledge of Tarot. The second is that

> In 1974, in order to allow astrologers to continue to offer their services for a fee, California Governor Ronald Reagan signed a law differentiating them from fortune-tellers.

they find a way for the recipient of a Tarot reading to be the one who actually picks the cards.

Sometimes when psychics claim to use Tarot, over the Internet or telephone, they pick your cards for you (sometimes they have pre-picked cards that go well with their script), and then give you their interpretation of those cards. Customers of psychic reading services are encouraged to believe that their reader is psychic enough to energetically synchronize with the client, and therefore it does not matter who picks the cards. However, considering all the possible distractions, hidden motivations and other forms of psychic interference, we have our doubts about this.

Although most Tarot readers who work over the phone would probably disagree with me, I believe that picking cards for another person is not authentic. It's possible that cards picked by the reader could stimulate a reader's intuition while she thinks about you, but according to the Synchronicity Principle, the cards picked for you by a psychic reader are more related to what's going on inside the reader, not you. Psychological factors like mood, desires, and personal histories can create interference. In other words, although an exceptional intuitive could possibly get it right, it is not likely. In the most authentic Tarot readings, you always pick your own cards. (There are ways to do this that accommodate telephone communications too.)

> Human beings have an innate desire to know the future, and profit-seeking hucksters have always been quite willing to profit from it.

In the last few decades, there has been a significant increase in the number of businesses offering tarot, Numerology, Palmistry, Crystal Scrying and other forms of fortune-telling. While some of these are legitimate, most are scams, offering such services as the lifting of curses for hundreds or thousands of dollars, conducting meditation sessions on behalf of the client, and psychically contacting victims of murder or missing children.

Associating divination with psychics reinforces a general misunderstanding in the popular imagination. The result of this confusion, which only benefits the marketers of psychic services, is ironically similar to the result of the medieval church's reasons for prohibiting divinatory practices. The overall result is that through a repetitive campaign of misleading propaganda, access to intuitive development systems has been hidden from,

True Psychic Friends

In response to a speech I gave some years ago entitled "Beware of Psychic Friends," I was shown an article by Juliet Nightingale, called "Psychic Hotlines: An Insider's Story":

"…There are now a few 'grassroots' groups of psychics who have formed their own psychic networks with integrity…in order to avail themselves to the public without false representation and charging outrageous fees. It is right that we should be accessible to as many people as possible, so that we may provide a valid and much needed service. This is not a 900 line and I was so honoured to be with this group of loving and dedicated practitioners, before moving on to running my own business. Everyone was sincere there. There was no pressure, no one tried to keep you on the line, because the client would decide in advance how long of a reading one wanted and the readings were guaranteed! The caller only paid $2.90 and the psychic was paid $.50 per minute! When the call was patched through to me, all I had to be concerned with was giving the reading and the callers rang back again and again, because they trusted us and knew that we were real! "

and effectively denied to, most people. When individuals believe they should plan their future according to the expensive mind reading of an intermediary, they miss out on an opportunity to gain insight into their present situation by means of tools that can actually strengthen their own intuition, such as classical divination systems like authentic Tarot.

There are many excellent Tarot readers and astrologers, but for the most part, psychic service businesses prey on human weakness by offering an easy solution to serious dilemmas—for which they take no responsibility. In reality, they are creating more problems for people by encouraging dependency, whereas the skillful use of divination systems develops greater personal independence and freedom.

Psychic reading has become big business, and is often a big scam. Psychic networks are owned and run by well-financed, and often unscrupulous, corporations. Theifs and con-artists can be very persuasive. They are co-opting classical divination in the popular imagination, much like the fundamentalists have co-opted the three great Western religions. For the purposes of power and financial gain, by promoting the idea of divination as fortune-telling, psychic reading services have done the world a great disservice.

When truly gifted intuitives give counseling, it can be a powerfully positive influence, helping people gain deeper insight into trends and patterns in their lives. Like a divination ritual used as a meditation experience, a personal counseling approach focuses on what's happening in the present, not the future. It is a shame that the valuable work of gifted practitioners is tarnished, along with all forms of divination, by commercial exploitation preying on people's gullibility.

SCIENTISM

As soon as questions of will or decision or reason or choice of action arise, human science is at a loss.
—Noam Chomsky, TV interview, 1978

There is another force, similar to religion, that opposes and discredits divination—the left-brained ideology of scientific rationalism. Scientism is defined by the *American Heritage Dictionary* as "the belief that the investigative methods of the physical sciences are applicable or justifiable in all fields of inquiry." Like doctrine-centric religions, scientism considers itself to be the only valid route to truth.

Let's face it, since the invention of literacy, we humans have been easily dominated by black-and-white thinking. Most formal education is focused on the left-brained realm of logic and linear thought, and science has become like a religion for millions of people. Anything that can't be measured doesn't really exist, or else doesn't matter. The great psychologist Carl Jung pointed out that intuition is something other than reason, so it is no surprise that the concept is not discussed much in scientific circles. This exclusionary approach to what's important provides a backdrop for modern society's rampant materialism.

On the other end of the spectrum, we have religious doctrine treated separately—and as more important—than the experience of a dynamic learning relationship with the Divine. Fundamentalists of all religions teach that if a belief doesn't coincide with the "good book" of doctrinal authority, it can't be right. Even though intuitive discoveries have been responsible for all the greatest discoveries and inventions of science, as well as religion, science has also become institutionalized and dogmatic.

Scientism considers science to be the only valid route to truth. It is defined by the *American Heritage Dictionary* as "the belief that the investigative methods of the physical sciences are applicable or justifiable in all fields of inquiry."

Since the Renaissance, the Western world has glorified reason—looking for a rational solution to all problems. The assumption was that if sufficient data were collected, good answers would result. With the advent of the Information Age offering instant access to virtually unlimited data, it was thought that logical decision-making would become so much easier and faster. Logic

Chapter 5: Enemies of Divination

A Shrink in a Box

"The Tarot deck, an early victim of rational science, has been derided for several centuries by a skeptical public as pure superstition; the province of Gypsy fortune-tellers and sidewalk psychics. ... Tarot's popularity today goes beyond the tabloids; its audience is primarily the extensive New Age book-buying public and a broad stream of Generation Xers. They look to it, not as a fortune-telling tool, but rather as a form of do-it-yourself therapy, a way of unlocking secrets of the self and providing directions toward specific life goals."

—*Trends Journal* article "Tarot: The Shrink-in-the-Box"

(see Appendix D)

and science would take their rightful place and the left brain would finally rule once and for all, making all our important decisions the right way—logically, of course!

Well, think again. Science, by definition, can only deal with measurable phenomena. It can hardly touch the fuzzier realms of morality, society, love, politics, creativity and wisdom. Whether taking things apart, analyzing statistics, applying probability theory, or toying with computer models, logical analysis is only appropriate when the subject is of a measurable (as opposed to intuitive) nature, and only as good as the quality of the information available. And that brings up a huge limitation of relying upon logical analysis to solve our day-to-day problems.

We've got *too much* information! It's more difficult than ever to tell the reliable from the bogus. Even the information we currently accept as true has a shorter shelf life, as new discoveries can quickly make our "facts" obsolete. We can delay decisions while awaiting more information (and often do), but then we are liable to miss increasingly brief windows of opportunity. So, how can we determine which information is true or relevant, so that we can make the decisions that need to be made in a timely manner? The answer is intuition.

In spite of all the scientific advances and powerful data collection technologies, good decision-making remains much more art than science. Ironically, by harnessing powerful computers—the ultimate models of left-brain processing—we have become aware of the limitations of logic. Will we finally admit that our commitment to any given course of action is based largely on gut-feel? Moreover, can we accept that this is how it is meant to be, the nature of things, and learn to trust our intuition? If so, we will appreciate that decision-making aids in the form of divination tools offer valuable help. Stimulating and supporting the intuition, they can reflect on motives, desires, fears, and expectations. Divination systems are intuitive decision-making aids, as well as a form of do-it-yourself psychotherapy!

Almost all rationalists are cynical when it comes to divination. They don't understand it and they possibly lack respect for intuition's role in discovery. In an age

that glorifies science, individuals experimenting with divination will encounter skeptics, who are willing to explain in great detail how divination is nothing more than a figment of the imagination—or worse, a hoax. As we have seen, skepticism is increased by the activity of the many charlatans who misuse or misrepresent divination for their own ends. These impostors provide evidence for skeptics that it's all a form of trickery, designed to prey on vulnerable people.

When faced with a skeptic, it's important to remember that there are often valid (though perhaps one-sided) reasons for their views on the subject. However, some rationalists are just like religious fundamentalists, committed to the black-and-white notion that you're either a rational human being or you believe in things like divination that science can't measure. In this regard, divination is often derisively lumped together with UFOs, aliens, conspiracy theory, ghosts, magic and the like.

There have been long periods in history in which the art and systems of divination have been accorded the highest respect. Divination always was the natural domain of shamans and sages, the "guidance counselors" of their times and cultures. But its popularity also gave rise to corrupt, willful and vicious opposition by fundamentalists who, fearing challenges to their beliefs, demonized divination systems as the work of the devil. This dark period of European history was followed by the so-called Age of Enlightenment, which glorified the logic of reason and scientific laws as the only valid source for answers, further dismissing of the sacred traditions.

Given this history, is it any wonder that misunderstanding about the true nature and benefits of divination is widespread to this day? Under attack from the dogmatic influences of science and religion, humanity's rightful access to divination has suffered greatly from fear and prejudice. In spite of all the confusion and attacks, divination's popularity is still on the rise, even in this modern age. Ironically, the dogmatic belief systems propagated by science and the church are causing millions to look for spiritual awareness in ways that are more personal, useful and helpful.

Happily for seekers of truth, access to authentic tools

> **Scientific Validation**
>
> "There is only one figure to my knowledge who has tried to evaluate astrology in anything like a scientific way: the French researcher Michel Gauquelin (1928-91). After scrutinizing thousands of birth charts, Gauquelin came to conclusions that discomfited both conventional scientists and astrologers. He discovered that prominent members of various professions did indeed tend to have certain planets in certain places in their charts. Control groups taken from the general population had no such correlations."
> —Richard Smoley, in "The Stars We Are," *Gnosis,* Winter 1996.

Chapter 5: Enemies of Divination

for self-discovery is more widespread than ever, despite the clamor of fundamentalist fears, scientific prejudice and the self-serving stimulation of self-proclaimed psychics. We still have the freedom to investigate divination for ourselves, to discover and use these sacred arts for the development of our own intuition and true wisdom.

CHAPTER 6
The Gift of Prophecy—Divination in the Bible

The lot is cast, but its every decision is from the LORD.
—Proverbs 16:33, New King James Version

Almost everyone whose faith depends on biblical scripture believes that divination is a sin condemned by God. Fundamentalists claim that astrologers and diviners are agents of the devil leading the weak to eternal damnation. They selectively quote the Bible to back up their condemnation of divination systems and intuitive powers—many of which were accorded high respect within many parts of the same Bible. Fundamentalists ignore the fact that the Bible, even after extensive early editing, still contains numerous verses that show God approving the use of divination as a way to decipher His will and make enlightened decisions. In fact, there are more verses in the Bible that are pro-divination rather against it.

> *The dogma of the infallibility of the Bible is no more self-evident than is that of the infallibility of the popes.*
> —Thomas Huxley

Part of my training to become a minister was to study the Bible. Having attended Catholic schools for thirteen years, Christian scripture was hardly a new subject for me. Fortunately for me, neither Catholicism nor the New Thought form of Christianity that ordained me—a branch that includes Unity, Religious Science and Science of Mind churches—insist on a literal interpretation of ancient scriptures. As a result of my own interest and curiosity, I have further researched the history of the Bible, how the books were chosen, and how much of it, including the Genesis creation story and virgin birth, was borrowed from the similar myths of even more ancient cultures.

The historical account of how the twenty-seven books of the New Testament were chosen—and other books rejected—more than three hundred years after the death of Jesus is fascinating. This history is rarely taught by any of the Christian churches. One would think that the true story of how the Bible's books were selected—which canons were chosen, which were rejected, and the debate that waged around these choices—would be of supreme interest to all who consider the Bible the ultimate scriptural authority, but nothing could be further from the truth. Why is this?

The question turns mainly on whether the strange Greek in which the four Gospels are written is simply the work of Jews thinking in Aramaic though writing in Greek, or whether it represents rather an effort to translate literally into Greek original Aramaic Gospels now lost.

—Ernest Sutherland Bates

The obvious answer is that a legendary status for the Bible as the direct word of God would be compromised. The authority of the Bible would be tainted by a recounting of the political battles at the first great council of bishops, the Council of Nicea in 325 A.D., and how books were discarded or chosen and censored. It might stain the Bible's pedigree to let people know that this council was presided over by the pagan Roman emperor rather than the Bishop of Rome, who did not attend. And it might confuse the people if they knew of all the debate that went on about pivotal questions—like Jesus' true identity, the trinity, the end of times.

Like all large organizations, religions are political. Since the earliest monotheists (the Zoroastrans and the Levites of ancient Israel) up and through Christianity and Islam, religions have ruled entire societies. Some continue to do so today. Since the mastery of writing by the Levites—the priestly ruling tribe of Israel who wrote the Torah, known by Christians as the first five books of the Old Testament—religious leaders have been eager to develop, edit and use the power of composing and citing *holy texts* in order to exert political control.

As Leonard Shlain points out in his monumental book, *The Alphabet Versus The Goddess,* the technology of alphabetic writing, which historically coincides with the emergence of patriarchal societies, changed everything. Considering that early mastery of this miraculous skill was the exclusive province of the high priests of Israel, any text they declared as such was deemed *holy scripture.* And, as Dr. Shlain points out, the primary thing that men focus on, when they first acquire the ability to write, are laws. But these were not just any laws, but *holy* laws, backed by the threat of divine punishment, including eternal damnation.

Once the letter of the law is established, with authorship attributed to God, ongoing control mechanisms include censorship and fear-mongering, which is where devils as an active force of evil in the world come in. As we saw in the Middle Ages, totalitarian levels of control may include persecution, torture and execution—whatever it takes to maintain a maximum level of psychological power over the population, all in the name of God, of course, as interpreted by his political representatives on earth.

In the case of Christianity, this is that much easier to understand when one considers that the Church was approved as a state religion by the politically crafty Roman emperor, Constantine, at the Council of Nicea in 325 A.D., which he convened and presided over—where orthodox Christian ideology and the books to include in the Christian Bible were voted on.

Omissions and additions to the original texts were authorized in order to come up with an approved version that would at the very least be compatible with Roman political needs. For instance, many scholars assert that most (but not all) mentions of reincarnation were censored out in deference to the church's promise of eternal heaven and, more importantly, to support a fear of imminent eternal damnation for non-believers. Blame for the crucifixion was shifted away from the Roman, Pontius Pilate, and placed squarely upon the Jews, fueling anti-Semitism for the next 2000 years. John's apocalypse, now known as the Book of Revelations, was chosen for its fearsomeness, instead of Saint Peter's apocalypse which tells a different story with a different ending.

> The prophets of the Old Testament receive wisdom in the form of voices or visions from a higher power, which is then conveyed to others.

According to the documentary film *Banned From the Bible,* broadcast on the History Channel, Peter's version of the apocalypse was left out of the Bible because it contradicted what the newly formed Roman church wanted people to think and believe. Interestingly, these epistles, ascribed to Peter, support some claims that Islam would later make—that Jesus was not killed on the cross, that the divinity of Jesus the Prophet and the Trinity concept supporting that idea were mistakes that flew in the face of the central tenet of monotheism, that there is only one God. The banned epistles of Peter are only a few of the banned (and later burned) scriptures that have been archeologically discovered in the last 150 years.

The Apocalypse of Peter was popular among large groups of Christians during the second century. Every bit as fervent as any modern day Bible thumpers, they believed it was spiritually inspired by God to Saint Peter. They had serious doubts about John's version of the apocalypse, which was finally selected by the proto-

orthodox church of Rome. The differences are stark and highlight the political process behind state-sanctioned Christianity's organization and selection of its dogma.

The Apocalypse of Peter tells a story that is very different from the horrific Revelations. According to it, after God fills both Heaven and Hell with inhabitants from humankind, and the people of Hell get tortured long enough, the people of Heaven will entreat God to forgive the people in Hell. God will eventually listen to their prayers, and order the gates of Hell to be opened and allow all the people to enter Heaven for good. In this regard, the Apocalypse of Peter fits perfectly with verse 7:40 in the Quran where Allah promises that He will eventually open the gates of Heaven to all disbelievers and empty Hell.

> "The Word of God is the universal and invisible Light, cognizable by the senses, that emits its blaze in the Sun, Moon, Planets, and other Stars."
> —Albert Pike, in *Morals & Dogma.*

Revelations of John and Peter's Apocalypse can't both be right. The point is to recognize that all the great religions have made deliberate decisions in choosing their scriptures, as they clung to the power of the word in the form of some writings, but not others, which they would anoint as "the unchanging word of God."

The final selection of the twenty-seven books of the New Testament was complete by around 367 A.D.—over 300 years after the death of Jesus. During this period the fledgling Christian church also appropriated the Jewish scriptures and claimed them as its own "old testament," in order to confer upon itself a claim to antiquity.

Soon after, and ever since, the canonization of sacred scripture, sentences that support various political and social arguments—including the condemnation of divination—have been routinely taken out of the context of the time and place in which they were written. At this point, these are narrow interpretations of an ancient text that has been translated many times, and which includes many words and concepts no longer spoken or understood. Free-spirited rational beings will naturally have healthy skepticism and, in the final analysis, trust their own intuition about what to cite from ancient scriptures and what to believe was really intended and why.

Because divination and other intuitive arts are now so widely criticized and condemned based on selective citation of scriptures, this chapter and Appendix C,

which contains an exhaustive set of the relevant verses, are this writer's attempts to set the record straight. In an earlier chapter we showed how Jewish, Christian and Islamic sects dominated the minds of their followers by discrediting and severely punishing the slightest challenges to their authority as the sole representatives of God. We shall scan the spectrum of what the texts of the Old and New Testaments still contain about divination and psychic arts—including God's favorite divination technique of the time, as well as omen reading, channeling, psychic seers and prophets.

Upon a careful examination of the chosen books of the Bible, one discovers that it is chockful of the mantic arts. And, more often than not, God is shown as being in favor of these activities. He even commands the Israelites on several occasions to use their sacred divination system as a way of ascertaining His will.

In this chapter we will focus on the references to divination as well as other psychic arts in the Christian Bible. All scriptural passages referenced are from the New King James version. Once we examine the record, it will be clear that even according to the Bible, God intended us to use our intuitive abilities—including divination systems—as a way of interpreting and cooperating with His will.

This will be news to the Christians, Jews and Muslims who have been taught to believe the opposite based on a few negative verses taken out of context and repeated ad nauseam. Admittedly, in a few books of the Old Testament it is obvious that God was displeased by certain practices occurring at certain times by certain people. Perhaps this had to do with the historical period during which a particular book like Deuteronomy was written. Perhaps God was upset over some misuse of divination at the time. Who can say?

> *The Bible may be the truth, but it is not the whole truth and nothing but the truth.*
>
> —Samuel Butler

In order to be open to the value of the intuitive arts, people need to know that the opposition of the religious establishment contradicts its own scriptural authority. If fundamentalist zealots should ever condemn your interest in or use of divination, a knowledge of Jehovah's mixed feelings on the subject, supported by chapter and verse, will provide good rebuttal and offer verification

of God's approval of divination as revealed in their own scriptures, for what that's worth.

PROPHETS AND DIVINERS

Organized religions' condemnation of intuitive powers is especially ironic considering that the Bible itself is considered a channeled work, transcribed by its human authors through what St. Paul later defined as "the gift of prophecy," which was available to all who believed in orthodox doctrine. It is an article of faith in scripture's authority that God spoke through prophets, who received His message using what we now call channeling, a free form psychic version of divination. The Bible describes this process in several places, including the following:

> I will raise up for them a Prophet like you from among their brethren, and will put My words in His mouth, and He shall speak to them all that I command Him. (Deut. 18:18)

> I have also spoken by the prophets, And have multiplied visions; I have given symbols through the witness of the prophets. (Hos. 12:10)

The prophets are psychic mediums who received wisdom in the form of voices and visions from a higher power, which they then conveyed to others. The God of the Old Testament gave prophets knowledge of the future to warn people and persuade them to abide by God's will. As it is recorded, the prophets who predict the future generally do so when a warning is necessary, but it is reasonable to assume that they do it at other times too.

The prophets were watchmen, guardians of the people, who looked out for the nation because they could foresee the dangers coming. Prophets were also known to interpret events that were happening in the present, providing insights into God's reasons for creating the conditions in question. Diviners and prophets were classed as similar functionaries. In Isaiah 3:2-3 diviners are ranked with judges, warriors and prophets as pillars of the state.

> The mighty man and the man of war, The judge and the prophet, And the diviner and the elder; The cap-

tain of fifty and the honorable man, The counselor and the skillful artisan, And the expert enchanter. (Isa. 3:2-3)

The book of Numbers (Chapters 22-24) contains the story of Balaam, a diviner who was known for the effectiveness of his blessings—and his curses. This story is the furthest thing from an illustration of an abomination, or even a parable illustrating the dangers of the psychic arts. Balaam was in the good graces of God and was chosen by God to speak for Him. He was obedient, dutiful, and fair. The Bible does not cast aspersions upon him or condemn his actions as a diviner. God freely spoke to him, in a friendly way, and considered him as His messenger.

The story of the prophet Moses is a classic example of mystical experience. Moses repeatedly ascended Mt. Sinai to communicate directly with God. Not only did he listen to God's instructions, he also was able to ask questions in order to confirm the divine plan. Moses also used the Israelite's Urim method of divination described below. It only makes sense that he would use it, because communicating with divinity is what the word "divination" means, and what all divination systems are created to facilitate.

"In the beginning God created the heavens…."

Human beings have always looked up to the heavens for guidance, which is why Astrology is one of the oldest forms of divination. Long before astronomy was formalized, ancient astrologers observed the heavens for cosmic patterns, as well as omens and signs of divine will. Comets, eclipses, planetary alignments, and many other observable phenomena were, over time, accorded special significance. This practice was established long before biblical Palestine, and was an integral part of the region's culture.

In spite of its ancient pedigree, fundamentalists condemn Astrology, largely because of a misunderstanding about how Astrology works. Historically, religious persecutors took the position that astrologers worshipped false gods because they supposedly considered the heavenly bodies as deities that control our destinies and reveal our future. Thus, Astrology is a form of idolatry,

Astrological Event

"Lo, the star, which they saw in the east, went before them, till it came and stood over where the young child was."
—St. Matthew 2:9

The classic five-pointed star (a vaguely human form) was originally a Christian symbol of the incarnation of Jesus.

the reasoning goes. But the argument is false.

While the image of deities has always been one way to characterize divine powers in many ancient religions like Hinduism and Buddhism, it is not the only way. I know a lot of astrologers and have yet to meet one who believes the stars are gods that control our fate. Using Astrology for reflections on personalities and events is based on an understanding, recently proven by science, of the interconnectedness of all things. We know that the moon and other celestial bodies affect cycles on Earth—such as the tides, animal behavior, and human emotional states.

In Genesis, the first book of the Bible, God specifically said that He was creating the heavens to produce signs, among other things. Considering that Astrology was a fixture of Middle Eastern culture when the books were written, it is completely reasonable to assume that the word "signs" was at least an indirect reference to Astrology in the following passage.

> Then God said, "Let there be lights in the firmament of the heavens to divide the day from the night; and let them be for signs and seasons, and for days and years;…" (Gen. 1:14)

What was the Star of Bethlehem, if not such a sign in the form of a celestial body that wise men followed? How is this different from Astrology?

THE HIGH PRIEST'S DIVINATION SYSTEM

Divination and the reading of omens are commonly used in the Bible when it comes to deciding all sorts of issues. Most that were recorded had to do with the safety of king or state. The prophet Elisha directed King Joash to throw two arrows through the window in order to find out whether the king would be victorious or not (2 Kings 13:14-19). Gideon's victory over the Midianites was signalled by God using omens. If the fleece of the sheep was wet and the ground was dry, it was a sign of ensuing success (Judg. 6:36-40). In 1 Samuel 14:9, Jonathan decides whether or not he should attack the Philistines by the words the Lord has them speak. There is nothing in the Bible that disapproves of the reading of signs sent from God.

But the Israelites did not have to rely on external signs. They had a sacred divination system, known as Urim and Thummim, given to them by Jahweh, the use of which is referenced in several verses of the Old Testament that were not edited out. The exact composition of the Urim and Thummim is not known, but most scholars believe that they were two sacred stone dice, probably made of precious gems. They were stored in a pouch that was kept behind the high priest's "breastplate of judgment," which he wore whenever seeking divine guidance with regard to important legal controversies or strategic decisions of state.

There is no way to confirm the exact details of how the Urim and Thummim were cast or read. However it worked (and we do not know exactly), the Bible makes it clear that the divination system was sacred, and that God controlled the answers it produced.

Abraham used Urim and Thummim, as did Aaron and the priests of Israel.

> He shall stand before Eleazer the priest, who shall inquire before the Lord for him by the judgment of the Urim. At his word they shall go out, and at his word they shall come in, he and all the children of Israel with him—all the congregation. (Num. 27:21)

As noted, Moses used the Urim and Thummim. Joshua was named as his successor using this divination system (Num. 27:21). After Joshua died, the Israelites used it to determine who would continue to lead them into victory over the Canaanites (Judg. 1:1). When David was considering whether or not to pursue the marauding Amalekites, the divination tool confirmed for him that it was advisable to do so (1 Sam. 30: 7-8). There are many more examples of the divinatory use of the Urim and Thummim which can be easily looked up in any Bible concordance.

Since there are so many instances in the Bible in which God provides answers to his followers through divination—either with Urim and Thummim or the casting of lots, as was used in the New Testament to pick Matthias as the replacement for Judas—we ask ourselves how and why it is that divination has come to be portrayed as evil by fundamentalist religions and sects.

The casting of lots as a spiritual practice:

"Then Aaron shall cast lots for the two goats: one lot for the Lord and the other lot for the scapegoat."
—Leviticus 16:8

"And they cast lots for their duty, the small as well as the great, the teacher with the student."
—1 Chronicles 25:8

"And they cast their lots, and the lot fell on Matthias. And he was numbered with the eleven apostles."
—Acts 1:26 (how the apostles replaced Judas)

The most commonly quoted verses in the Bible used to condemn divination:

"There shall not be found among you *anyone* who makes his son or his daughter pass through the fire, *or one* who practices witchcraft, *or* a soothsayer, or one who interprets omens, or a sorcerer, or one who conjures spells, or a medium, or a spiritist, or one who calls up the dead.

For all who do these things *are* an abomination to the Lord, and because of these abominations the Lord your God drives them out from before you."

—Deuteronomy 18:10-12

The Biblical Case Against Divination

Considering that the God of the Old Testament sanctioned and recommended divination in more passages than otherwise (see Appendix C of this book for a full listing of verses), it is a travesty that Judaism, Christianity, and Islam have condemned divination systems. In spite of all the passages noted herein (and listed on Divination.com), the fact that Christian fundamentalists continue to cite the Bible as proof that God condemns diviners is incredible.

The most commonly cited verse in the Bible used to assert that divination is a terrible transgression against God's will is Deuteronomy 18:10-12 (see sidebar).

Before taking this at face value out of context, it's important to note that the book of Deuteronomy contains countless laws that were themselves abominable and are no longer respected or practiced by anyone, let alone used as grounds for persecution. For instance, "At the end of every seven years you shall grant a release of debts" (Deut. 15:1). There would be countless people in a much better financial position if this law were enforced!

Women might be interested to know that they are an abomination to the Lord if they wear men's clothes (Deut. 22:5). Also according to this law, any bride who is not a virgin on her wedding night shall be stoned to death on her father's porch (Deut. 22:21). This book also instructs what women should do in the event they are captured during battle.

> When you go out to war against your enemies, and the LORD your God delivers them into your hand, and you take them captive, and you see among the captives a beautiful woman, and desire her and would take her for your wife, then you shall bring her home to your house, and she shall shave her head and trim her nails. (Deut. 21:10-12)

Over the centuries, churches, temples and mosques have narrowly selected which parts of their scriptures to heed, and which to ignore, but in this modern age we are free to review scriptures for ourselves with fresh eyes. In so doing, we need to remember that the true value of scriptures does not lie in lists of ancient laws

and "shalt-nots," but in parables of virtue and timeless principles that are relevant to the cultivation of wisdom. If religious organizations have been hostile to divination, it is because they are not interested in cultivating the types of mystical experiences that inspired the formation of those religions in the first place.

We cannot be sure why there are some verses in the Old Testament that seem to forbid divination. Perhaps there were fraudulent psychics at the time of Deuteronomy, just like there are today. Even so, why should we ignore the even more numerous verses in which God approves of divination, or even dictates its use? As we have noted, the Bible is full of such phenomenon (see an exhaustive list in Appendix C of this book).

Based on a fair and balanced look at the biblical record, it is safe to conclude that our Western God intended us to use divination systems to better interpret a divine plan. In ancient times, only the high priest had the power of direct access. Luckily, all spiritually inclined people alive today have access to better divination systems—like the I Ching and Tarot. We are now able to access divination systems directly on our own, bypassing religious and political hierarchies altogether.

In the first century of the common era, as he was defining orthodox Christian beliefs, St. Paul labeled the ability to decipher the mind of God as "the Gift of Prophecy"—one of the gifts of the Holy Spirit supposed to be available to true believers. It was a form of channeling. Nowadays, thanks to universal access to authentic divination tools, everyone—Christian and non-Christian alike—who approaches the process with sincerity can go direct, without being expected to channel (or speak in tongues, for that matter). When it comes to communicating with the divine, we are truly the chosen people.

Numerology is not the only system for finding meaning in numbers. Christian symbolism attributes significance to these numbers:

1 = singularity of God

2 = divine and human duality of Christ

3 = Holy Trinity

4 = four gospel writers (Evangelists); also the four seasons

5 = Christ's wounds on the cross; sacrifice

6 = days of creation

7 = consummation, perfection, and rest

8 = the kingdom of grace following the world's creation; regeneration

9 = the choirs of angels, the holy spirit's gifts

10 = God's commandments

13 = Betrayal (Judas)

CHAPTER 7
Divination Practice Today

Wheel of Fortune
Change, fate, luck

The Art Nouveau Tarot
© US Games Systems Inc.

If used mindfully, [divination] will help you to see the mountains you must climb, not avoid them.

—Sandra Mizumoto Posey, Ph.D.

hroughout history, including modern times, emperors and heads of state have sought wisdom from divination systems and rituals to help guide their decisions. Nowadays, a vast and growing number of people use divination to help themselves make better choices. For instance, I have heard from Wall Street stockbrokers who use the I Ching to aid their intuition in choosing companies with growth potential. In defense of his use of Astrology, J.P. Morgan once said, "Millionaires don't use astrologers, billionaires do."

Despite how divination may have been represented to you in the past, authentic divination does not pretend to predict the future, nor does it claim to offer specific answers to problems. This is what fortune-tellers and mind readers purport to do. It is not necessary to be psychic to use divination to stimulate and support your intuition, to learn to read between the lines and find the answers you need within yourself.

In helping you understand how to use divination tools, I don't want to just hand you a fish, as the proverb goes. Rather I'd rather convince you that you can learn how to fish, and then show you how. There is a deep well of divine wisdom within you, stocked with all the answers you will ever need, which you can fish from using your intuition whenever you want or need to. Divination tools just make the fishing a lot easier.

Before cultivating a divination practice, it is important to get clear about what you hope to gain from the experience. Put serious thought and energy into how you frame your question, as well as how you approach and interpret your reading. Let yourself be open to the wisdom of the reading you manifest. Ultimately, we need to take personal responsibility for the choices or decisions we make. Divination is a powerful tool that needs to be used correctly. It is not a crutch. Divination does not

"I never rely on Tarot cards or the I-Ching to tell me what to do, but I have found that they do help me think outside the box, to view situations and relationships with greater creativity and wisdom."

—John Gray, "Tarot and I-Ching for Relationships" (see Appendix F)

> No one is born under a bad star, there are only those who do not know how to read the sky.
>
> —Dalai Lama

predict the future. You ultimately have the power within you to manifest your destiny. Some unprincipled people use divination to take advantage of others, so it's important to pick counselors carefully. Finally, any authentic divination system will give you a reflection of the energy you put into it, and the spirit in which you do it.

Whether you are experimenting with divination for the first time, or looking for ways to make your use of divination more fruitful, you are likely to encounter some of the following questions: when to use divination, which divination system is best for you, how to ask an appropriate question, and how to put together a personal divination ritual for yourself. This chapter will strive to provide answers to these and other questions regarding the practical and effective use of divination.

WHEN TO USE DIVINATION

Divination is a useful problem-solving or decision-making aid whenever you have a dilemma that logic can't handle, or would just like some new insights into a particular situation. There are plenty of important areas in life where logic cannot do the job by itself—such as relationships, negotiations and timing issues, to name a few recurring ones. Certainly, if logic can solve a problem, it is a great tool and common sense dictates that one should use it. Logic is like surgery—even if you are an ardent believer in holistic medicine, there is a time and place for surgical interventions. Using a divination system is never an excuse for ignoring what you can figure out—the facts are every bit as important as your intuition. They always deserve attention and respect.

This seemingly obvious observation is sometimes ignored by people who have taken the maxim "you create your own reality" too much to heart. While there is an important truth behind this saying, the exercise of left-brained analysis and reasonable compromises is all that is required to deal with some obstacles. To benefit from our powers of logical analysis, a realistic acceptance of the present situation helps. No matter how strong you may feel your creative powers of manifestation are, denial of the facts in favor of wishful thinking almost always sets you back. We have to deal with situations

and challenges the way we find them. We cannot override our karma through wishful thinking or even raw will power.

Even when we carefully consider the reality of a situation, analysis often cannot provide enough information to sort things out. Sometimes there are too many unknowable factors. This is when wisdom, not just sheer intelligence, is called for. By supporting the intuitive part of our brains, divination can stimulate practical wisdom for any kind of issue or situation that can't be solved through logic alone.

> People who lean on logic and philosophy and rational exposition end by starving the best part of the mind.
>
> —William Butler Yeats

For instance, in times of low self-esteem when you are most in need of support and reassurance, divination can help you make better choices. An authentic reading can help you come to terms with challenging situations, in spite of patterns from your past that still give rise to confusion or conflict. Some forms of divination can even be used to identify these previous influences. One example of this is how the most common Tarot spread, the Celtic Cross, includes positions that reflect old patterns, relating to one's personal history leading up to a current confusing situation or predicament.

Given the pressure of decision-making in modern times, is it any wonder people feel overwhelmed? Choose a cell phone plan. Choose an Internet service provider. Choose a car insurance company. Choose a career. Choose an appetizer. It's hard enough to manage all the small details of life, but when you are faced with critical personal choices, the challenge of making the right decision can be frightening. In cases like these, an authentic divination experience can provide much needed perspective.

The need for intuitive support can seem almost urgent in times of uncertainty, high anxiety or stress. Unfortunately, it is precisely when you are feeling most depressed or anxious that it is best not to rush a reading. Extreme emotion can interfere with one's ability to make an accurate interpretation. During these times, it may be preferable to seek out a gifted practitioner, ask skilled friends to help you interpret your reading, or wait until after a few minutes in meditation or deep breathing to give yourself an online reading. Having an objective

interpretation is particularly important when you are experiencing high levels of stress.

Questions to ask yourself when choosing a live reader:

• What do *you* want out of the reading?

• What are you willing to pay?

• Do you intuitively feel comfortable enough to trust this person?

CHOOSING A LIVE READER

While the five classical divination systems presented here are based on ancient wisdom traditions, there are an astounding variety of ways in which they are practiced in our highly diverse world. Since literacy and books were rare in ancient times, almost all divination was dependent upon a skilled intermediary—usually a medium, reader, psychic or shaman. Most ancient divination systems were shared in the oral tradition, so seekers had to rely on wise elders, their priestesses and shamans. Today, however, if a person can use an Internet connection, he or she has direct access to more systems of divination than ever before in history.

Most people still think of divinatory readings as an interaction between two people—the client and the reader. Traditionally, the two have had to be in the same place, but nowadays readings are commonly given over the phone, or even by e-mail, which can reduce the counseling value of the personal connection. No matter what form of communication you use—whether it's a live reader or an interactive do-it-yourself system—it is absolutely critical that the interpreter be trustworthy, experienced and knowledgeable.

It is my conviction that the seeker, not the reader, should be the one to pick the cards in the case of a Tarot reading, flip the coins for I Ching, or toss the Rune stones. This idea is a bit controversial, since there are many readers who depend upon their ability to deliver services by phone, and who will claim that they are so adept at tuning into your energy that they can cast an oracle for you. But there are ways a reader can have a client pick their own cards for a reading over the phone, even if they don't have a deck handy. For instance, the client could tell the reader when to stop shuffling or that the card they want is, say, three cards from the top. Every little bit helps!

As we saw in chapter 5, "Enemies of Divination," there are so many con artists out there operating as psychics that it can be difficult to trust that someone you don't know is on the level. A gifted reader provides a form of spiritual counseling that can touch on the most sensitive areas of your life. So, take great care in selecting a reader, just as you would a counselor, a mechanic, doctor or babysitter.

Beware of becoming emotionally dependent on a psychic or spiritual counselor. Such a relationship could turn into a dangerous form of co-dependence,

> **It is best to avoid psychic readers who:**
>
> • Believe in curses, hexes, demonic possession, or exorcism. This is the common spin of frauds.
>
> • Are unwilling to discuss—free of charge—their beliefs, method, background, or experience.
>
> • Cannot quote a specific price for their services.
>
> • Cannot provide a code of ethics, a personal policy statement, or a similar document of standards.
>
> • Seem too theatrical—i.e., they are costumed, veiled, and preoccupied with ambience.
>
> • Will not allow you to tape-record the reading, or will not give you the only copy of the recording.

actually setting back your healing process. If emotional issues keep coming up for you, seek out a psychotherapist or a licensed counselor to help you. Divination has been described as "do-it-yourself psychotherapy"—and it certainly can perform this function up to a point—but it is more a tool for self-help or spiritual counseling than it is for healing deep emotional wounds.

The process of choosing the right reader is all about you. What do *you* want out of the reading? What are you willing to pay? Do you intuitively feel comfortable enough to trust this person? Finding the right counselor for you can take time. While it is helpful to get referrals from friends, co-workers, or relatives, the psychic who's best for you may not be right for someone else and vice versa. Do your best to make a well-researched, informed decision. Trust your instincts, and don't be afraid to walk away.

If you get a reading, be straightforward and honest if nothing in it had any meaning for you. Feel free to experiment with finding the right reader in a trial-and-error process. Don't ever forget that the responsibility for your spiritual progress is all yours. Under no circumstances should you ever give your personal power away to a reader. If you feel compatible with him or her, and your reading has the ring of truth, then consider the wisdom that is stimulated within you. See if it works for you in terms of making better choices. If so, you might

Heaven   Water/River

Thunder   Mountain

Lake   Fire/Wood

Earth   Wind/Grass

The eight Trigrams represent the eight elements of Chinese philosophy and combine to make the sixty-four hexagrams used for I Ching readings.

want to try that reader again. But never forget that like doctors and mechanics, a reader is working for you!

It's always important to remember that nobody can predict the future. Any psychic claiming to do so is a fraud. If he or she is making flat-out predictions, especially negative ones, just leave. Until you have reason to trust a reader's skill, take all advice with a grain of salt. At the same time, be prepared to hear things you don't want to hear, or may be resistant to. If a reading seems inaccurate at first, you can give it a little time—see how it ages. Occasionally, an accurate reading cuts through our ego defenses in such a way that it is tough to accept.

DO-IT-YOURSELF DIVINATION

If you have contact with a gifted reader who understands the archetypes of a divination system—and you can afford the service—by all means, go for it. If you don't, experiment with do-it-yourself services like the Tarot.com or I-Ching.com web sites. These are among a handful of authentic divination sites and software programs that let you give yourself an accurate reading, based on interpretations by scholars. While online or computer-generated reports will never match the richness of a personal session with a gifted reader, they have the advantages of being inexpensive and always available. When they are authored by a mystical scholar of the divination art, they are totally consistent in their high quality.

There are readers who insist that a divination system facilitated by computer or Internet is not the real thing, but it can be just as accurate as a face-to-face reading, and depending upon the emotional state of a reader, often more so. Astrologers and numerologists have used computers for more than thirty years now, because it is more efficient to let the computers calculate charts and tables. It makes sense to use a computer to look up an interpretation for a particular image or pattern from what is essentially a nonlinear encyclopedia of all the possible permutations. It's no problem to use a computer to pick cards or toss coins either—this can be programmed so that the computer will not affect the results and be just as transparent to the process as a cup that is used to toss coins or dice.

Superior software and web sites that are designed by someone who truly understands divination not only make it easy for you to pick your own cards or cast the coins without interfering, they also provide an instant and permanent copy of your reading that is often more extensive than what one takes away from a private session. One advantage of accumulating a divination journal is that it is helpful to be able to analyze patterns that run through your readings over time. (There is a free feature on Tarot. com that can perform such an analysis.) Even if you are going for a personal session, it helps to print out an online reading first, so you can then ask questions, clarify, and arrive at deeper meaning through a more informed interaction with your reader.

The following true story of Karen, a Tarot.com customer, illustrates how computer-assisted divination can be profoundly helpful. Karen had a tendency to try to rescue others, whatever their situation. For Karen, who worked in show business for many years, there was never a shortage of people living in dramas of their own making and needing help. So, when a well-known acquaintance and sports figure got unfairly crucified in the press, Karen found herself involved in a nine-month effort to help him repair his public image. The situation did not improve. At one point, she sought Tarot.com's guidance.

The do-it-yourself Tarot reading she gave herself included the Hanged Man card appearing in the "Other" position. "Some unconscious aspect of one's reality is occasionally publicly exposed. It is the other person's turn in the stockades." In short, this was not really her fight or her problem. According to Karen, "That little

reading was the most accurate one I have ever received and it really helped me become more realistic about the situation and my role."

Another card suggested that Karen "cease all attempts to rescue, defend, or explain the situation because whatever distress this person is experiencing is unavoidable." The reading was so uncannily accurate that it awakened Karen to her own narrow thinking, which had been producing feelings of failure within herself.

"Much like the guy I was trying to help," she says, "I had a problem with intolerance. I used to scoff at whether a reading could be accurate without the presence of a live reader. In other words, I doubted the validity of a computer's ability to facilitate that kind of insight. It took that passage to wake me up and make me notice it."

The insights she received from her reading released Karen from always trying to rescue others, or solve problems that weren't really hers. "It's like I'm free," she says. The experience also helped Karen recognize that do-it-yourself divination methods can be accurate and helpful. "If it is late at night and you need help, [computerized readings] can help you pretty much like a human counselor sitting in the room. I'm not excluding it anymore. I've come to a happy acceptance, a welcoming, actually."

In addition to personal readers and software, there is also the option of divining the old-fashioned way. Buy the *I Ching* book and some coins, a Tarot deck or Rune stones, and a few books on interpretation -- and then study! If you have the time and energy necessary to master a system, it can be highly satisfying for your own life and offers the benefit of being able to help others too. The reality is that most of us in this fast-paced world don't have time to become an expert at divination, which is perfectly okay. Unless that is a personal goal, allow yourself to experience divination the way that feels most compelling, easy, and natural for you. For information on how to use a classical divination system the traditional way, see Appendix B, "How to Give Yourself a Reading."

> We are born at a given moment, in a given place and, like vintage years of wine, we have the qualities of the year and of the season of which we are born. Astrology does not lay claim to anything more.
>
> —Carl Jung

Choosing a Divination System

When people try different kinds of divination systems, they usually feel more drawn to one than another. This is to be expected. Many people like to use more than one. Others switch to a new type of divination after spending years working with another. Aside from whether a particular system aesthetically or culturally appeals to you, the primary factors in choosing which form of divination to use are whether the author or reader speaks to you, whether it has a "voice" that you resonate with, or the system is particularly well-suited to your type of inquiry.

Numerology often appeals to analytical people, says Hans Decoz, professional numerologist, author of *Numerology: Key to Your Inner Self,* and Numerology report author for Tarot.com. Because its foundation is numbers, and people associate numbers with objectivity, there is a universal sense that Numerology is unbiased, clean and specific. "Numbers don't lie," Hans playfully reminds us.

Numerology is especially useful for career and lifestyle questions because it can deliver a blueprint of your talents, shortcomings, and temperament from birth to death. This information helps us to pursue the careers that suit our true nature, and find a range of potentially rewarding pursuits.

Hans believes that using Numerology for personal profiles, compatibility reports and future forecasts is a minor benefit. In its grander sense, he says, Numerology opens up a universal way of thinking about and understanding life and the world around us. Through the power and magic of numbers, it helps us recognize patterns in people, time, and places.

Astrology is the oldest and perhaps the most familiar of all the divination systems, because of the popularity of daily horoscopes. Master astrologer, Rick Levine, who

Hans Decoz was a precocious child. He loved to figure out complex mathematical problems and, once completed, put aside such work for hours at his easel where he produced drawings and paintings. These abilities eventually led to fascination with computers. He sought to put these disciplines in the service of making Numerology more accessible and user friendly. In 1985, Hans developed the renowned computer software program known as the DecozChart.

That program is still the only Numerology program capable of producing a complete chart with fifty years of forecasting cycles. The chart—a beautifully designed layout—appears on a single page, visually capturing a lifetime of cycles and changes. DecozCharts have been featured on Tarot.com since 2001.

Presidential Astrology

Ronald Reagan, at the advice of his wife's astrologer, chose 12:42 AM as the time for his gubernatorial inauguration.

writes the horoscopes for Tarot.com, says, "Astrology is the most scientific of the divinatory arts, because it is based on the movements of the Sun, moon and planets. At the same time, Astrology is also an intuitive art that can give a reflection of an entire lifetime, or focus in on a particular issue or relationship. It can also be used for selecting the best times for planned events." Rick reminds us that while there are no bad times to do a good thing, and no good times to do bad, people consult Astrology for the ideal time to get married, change jobs, buy a house, sell a car, move to a new state, and so on.

Rick also points out that Astrology has played an important role in the development of the sciences, arts and even religion. Many of the greatest scientists throughout history had astrological interests, including Johannes Kepler, the father of modern astronomy. Physicians still take the Oath of Hippocrates, overlooking that he also wrote, "He who practices medicine without the benefit of the movement of the stars and planets is a fool." To see how deep the relationship is between Astrology and the Church, all one needs to do is go into the Vatican's Sistine Chapel and look up. The twelve signs of the zodiac are quite prominent.

An Astrology reading can provide information on relationship dynamics, career possibilities, personal psychology, life goals, and family issues. It's possible to compare patterns from the past to the present and a probable future. Even though Astrology can deliver many types of reports, Rick says, "Most people are interested in sex, drugs and rock-and-roll—in other words, love, our Heart's Desires and meaningful work."

Tarot, the I Ching and Runes differ from Astrology and Numerology in that they are interactive divination tools that can help you derive insights or decision-making support for something that is happening *now*, based on the actions you do in the present—picking cards, tossing coins, choosing a stone. Even though these three systems can reveal patterns and suggest future tendencies, they are primarily focused on the present dynamics of a particular situation or relationship. For this reason, many people give themselves a daily Tarot or I Ching reading as a form of meditation on their day, inquiring about no particular subject at all.

Best-selling Tarot author Mary Greer recommends Tarot as a way to explore new options, clarify goals, and make better decisions. Mary points out that Tarot, like Numerology and Astrology, can help us to look at patterns and connections in different parts of our lives. Because Tarot uses pictorial metaphors that are derived from mysticism and folk wisdom, visually oriented people may respond more strongly to Tarot than other divination systems. An artfully designed deck makes it possible to see connections from one card to the next, simply based on the characters, colors, and imagery. "Tarot cards amplify the symbolic aspects of events," says Mary. "The Tarot reflects a profound sense of what's going on in your life. The cards help you to more clearly see aspects of a situation that may have been blind spots for your ego." The solution to your dilemma or situation depends on how well you adapt to the underlying conditions—both personal and impersonal—that the reading is making more visible.

Even in the ultra-practical world of business, Tarot is proving to be a useful way to understand personalities and interpersonal dynamics, for team building, counseling and hiring. I recently used the Tarot to assist in hiring for a position of responsibility at Visionary Networks. I asked the Tarot, "What values are the candidates likely to bring to the company?" I drew three cards for each candidate. For candidate number 1—the more task-oriented of the two—I drew the 3 of Wands, 6 of Cups, and 9 of Cups. For candidate number 2—the relationship-oriented candidate—I drew the 5 of Coins, 4 of Coins, and 4 of Cups. As you can guess by the card meanings in the chart in the margin, I chose the first candidate.

> ### Job Candidate #1
>
> 3 of Wands: solutions, enterprise, virtue
> 6 of Cups: pleasure, the future
> 9 of Cups: success, abundance
>
> ### Job Candidate #2
>
> 5 of Coins: material difficulty, painful outcomes
> 4 of Coins: poverty consciousness
> 4 of Cups: mixed happiness, dissatisfaction

The I Ching, since its Western revival in the 1960s, has been categorized as New Age in the media. It is, however, anything but new—having been used by emperors, sages, and Chinese military leaders for more than three thousand years. Today, this ancient oracle

> "I use the I-Ching from time to time. I have no cultural connection to it, yet the coins sing to me. When I first held them in my hands, it was as if I had come home. The joy in my soul was incredible. If I had worried that I was not fit to use them, I never would have felt that joy. I use divination primarily to shed light on current problems and situations. I try to find out what I might be overlooking. Sort of like using a flashlight in the dark."
> —Posted by "Lucida" in a divination web forum

continues to be put to practical use by stockbrokers, business owners, psychotherapists, physicists, and many other enlightened yet practical individuals. Some say it is the most authoritative of all divination systems.

Some women have found traditional translations of the I Ching too masculine and politically oriented. In my early work developing the first I Ching software product, I found that rephrasing the "Judgments" section created a new level of accessibility for this ancient source of wisdom. We made it a point to reinterpret patriarchal language such as "the superior man" and to translate the military hexagrams to reflect ideals of organization and teamwork. Nevertheless, compared to other divination modalities, the I Ching lends itself to the executive function of decision-making. Because its wisdom speaks so directly, it also lends itself to group orientation and problem-solving. An Oregon story illustrates this.

On the 4th of July weekend in 1974, a statewide conference called "Bend in the River" was held in Bend, Oregon. More than 100 delegates from around the state gathered to help shape the state's future. They were there to talk, listen and offer resolutions in the hope of building on Oregon's reputation as a livable place, supported by its groundbreaking land-use planning laws.

Author and famous "merry prankster" Ken Kesey gave the opening remarks, while public radio and television broadcast the event. Poets served as delegates. The I Ching was consulted to smooth over procedural differences. That an ancient source of divinatory wisdom was used in the 20th century at a conference presided over by the governor of an American state makes me proud to be an Oregonian!

How to Frame a Question for Divination

Would you ask an electrician how to change the transmission fluid in your car? Would you ask a mechanic for stock tips? Of course not. Asking the right questions of a qualified source is the only consistent way to get answers you can trust. In the same way, divination tools are useful only for certain kinds of queries. They work best when you are looking for insight, wise advice or a sense of which way the wind is blowing. They are

146

not designed to answer questions asking for data, yes/no answers, or to precisely predict the future. Think of the process of divination as consulting a wise friend or mentor. Even so, no matter how good the advice, you have to make your own choices, your own bets, and the way things turn out will still be up to you.

Divination is a way to gain perspective on what's happening in the present moment, to receive new information in the form of insights. So, form your inquiry with the pursuit of wisdom in mind. The words are important, because they influence your mind and your energy as you perform the ritual. Ask for insights, not predictions. "What is the best approach to take vis-a-vis 'xyz'?" After you have had a chance to glean the primary gems of insight from a reading—the thought-forms that stimulate new ideas and a broader perspective—then you can make a more informed decision, knowing that you have done your best to create a glorious future that is in alignment with your true destiny. That is the best anyone can do.

There are two classes of divination queries—the big picture and the snapshot. Big picture questions work well when you are not in a specific crisis, but are interested in personality traits or trends in your life, or your compatibility with another person. Beware of overly broad questions such as "what is the meaning of life?" The archetypes of any divination system were never designed to deliver a philosophical treatise.

A snapshot question works best when you are faced with making a decision for a given dilemma, and are looking for a new idea or a bit of good advice. When dealing with an immediate problem, it is best to ask the oracle about the attitude, method or approach to take rather than specific details on what is going to happen. Avoid asking for data like, "Where will I get a job?" or, "Who is the man of my dreams?" Notice the difference when these issues are rephrased: "What is the best course of action for finding a satisfying job?" and "What should I look for in a suitable mate?" If you ask the appropriate kinds of questions, you are more likely to have a satisfying divination experience.

As much as humans fantasize about the ability to

Types of questions that work well using Tarot and the I Ching:

- "What is the best approach to take in my relationship?"

- "What is the most skillful way to relate to (a person) at this time?"

- "Please give me a reflection on what's happening with this situation."

- "What is the best way to approach a situation?"

Types of questions that do not work well:

- "Where should I go on vacation?"

- "Is my love interest really the one for me?"

- "What is the meaning of life?"

> *A prudent question is one half of wisdom.*
> —Francis Bacon

foretell the future, divination systems cannot reply to questions asking for specific data or predictions. What they can do is provide a better sense of direction, with insights and advice based on timeless wisdom. It is not even necessary to formulate your query as a question. It's usually better to focus on a specific subject during the divination process. Just write down the name of a situation or person with whom you are in a relationship. The extra clarity will help to produce a more informative reading.

Certain areas of life present the kinds of problems that are beyond the ability of logic to resolve. These were described to me by Christine Payne-Towler, one of the world's leading Tarot scholars who is the author of the interactive readings on Tarot.com and a book, *The Underground Stream: Esoteric Tarot Revealed.* In an interview (on February 25, 2003), Christine described to me the three most common categories of questions she receives when giving readings.

Questions about romance and intimacy are the most common. In addition to people who are dating, these queries may come from people who have been married and are confused by a recent profound connection with a stranger or old flame, a form of the "grass is greener" syndrome. In either case, they want to know what kind of approach to take toward their social lives, or whether a real connection is possible with another person.

Career and work-related questions are the second largest category. Often individuals are wondering what is next after losing their jobs, are looking for ways to improve their career, or are simply seeking wisdom about their true calling. These questions focus on the individual's connection to the outside world, passion, purpose or vocation.

Self-improvement and introspective inquiries are less frequent. Christine points out that if more people used Tarot in this way, they wouldn't end up in the dire straits they're in by the time they turn to readers for advice. These questions focus on the individual's connection to themselves, their goals and dreams, and their destiny.

Whatever your focus, avoid disrespectful or frivolous questioning when you go for any kind of reading. As

the Chinese say, "Sincerity makes for accuracy." If you want divination to be accurate for you, you must be totally sincere in your attitude, approach, and the type of question you ask. Don't do what I did when I first tried the I Ching; don't fool around. Remember, the goal is not to predict the future—which, after all, is ours to create—but to make the most creative decisions and the best choices along the way.

Often individuals will try to ask an oracle about how other people feel or will act. This is not recommended, although Numerology and Astrology can be used to learn about characteristics of another person. For instance, it is common to calculate the astrological birth chart of a baby, or to use Astrology or Numerology to judge the compatibility of a couple. They've been doing it this way in Asia for centuries (where the newspapers pioneered personal ads decades before the practice became popular in the West). But even when trying to use divination systems to inquire about others, the oracle will respond to your dominant personal issues—such as fear of confrontation, insecurity, or lack of trust—instead of reflecting anything about the other person.

Might you be asking about another's intentions because you're feeling jealous, afraid, hopeful, or shy? You will find more meaning by examining the feelings *you* have at the time of divination, and asking about how to deal with your own emotions. If a friend or loved one is asking you for help, or requesting an opinion, suggest they get a reading for themselves.

No matter what your issue or concern, the attitude with which you approach divination is a critical factor in a reading's effectiveness. There are times when we turn to divination because we are experiencing anxiety, doubt, distress. When we are confused and don't understand why things are turning out the way they are, it's easy to be afraid, perhaps even a little paranoid at times. But fear thoughts can easily dominate your consciousness and interfere with our creative powers exactly when we need them most.

At such a time, it is important to take a few moments to affirm your faith—honestly and confidently—that everything will work out the way it is supposed to. If you

The attitude with which you approach divination is a critical determinant in a reading's effectiveness.

A Ritual Checklist

Environment: Use music, candles, incense, and so on to create a ritual space.

Affirmation: Believe that you can access your intuitive knowledge.

Attitude: Pray for a humble attitude that doesn't try to force the outcome.

Herbal Aids: Burning special herbs at the beginning and end of your divination rituals can help define your sacred space and cleanse it of unwanted energies.

• **Sage** is a cleansing and purifying herb. It's used to banish negative energies.

• **Cedar** needles are also used to cleanse, as well as bring emotional balance.

• **Lavender** flowers can be burned to promote forgiveness and to offer a spiritual blessing.

• **Sweetgrass** brings harmony and beauty into the space, as well as one's life.

are simply overwhelmed by strong emotion, you have no choice but to inquire about that feeling state itself, or not inquire at all, and just wait for a bit.

There's no point in inquiring about anything else unless you can retain some semblance of balance. Be as calm, focused, and open as you can when approaching any divination ritual. The more clearly you can focus on an issue or inquiry, the more clearly understood the result will be for you. If you are comfortable with the divination process, it is more likely you will find the reading accurate and helpful. Perform whatever centering exercise works best for you prior to any process of divination. It is important that you be as close as you can be to a state of relaxed concentration.

Creating Your Own Ritual

The idea of engaging in a ritual may seem foreign or even slightly intimidating to some people. In general, rituals have been associated with religious and cult activities. In truth, everyone has his or her rituals—mundane as well as spiritual. The *American Heritage Dictionary* defines ritual as "a ceremonial act or a series of such acts; a detailed method of procedure faithfully followed." The word "faithfully" is key here, because consciousness is what separates ritual from mere habit. Whether it's taking a yoga or dance class, playing golf every Saturday, or taking the kids to the park. These can all be considered rituals, if the habits are practiced with conscious reverence as well as regularity.

Commitment begins with intention. If your intention is to establish a regular practice of self-improvement, you have the ability to spiritually evolve through any positive and systematic practice that makes sense to you. For instance, if you take the kids to the park every week simply because you have agreed to, that is a commitment but not a ritual. Perhaps you even dread going, because you would rather be doing something else. However, if you approach the weekly event with the intention of letting go of all your worries and celebrating playfulness—a virtue that children excel at—you will find the time more rewarding and could turn it into a bonding ritual that you and the kids engage in together.

When it comes to rituals, deciding what you hope to realize is the first step. With divination, your goal could be to strengthen your intuition, become more conscious in your choices, to commune with the divine, or simply to reduce stress. These are not normally the goals of the ego. In fact, ritual could be defined as any intentional process that helps us to move the ego out of the way.

In the development of your own divination ritual, it is important to factor in what you know and are comfortable with. You may want to draw inspiration from established practices or divination experiences you've had. You might feel compelled to create an elaborate procedure, or perhaps "short and sweet" is more your style.

When you are creating a meaningful ritual for yourself, do not compare it with the rituals of your parents or your inherited religion. Doing what you feel guided to do is a good exercise. Write down your procedure. Refine it for yourself over time. Trust yourself, but be systematic. You want to develop a repeatable process that feels right for you even if it is completely unique. The goal is to create a direct channel between you and divine wisdom that works for you, but there are a few general guidelines that apply to everyone.

Divination should always start with a calming first step. For some, taking a bath is a good way to get centered before beginning a ritual. Meditation is an excellent all around calming technique because, in addition to producing a relaxed presence, it also supports greater clarity. One aspect of the preparatory meditation is to let go of having attachment to receiving any particular answer or outcome. By giving the mind a vacation—"to vacate" or empty itself of its usual preoccupations—you increase your receptivity to the universal archetypes that operate within and through you, and that may have messages for you.

Some people have the time for and prefer an elaborate divination ritual that might include a certain time of day, special garments, amulets, or some particular form of chanting. This might include performing the divination in a traditional labor-intensive way. (Some astrologers even report that calculating and drawing

Where Rituals Get Their Power

"What makes a ritual powerful is its coherence with what you consider sacred. Take the knowledge you get from others, and study it for a while. Make your own associations and leaps of inspiration. What makes the runes vital is the way their meanings and uses evolve from person to person. Beware of the contention that there is one pure way, based upon some sort of holy writ. This is the problem that has robbed Christianity of much of its mythological vitality."
—Posted on an Internet Runes forum

A serene landscape photograph like this one can help create an atmosphere of focus and introspection for your divination rituals.

charts by hand is a ritual that helps them develop a better reading.) For others, simply lighting a candle, burning incense or taking a few deep breaths with eyes closed provides them the state of focused relaxation. Above all, choosing what feels the most comfortable for you is the important thing. Whatever method you choose, find a way to relax, center yourself and mentally prepare to enter a state of intuitive readiness. When you find a way to do this that works for you, just stick with it!

Consider creating a special place at home for your divination rituals. This need not be an elaborate indoor fountain with palm ferns and Buddha statues, but if that feels right and you have the resources, beautiful art is psychologically supportive. Some people need dramatic rituals to help focus their minds away from the mundane tasks of day-to-day life, and toward clarity.

It is not necessary that ritual space be dedicated only to divination—in fact, you can simply close the door or burn incense to define ritual space no matter where you are. An inspirational photo—perhaps of an ancient temple, wild landscape or goddess image—is a portable device that can help you establish the serenity you need. Take care not to attach too much meaning to the physical artifacts of your ritual space or the divination system you use. The information you receive from the reading comes from within you, not from the tools you use. Take the process seriously—without venerating any book, card deck, set of coins or stones—and you will experience better results in the long run.

The Results

Whenever you give yourself a reading, be sure to set aside enough time to do it carefully. A rushed reading can cause you to easily lose focus as well as overlook key elements of its meaning. This doesn't mean that you should overanalyze the meaning of a reading. Often your first instinct—what first pops into your head—captures the core message or central truth. Too much analysis can create confusion. It is helpful to take notes, so it is a good idea to have a pen and paper or tape recorder ready before you start your reading. Live readers often encourage this, and the best online divination services provide electronic journals of your readings so you can evaluate and compare them easily in the future.

Make a strong effort to really listen to the oracle, and avoid jumping to conclusions. It is not unusual for an oracle's response to be about something more important than the question you explicitly posed. The first time I tried the I Ching, it completely ignored my irreverent question and reflected my intent, which was not sincere at all.

Do not be too eager to repeat a reading just because you don't like the results. Remember that divination's report may not be what you were hoping to hear, but it could be what you need to hear. Before beginning the process of a reading, it is good to ask yourself whether or not you are ready and willing to see beyond your desires or expectations. Answer this question truthfully. If, after you have completed a reading, you feel that you were not focused enough, it is perfectly acceptable to discard that reading and pick new cards, cast the coins again, or pick new Runes stones. Trust your sincerity as the channel, and be open to all possibilities.

If the meaning of a reading is not immediately clear, give it some time—take care of some other business and come back to it later. One I Ching seeker described the perplexing results of a reading he received when asking about his failing marriage. When the meaning of the hexagrams escaped him, he sought deeper levels of meaning. Every succeeding layer of depth only brought more confusion. Later, looking back on the results, he found that the very titles of the hexagrams were an answer to his question—one he refused to hear because of his emotional attachment to receiving a certain answer. Only with time and reflection was he able to see the true meaning of the hexagrams.

Sometimes a reading appears to be accurate because it is a confirmation of what you intuitively know to be true. For instance, a set of identical twins always suspected a substantial difference in their astrological charts, but had never had a reading. They received a gift of an astrological reading for their twenty-fifth birthdays. Sure enough, the first twin was born in the last few seconds of Aries rising, while the second twin—born seven minutes later—was born with Taurus rising. The rising sign, or

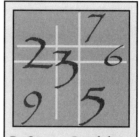

Be Open to Possibilities

Occasionally, an accurate reading can be tough to accept. Hans Decoz, a professional numerologist, once did a reading for the parents of a child who had committed suicide. Why was their son unhappy? What brought him to suicide? The reasons practically jumped out at Hans: the boy was gay, scared, and vulnerable. The family found this impossible to believe—until the boy's friend confessed that he was indeed gay, and tortured by this fact.

Listen to the Oracle

Angie had been in business for a year when she was hired to cater a large conference. Registration was on the day of the event, so there was no way to predict how many people she would be serving.

If she counted on too many people attending, bought too much food and hired too many people, she would lose money. But underestimating and running out of food at an event is even worse. Angie was stuck, and decided to do a Tarot reading.

All signs from her reading pointed to a small turnout. Angie was disappointed, wanting to believe that this was her chance to get ahead. After all, she was being paid $20 a head and the capacity for the conference was 500 people. Plus, she did not want to underestimate.

So she planned for 350 people. Only eighty-five showed up, and Angie lost money on the conference. However, she learned to trust her intuition, and not be as attached to desired outcomes.

ascendant, is indicative of personality type, and is one of the most significant factors, after one's sun sign, in Astrology.

USING DIVINATION FOR BUSINESS DECISIONS

Anxiety afflicts all parts of life, but the business world can be particularly stressful because important decisions often need to be made on a daily basis. Lacking the guidance of a trustworthy internal pilot, we can easily get stuck in a bog of confusion, mistrust, false expectations, stress and indecision. No matter how skillful we may be at logical analysis, it seems like there is never enough information, and pros and cons rarely can guide us through a chaotic situation. Parched for guidance and wisdom, many resourceful leaders turn to tools like the I Ching and Tarot—decision-making aids with an ancient and honorable pedigree—to stimulate their intuition around business problems.

Robert Aughenbaugh, a successful entrepreneur in Portland, Oregon, started a new company called Via Training a few years ago. While it was an exciting business, growing a new company creates a lot of stress, and Robert found himself consulting different Tarot spreads on Tarot.com every few months or so.

Early in the company's history, Robert faced a particularly difficult crisis. His fledgling company was bidding on a large project and, at the time, its future seemed to depend on its ability to win this account. At the height of preparation for the bid, the account manager handed in her letter of resignation. Kim (not her real name) was not only leaving the company at a critical time, but she had accepted a job with the only other company that was competing for the desired account, a company that was better established than Via.

Sabotage, thought Robert. How was he going to swing this one? If Kim left, they would not only lose the account, but the competition would have access to Kim's intimate knowledge of their technology, other customers, and so on. Via Training wouldn't stand a chance.

In an effort to quickly stimulate new insights, Robert turned to Tarot.com for guidance. Instead of

doing a business reading, he chose to do a relationship reading because he realized the issue was as much about their teamwork as anything else. Kim was the first employee of the company, after all, and had worked with him side by side in its formation. One clear message of the reading he got was, "You're not finished with this person. You still have a lot of work to do together."

Encouraged, Robert printed out a copy of the reading and asked Kim to join him for coffee on one of her last days in the office. Reluctantly, she agreed. The meeting started off tense and her body language expressed her lack of interest. It was a done deal after all. What more was there to say?

"I did a Tarot reading," Robert informed her. Unexpectedly, Kim—who had no experience with Tarot—perked up. He showed her the Tarot.com printout and explained how he was interpreting it with regard to their relationship. All of the things they had been needing to talk about were present in the reading, and it served as a safe, unbiased, way to broach some difficult issues. "We started this thing. If we continue and stick to it, we will succeed," he told her. It was in the cards. Because it came from a third party, Kim was able to be more open to the idea, and a healing occurred in their relationship. If Robert had told her all of this without the reading, she probably wouldn't have listened.

As Robert left the meeting, he could sense that Kim was not going to leave. Needless to say, Kim stayed and Via Training got that big account. Since that auspicious beginning, the team that began with Kim and Robert has grown to more than 135 employees, has won many more huge accounts, as well as awards for being one of the fastest growing companies in Oregon.

Paul Wenner is another successful entrepreneur, and a man with a cause. In 1985, he founded Gardenburger, Inc., to provide healthy vegetarian alternatives to fast food. Much sweat equity and thousands of decisions later, Gardenburger rose to become one of the fastest growth stocks in the food industry. Today Paul is a suc-

The Oracle of changes

The I Ching CD-ROM and I-Ching.com were successors to *Synchronicity*, the first published divination software program.

cessful multimillionaire and the author of a book on vegetarianism, *Garden Cuisine: Heal Yourself Through Low Fat Meatless Eating.*

One of Wenner's secrets was to stimulate intuition and support critical decision-making by consulting the I Ching. He purchased my first interactive I Ching program software product called *Synchronicity* (now known as I Ching.com). A few years ago, Paul said, "The *Synchronicity* program played a major role in my company's success and growth. I made over 300 important decisions using it."

Randy Komisar is another businessman with a respect for authentic classical divination. Like Paul Wenner, Randy had also purchased the *Synchronicity* program, because he liked using the I Ching to help himself think outside the box and make key decisions in his life and career. A few years ago he was offered a job as head of a major animation group owned by Dreamworks, the exciting movie studio founded by Steven Spielberg and others. The animation studio was in the process of splitting off from Dreamworks, and Randy was enthusiastic about the projects it was working on, as well as the people in the animation group.

He had reservations about working for any company with a distant and powerful chain of command, so he needed to be sure that the process of splitting off the animation group into a separate company would go forward. As its full-time CEO, Randy did not want to be required to answer to a parent company for very long. His potential employers assured him that the animation studio would indeed become an independent entity, and if he took the position, he would not have to report through the larger company's bureaucracy. These assurances helped him rationalize his attraction to the opportunity, but he still could not rid himself of the nagging feeling that something wasn't quite right.

Randy had used meditation and reflection for years, so he knew how to tap his intuition. However, in this instance, he needed a bit of help to step back from his desires, think clearly about the job offer, and pay attention to his sixth sense. He turned to the I Ching program. The first reading he got warned that there were

> *If you know yourself, you'll find that there's not just one passion but many passions. Then the question becomes which ones do you indulge when. And that's a matter of matching passion and opportunity.*
>
> —Randy Komisar, Virtual CEO

storm clouds on the horizon—not the best sign.

Since he was quite taken with the promise of what seemed like a dream job, he found himself unable to accept the first reading at face value. He asked the I Ching again, but the reading was more negative on the question than the one before. Still resistant to accepting the reflections of the oracle, he asked a third time, and once again was alerted to risks in the offing. Each time his reflection on the I Ching's reading brought him deeper into the question and closer to his own intuition.

> *Success or failure in business is caused more by the mental attitude even than by mental capacities.*
> —Sir Walter Scott

Finally, he could not ignore his gut any longer and his fantasies about the job lost their power over him. It was difficult, but he turned down the position. Shortly afterwards the studio was rolled back into the parent company, eliminating its independence altogether. To this day, Randy credits the I Ching program with helping him make the right decision and avoid what would have been a wrong turn for him.

It is not always easy to hear the quiet voice of intuition, or to give it credit when we do, but we need it in order to make the best decisions and dance with our destiny. Sometimes, as in Randy's case, we have to go back to the well more than once to get the clarity we need. But getting in touch with our intuition in order to get that clarity of purpose is central to the achievement of success and happiness in life. As we have shown through the stories of a few individuals, the skillful use of an authentic divination system can help guide us toward what is right and fulfilling for us so we can avoid making unnecessary missteps. I encourage everyone to give it a try, to approach divination sincerely with an open mind, heart and soul.

CHAPTER 8
The Evolving Technology of Divination

The High Priestess (with laptop)
Mystery, intuition, receptivity

Rider-Waite Tarot
© US Games Systems, Inc.

Our need for a practical philosophy of self-knowledge has never been greater as we struggle to make meaning from our lives on the [computer] screen.

—Sherry Turkle, MIT professor and clinical psycholgist

nformation technology in preliterate societies was primitive, which hampered the spread and use of all ideas, including divination. Until recently, there simply were no channels other than word of mouth for the passing on of esoteric knowledge. Books were made by hand, and literacy was extremely rare. Any information that was passed on was done so selectively, and guarded as something very special. Until the advent of printing, transportation, and communication technologies, information was difficult to save and hardly distributed at all.

In our modern high-tech age, we tend to forget that books, coins, and cards are technologies too. The use of the I Ching depended upon the ability to forge and manufacture coins, cultivate and harvest yarrow stalks, make paper, and bind the ancient hand-written texts. Tarot required the production of playing cards. Before the widespread use of the printing press, the reproduction of seventy-eight images by hand was painstaking to say the least. Astrology depended upon the technologies of cataloguing positions and patterns of heavenly bodies and the printing of books. It may not seem like much to us, but all of these developments represented major advances in the evolution of technology.

New technologies and electronic media have overcome the availability problem. Thanks to printing and distribution, thousands of books are published and distributed, sometimes electronically, and the world's divination systems are now available to almost everyone. There are dozens of versions of the *I Ching* published today, and over one thousand Tarot decks to choose from, with more on the way all the time. Personal computers and the Internet bring authentic divination systems directly into the homes and offices of millions of

Gottfried Wilhelm Leibniz (1646 - 1716)

This mathematician was a pioneer in early Western study of binary numbers. Leibniz became acquainted with the I Ching and found that the book's 3000-year-old system of opposing dualities—yin and yang—preceded and provided validation of his binary numbers scheme. His work with binary numbers was a vital contribution to the invention of modern computers.

people, twenty-four hours a day. This chapter explores the continuing evolution of divination technology, particularly the development of interactive software, and the contributing role I was fortunate enough to play.

In 1972, I was living the carefree life of a student at the University of Oregon in Eugene, having transferred from UC Berkeley. Like every teenager, I faced perplexing dilemmas. Considering the radical social changes like the rise of the women's movement and the sexual revolution, relationship issues were easy to come by. I consulted the I Ching often.

Jack Delay was a friend of mine who had immersed himself in the strange new profession of computer programming. He worked for the non-profit Oregon Research Institute (ORI) developing communication software for a new kind of machine—the time-sharing minicomputer. It was the first type of computer that could serve many people at the same time, making it appear that each user at a computer terminal had the entire machine to himself or herself. ORI's computer was one of the first that didn't need to be fed punch cards like the big computer at college. It was a predecessor to the web servers of today.

It was called a "minicomputer" because it was smaller than the IBM behemoths that preceded it, but the machine still took up a large air-conditioned room. IBM mainframe computers were so gigantic that they required a small building, and their input devices consisted of huge punched-card readers and reel-to-reel magnetic tapes that were one meter across.

Harvard University Computer Lab (1944)

Times have changed since then, and we now have the same computing power in a laptop PC.

The advent of time-sharing systems like the one at ORI, and the new technology known as "networking" vastly increased the ways computers could be used—for communications, education, collaborative research and countless other new applications. Time-sharing over networks meant that thousands of people equipped with a simple computer terminal and a modem could all use the same large computer—now called a "server"—at the same time. Before this, computers could only take in one stream of data, perform some calculations on it, analyze them, and generate a batch of "output," one job at a time.

One of the first time-sharing systems was called Unix by its developer, Bell Labs. (Linux, one of the most popular operating systems used to run web servers today, is an offspring of Unix.) The same technologies we were using at Oregon Research in the early 1970s evolved to make it possible twenty-five years later for millions of people to use personal computers to connect to millions of web servers, and each other, over what we now call the Internet.

But, as important as these new technologies were, it wasn't time-sharing or even networking that inspired me to want a job, any job, at ORI. It was something that Jack was playing with on the side. In addition to his professional duties at Oregon Research, Jack installed a game that we could play using our large computer's one resident video terminal. The game *Space War* had been invented in the labs of MIT. It involved two tiny space ships (consisting of only seven or eight screen-dots, or "pixels") that could be made to move, turn, and shoot simulated single-pixel photon torpedoes at each other. It was fun.

When ORI's gigantic machine wasn't being used to transmit reams of research data, Jack and I spent many long evenings playing *Space War*. This was in 1972, at least five years before microcomputers hit the market, along with *Pong*, an electronic ping-pong game that was the first commercially popular video game. Jack and his cohorts at MIT were way ahead of their time.

The game was intoxicating. Beyond the enjoyment of being able to play such a game, I became hooked by the idea of software, this new way that a person could conceive and create a captivating experience from nothing but ideas and computer code. I realized that the software skills that people like Jack had developed were a modern form of wizardry, a new form of very engaging creativity.

Inspired by my enjoyment of that game, I made it my goal to get a job at ORI. Because I knew Jack, and I could type fast, I got a job as a secretary there in 1973 and spent my free time taking night classes in software design. As it turned out, serving as a secretary would be the first step down a career path leading to the creative freedom I now enjoy and feel so grateful for.

> **Computers and Cultural Transformation**
>
> "The effective interaction that today's computers allow makes it possible for the user to switch back and forth among various roles of creator, transformer, communicator as well as receiver of knowledge. The information that just a decade ago involved effort and time to get together to finally work with is now literally at our fingertips. The time and effort spent on gathering information can now be spent on using it in creative ways."
>
> —Jaishree K. Odin

First Astrology System

The drive to create personalized astrology systems was pioneered by Alan Leo, a professional astrologer from London in the early 1900s. Leo's reports consisted of pre-written descriptions of planetary alignments, positions, and meanings that were assembled based on the client's time and place of birth. These formula reports were controversial, yet popular at the time.

In *Astrology, the Divine Science,* Marcia Moore and Mark Douglas wrote:

"During a three year period, Leo mailed out 20,000 of his prefabricated 'test horoscopes,' initiating a trend which has grown continuously and which has now metamorphosed into computer astrology."

Fulfilling one's destiny—professional, interpersonal or spiritual—is a mysterious and often arduous journey, usually involving circuitous routes. To make it more challenging, the day-to-day stresses of life don't leave nearly enough time to sit, think, and reflect. Even worse, most of us have been taught to suppress our instincts and intuition in favor of what we were told to believe. Like most people, I was trained from birth not to trust my own judgment, especially about life's most important matters.

DIVINATION SOFTWARE IS PUBLISHED

Since I first tried the I Ching at the age of 18, there have been pivotal times in my life when I have successfully used it or Tarot to overcome self-doubt, to strengthen my sense of direction, and to steer myself down the right path. One life-changing example was how I was stimulated by the I Ching to find the right livelihood in following my natural interests, specifically by allowing my interest in computers and divination to converge. As a result of several I Ching readings, and the way I interpreted them, I came to invent a new category of software—divination software—against all odds.

Fifteen years after taking the secretary job at ORI (a period which included a three-year spiritual pilgrimage to India and beyond), I had a position as vice president of marketing for a high-tech software firm. Not only was I making a six-figure salary, I had an active social life and an elegant home. I was in a good relationship, and was raising an intelligent, beautiful son. Yet I felt an emptiness inside. Something was missing. I was at a personal crossroads with no strong sense of direction, and I saw many of my peers in similar situations. We were zooming through busy lives on autopilot—without the passion, excitement, and drive that comes from being inspired by one's dreams.

At the time, I was also unhappy with the negative culture of the company I worked for, and the CEO's scapegoating management style. After a couple of great years, it was my job to sell a string of ill-advised new products. My marketing department had been allowed no input in their design, and it was obvious to me

that, as technically clever as the new software utilities were, our customers did not need or want them. But the owner—who was not only CEO, but also the chief engineer—didn't want to hear objections and held the marketing department responsible for the poor sales results. It was my turn to be the corporate scapegoat. The slings and arrows of outrageous fortune were flying under the radar and in all directions.

> *If confusion is the first step to knowledge, I must be a genius.*
> —Larry Leissner

The politics became so confusing for me that much of the time I didn't know what to do, whether I should do anything at all to defend myself, or how to react. On the one hand, I was earning a lot of money and if I could suffer through the situation until he developed a sensible new product, I would continue to enjoy the salary and perks of my position. On the other hand, I had lost respect for the CEO and saw little hope of the company changing its arrogant culture. So I turned to the I Ching for counsel.

During one tough week, I needed moral support so badly that I brought my large *I Ching* book to the office, so I could consult it if I felt the need to. After using it a few times, I perceived that the oracle was encouraging me to leave the company. At the time, however, such a move would require quite a leap of faith, since Portland was a tiny market for software marketing positions and I had nothing lined up. However, the I Ching's advice was persistent: I was stuck, it told me, and I needed a "breakthrough." The following day, I turned in my letter of resignation.

Destiny can work in devious ways, and I was surprised by what happened next. The senior member of the Board of Directors, whom I greatly respected, called me into a meeting and asked me to reconsider. He asked me to think about what the company could offer to keep me from leaving, and to please let them know the next day. I was so ready to make a change that, despite all uncertainties, I had stopped thinking about the possibility of working things out. I turned to the I Ching for guidance again that night and received hexagram sixty (Limits and Connections), which recommends biding one's time while reasoning through issues and making plans. Not a signal for taking rash action!

The next day I submitted my conditions, which included better working conditions as well as a hefty raise. I was sure they would never accept this and that I would be on my way. But after meeting privately, they agreed to all my requests, except the amount of the raise. They countered by offering me 20 percent more than I had asked for! I was surprised at this and asked them why they would want to pay me more. The senior director replied, "Because we want you to be happy."

Impressed by this vote of confidence, I accepted the offer, saying "Well I can't be bought, but I can be rented." This broke the ice. We all laughed and shook hands. This was the breakthrough I was seeking: resolving an issue and moving forward productively, instead of prematurely bolting when things were not going my way. But the I Ching would soon stimulate much bigger, revolutionary breakthroughs in my life and career.

> *The computer is the first metamedium, and as such it has degrees of freedom for representation and expression never before encountered and as yet barely investigated.*
>
> —Alan Kay

My experience of using the I Ching at work had planted a seed in my mind. Since tossing coins and using the large book was conspicuous and finding a private space difficult at work, it occurred to me that a software program might be designed to provide those services via my Macintosh computer. I began to envision a program that could faithfully replicate traditional I Ching casting methods, do all the busy work of recording the lines and such, and even provide interpretations that were more relevant to modern life than what I found in the best translations of ancient Chinese text.

I wanted to be able to discreetly perform an authentic I Ching consultation on my computer. I looked around but could not find divination software of any kind for sale anywhere. I knew there was a need for such a product, even if the market for it only consisted of one person—myself!

"Necessity is the mother of invention," the saying goes. The more I thought about how much this idea might make sense, the more my personal desire for such a program, coupled with my curiosity about how well it could work, were strong enough motivations for me to create one, even though I had never actually designed a software product before.

In spite of a multitude of logical reservations, I had

to give it a try and see what happened. I took it upon myself to design an I Ching program that would work in an authentic way, and perhaps even add a touch of magic to the consultation of the I Ching. It was obvious how computers could take the busy-work—the calculating and looking up of hexagrams, for instance—out of a divination ritual. More importantly, I had to find out if a computer could be programmed to cast the coins in both a mathematically and energetically authentic way, so as not to interfere at all with the personal connection required to synchronistically generate an I Ching hexagram.

My new product development project didn't make any practical sense from a marketing or business point of view, and I am not an impulsive person, but I was more compelled to follow this creative urge than anything I had ever been attracted to doing. Whenever I was asked to explain why I was spending my life savings on this project, I would recite my new motto, "Wherever God drags me, I will follow."

Designing and developing software or sophisticated web sites is not easy, and I have learned that just about any software project takes three times longer than you expect. And, in my case, I still had a full-time day job. By the time the program was finished, I had invested my entire savings and then some—most of it to pay a programmer and an artist to help me produce an authentic and engaging I Ching experience.

As it turns out, I was not only creating the first divination software product, but the inclusion of graphics, animation and sound effects also made it one of the very earliest multimedia titles. I named my first software creation *Synchronicity* after Carl Jung's principle that explains how divination works. As it turned out, *Synchronicity* was the first divination software title ever published. As a result, *Synchronicity* customers and famous divination authors Monte Farber and Amy Zerner would later dub me "the father of interactive divination."

Six months into moonlighting on the development of *Synchronicity*, I finally resigned my VP position, while arranging to work for the company as an international marketing consultant. This gave me extra time as well as

> "There is a perceived polarity (however artificial) between technology and the humanities, between science and art, between right brain and left. The burgeoning field of multimedia is likely to be one of those disciplines, like architecture, that bridges the gap."
> —Nicholas Negroponte, in *Being Digital.*

Chapter 8: The Evolving Technology of Divination

some cash flow to start up a new company, Visionary Software (now Visionary Networks). I had no entrepreneurial intentions, but using the I Ching at work had inspired a whole new career for me—to create more convenient ways to access the sacred oracle that had helped me so much, with the help of software.

Thus the desire to share the experience of authentic divination with the world by publishing a software version of the I Ching arose as much out of gratitude to the oracle as anything else.

The use of the I Ching while working in the software field had steered me toward re-inventing it in software form. How perfect! Even though I never had an intention of starting my own business, my I Ching practice ultimately led me to do just that—I like to think for its' sake. I learned firsthand how divine providence can work in unexpected and ironic ways. Even though it was difficult taking my turn as the company scapegoat, it turned out to contain a great blessing.

My path to right livelihood was not found by browsing the business classifieds searching for an entrepreneurial opportunity, nor was it based on the formulation of a logical business plan. Instead, my old-fashioned divination practice supported the courage to make a leap of faith, and continued to support the faith that I would land in a better place no matter what happened. For me, that place turned out to be my life's work, which perfectly combined my business experience in software with my spiritual sensibility. There are no accidents!

It wasn't easy, however. In fact, it was an extraordinarily difficult path the first few years, which tested my determination and perseverance, as well as my ability to sleep. Visionary Software almost went bankrupt several times, but I never gave up as I discovered there is nothing more psychologically or spiritually rewarding than following one's true destiny.

Designing and publishing divination software and web sites has been my life's work ever since. I come to my work feeling inspired and go to sleep grateful to be of service to the world in my own way. This joy spills over into every part of my life, helped by my continued use of divination to live beyond ego and relate better to the people I care about. I trust my intuition more than ever, knowing that it is supported by the wisdom of thousands of years that has gone into all the classical divination systems I use today—Astrology, the Tarot, Numerology, the Runes and, of course, the I Ching.

In the years I ran Visionary Networks, we developed divination software and web sites for Tarot, Numerology and Astrology. This small company, which began with the unwitting development of multimedia inspired by my respect and gratitude for ancient divination, found itself right in the middle of the exploding new world of interactive media, an art form that was just defining itself.

At authentic divination web sites like Tarot.com you can access interactive versions of Astrology, Numerology and I Ching.

The Magic of Interactive Media

One of the main reasons multimedia attracted so much attention and capital during the 1990s dot-com era was the emerging recognition of computer and networking technology's potential to serve people in more personal ways. Much has been accomplished, but most of the potential is still unrealized.

During the heyday of the dot-com boom, I served as Executive Director of the Oregon Multimedia Alliance for two years. The OMA was a non-profit organization sponsored by the State of Oregon and several large Oregon corporations with the goal of developing an interactive media industry in the state—for the sake of education, social welfare, and jobs. During my tenure, I invited companies like Netscape, Microsoft, Yahoo, Cybercash and other Internet pioneers to give presentations on how interactive media was expected to revolutionize our lives in the future.

Interactive media is uniquely able to provide guided learning experiences that one can navigate at one's own pace. The advantages of self-paced learning include accessing information exactly when you want at your own speed and, depending upon how well-designed the user interface, in your own way. Self-paced learning is a

> *Any sufficiently advanced technology is indistinguishable from magic.*
>
> —Arthur C. Clarke

wonderful example of personal convenience—and more effective education—for a low price. The progress of interactive learning systems has been slower than initially predicted. Systems for delivering educational and business instruction via the Internet are growing rapidly. Tarot.com is also developing online educational content in the areas of personal and cultural development, including how to read Tarot cards, how to interpret Astrology and Numerology charts, and so on.

Studies show that interactive media increases one's ability to learn by accommodating different personal learning styles. Although traditional education based on the "school as factory" model ignored the fact, each of us has a particular way of learning that suits us best. There are also general factors that affect learning. According to a Ferris State University study, "learners who listen to information will recall 25 percent of that material. If they hear and see the material, they will remember 50 percent. However, learners who hear, see, and interact with the material during the learning process will remember 75 percent of the material." Although the personal touch of an instructor or "coach" still adds tremendous value, interactive media can provide strong advantages.

Multimedia can also be used to add a mood or ambiance conducive to an interactive experience. Tarot.com demonstrated, with their *Oracle of Changes* and *Tarot Magic* CD-ROMs, that it is possible to produce an engaging computer-based experience using music, art, film and animation. Although the multimedia experience genre is still underdeveloped, there are programs called virtual reality that represent the cutting edge, and some, like the game *Myst,* have been commercially successful. Although *Myst* was a fantasy adventure game, the beauty of its art and the elegant simplicity of its navigation was a turning point for multimedia because it succeeded so well in delivering a unique experience of navigating a new world.

In general, computer-assisted media open new doors to information. Because computers can provide easy access to vast volumes of data, they offer a huge advantage over books. This is why the sales of CD-ROM encyclopedias now far outsell those heavy tomes many

of us grew up with. To use the Tarot.com web site as an example, if its thousands of possible Tarot card interpretations were published in book form, it would be more than 1500 pages long—heavy, expensive, and cumbersome to use. There are countless other examples of how the Internet provides easy access to incredible quantities of information, with sophisticated cross-referencing and search capabilities.

Using the Internet or software to perform divination provides every one of the benefits of interactive media—information access and self-paced learning, as well as mood setting. If a divination program is done correctly, the computer will take over the busy work parts of the ritual. For instance, the chores of recording the lines of an I Ching reading, deciphering which hexagram you received, and looking it up in a large book are all rote tasks that distract from one's intuitive focus, the subject of the consultation.

Many traditional divinators find it difficult to accept the fact that their favorite oracles could be authentically accessed using software or the Internet. Some claim that computers are too cold, or that by using a computer, one loses the ability to have a real energetic connection. They prefer older technologies like cards, coins, or carved stones (although I remind them that cardboard is not such a good conductor of energy). The attitude persists in spite of the fact that computers have been used to generate astrological and numerological charts for more than thirty years. And, more recently, authentic sites like Tarot.com have proven that it is possible to develop a computer-assisted Tarot, I Ching or Runes reading that is both mathematically accurate and energetically authentic.

Divination readings and reports are forms of information. Since information technologies have made it so easily available, the cost of information has come way down. Those of us who value divination information are also benefitting from this trend. In addition, the Internet also provides greater access to experts, who in the pre-wired era were only available to a select few. For example, most of the research needed for this book was found on the Internet, rather than in a traditional library.

> "The post-information age is about becoming acquainted over time: machines understanding individuals with the same degree of subtlety (or more than) we can expect from other human beings, including idiosyncrasies and totally random events, good and bad, in the unfolding narrative of our lives."
> —Nicholas Negroponte, in *Being Digital.*

William Butler O'Connor, a veteran of new media, describes the new cultural landscape:

"The move toward a more expressed culture will ... inspire entirely new forms of and ideas about culture, and enrich the life of the so-called 'average' person enormously. In short, what we might call the 'Big Bang' of the Internet's birth is bringing into being a new Cultural Renaissance."

In order to put this all in a larger context, let's look at how new technology can support creativity. Nicholas Negroponte wrote *Being Digital,* an influential book on technology's new role in our lives, and its possibilities for the future. As a *Wired* magazine columnist and former director of the Media Lab at MIT, Negroponte is an expert on how software can be a positive force. In his book, he describes two routes of invention: technological imperatives and expressive ones, and the convergence between them that is provided by multimedia. His observations clearly describe the creative process, even as it applies to interactive divination.

Television was invented through purely technological imperatives. When pioneers like Philo Farnsworth and Vladimir Zworykin looked at postage-stamp–size electronic images in 1929, they were driven to perfect the technology purely on the basis of its own merit.

…Photography, on the other hand, was invented by photographers. The people who perfected photographic technology did so for expressive purposes, fine tuning their techniques to meet the needs of their art, just as authors invented romance novels, essays, and comic books to fit their ideas.

Personal computers have moved computer science away from the purely technical imperative and are now evolving more like photography. Computing is no longer the exclusive realm of military, government, and big business. It is being channeled directly into the hands of very creative individuals at all levels of society, becoming the means for creative expression in both its use and development. The means and the messages of multimedia will become a blend of technical and artistic achievement.

Fear of the unknown is a psychological barrier to evolutionary change. But as most people realize the benefits of computers, and become more comfortable using them, interactive divination—along with other worthwhile pursuits facilitated by computers and the Internet—will become an integrated part of their lives. According to an April 26, 2006 study by the Pew Internet & American Life Project, 73 percent of American adults use the Internet, while 87 percent of American teenagers are online.

NETWORKED SPIRITUALITY

Today there are many books and web sites on the subject of how to read Tarot cards, give yourself an I Ching reading, and so on. For the sufficiently motivated, or even the casually inquisitive, the resources for learning how to perform divination are more available than ever. While some of these are a blessing to the savvy researcher or dedicated seeker, the sheer volume of information presents a sorting challenge. Search engines on the Internet are helping.

In a 2004 report called "Faith Online," a Pew Internet & American Life Project study found that 82 million Americans have used the Internet to get religious and spiritual information and connect with others on their personal journeys. Nevertheless, finding trustworthy information and the resources you are looking for still takes some work. And it takes intuition to sort out the good information from the bad.

As the result of research and development efforts since 1988, Visionary Networks has created Internet versions of the four most popular forms of classical divination on its Tarot.com family of web sites. The years of research required to develop these do-it-yourself divination experiences led me to a deeper understanding of divination and its place in human society. Starting from a place of personal need and intense curiosity, I came to realize that it was my mission to bring authentic divination to as many people as possible through the Internet, and a desire to continue this in educational realms led me to start the Divination Foundation after selling Tarot.com.

The quality of a computer-assisted divination experience depends entirely upon the design and programming of the software. One important but often overlooked element is whether or not the computer allows people to control the picking or casting process involved in generating a personal reading. In addition, multimedia aspects of the program can lend support to the right kind of meditative mood. Taking advantage of new developments in multimedia and the rise of the Internet, we were able to conceive how a computer might accomplish these goals for an interactive divination experience of high quality. Not only did we figure out how to make

> *Science and technology revolutionize our lives, but memory, tradition and myth frame our response.*
>
> —Arthur M. Schlesinger

the computer transparent when it came to picking cards or casting coins, we commissioned beautiful art and music suitable for a personal ritual delivered via CD-ROM or broadband Internet.

An interactive divination ritual is self-paced, which means that you can move at your own speed. It is continuously and universally available. The best programs and web sites also allow you to save your readings for further reflection at your convenience.

Thanks to advances in information technology, it is now possible for anyone with access to the Internet to enjoy an uplifting divination experience at any time. You can have an instant connection to the highest caliber of information—timeless wisdom. The power to get profound advice whenever you want, without being dependent on others, is a revolutionary value.

Not All Web Sites are Created Equal

There are only a few high-quality divination CD-ROMs published today. The most common way that this kind of software reaches people is through the Internet. Regrettably, most divination web sites cannot offer an authentic experience because they let the computer pick the cards or toss the coins for you, using what's called a "random-number generator" program. In this case, the computer is doing the casting—not you. This common mistake is a case of technology getting in the way of the process it should be serving.

Interactive Divination

In the year 2000, eleven years after the publication of the *Synchronicity* program—during which time a few other divination software products had hit the market—I felt it was my duty as an inventor of the medium to define some guidelines to distinguish between the authentic and the fake. To this end, I defined three criteria by which to judge a divination program's authenticity: mathematical authenticity; energetic authenticity; and emotional authenticity.

Mathematical authenticity means that the computer-assisted process of casting an oracle embodies the precise mathematical odds of the physical method it is based on. This is not a trivial requirement, especially in the case of Tarot, which requires sophisticated algorithms to capture the mathematical probabilities of card

movement in shuffling, cutting, and so on. Similarly, in the case of the I Ching, simulating the picking of yarrow stalks or the casting of coins with a computer keyboard and/or mouse requires careful programming. It is vital that the software is programmed to match the traditional odds exactly, not just to turn up something that looks like a traditional result, which is much easier to do. Computers excel at math, so there is really no excuse if the probabilities are not exactly replicated.

Energetic authenticity means that, no matter what computerized card-picking or casting technique is used, the program depends on the user's energy alone to determine what turns up. In other words, the actions of the user are solely responsible for the result of casting the coins or selecting the cards. A program or web site is not energetically authentic if the computer is doing the selecting—using a random number generator program that is triggered when the user clicks on something or hits the Enter key. This is the easiest technical approach, but anyone who understands synchronicity understands that the use of such a program is not energetically authentic.

Emotional authenticity is the most subjective of the three criteria. It refers to the use of art and multimedia to create an appropriately meditative mood or ambiance. This includes the graphics, animation, music, sound effects and, most subtle of all, the psychology of how the interactive ritual is designed. This is an art form that Tarot.com is always trying to refine, using tools that are constantly getting better.

> **Three Criteria for the Authenticity of Interactive Divination:**
>
> 1. Is it mathematically the same as the original casting method(s)?
>
> 2. Do the actions and energy of the user determine which cards or stones are picked or how the coins land?
>
> 3. Does the presentation of the interactive experience support a state of focused relaxation?

The Positive Role of Technology

Even though many Tarot.com customers use the services of a favorite personal reader on occasion, they still find a do-it-yourself reading convenient and helpful. Many do so on a daily basis. Whether it is for seeking advice or simply as a form of meditation, this makes perfect sense. It is not an either-or proposition. No matter how good a computer-assisted divination experience might be, it cannot compare to a reading delivered in person by a gifted reader. Certainly, as long as wisdom is present, there is a place for both.

There are some people who still find computer tech-

One customer of Visionary Networks claims to have closed a $3 million deal with Intel Corp., using the I Ching program to re-orient himself during the lengthy negotiation process. Before every meeting, he would consult the oracle on his PC to center himself, stimulate his intuition, and calibrate his sense of timing and patience.

nology and the Internet intimidating. But for all the abuses perpetrated by scam artists and fake mediums, the personal and community empowerment supported by the Internet is having a positive impact on human society. Every one of us now has unprecedented access to ancient information systems, as well as modern ones. We can communicate at rates and distances previously unimaginable, and have the ability to share what we've learned with communities both global and local. And the benefits of authentic divination are becoming available to a growing audience of individuals ready to take a closer look at their lives and the choices they make.

The Internet can support culture much better than the passive type of consumer experience that television and other forms of broadcasting foster. Computers make it possible for just about anyone to publish a book, capture an image or disseminate a work of art. The Internet is the distribution channel for new thoughts and works, allowing instant, worldwide access. The ability to both create, participate in, and observe culture enables us to enrich both our physical and spiritual worlds.

As time moves forward, the use of personal computers for spiritual and personal development will continue to be an exciting area of development. Of all the thousands of ways that interactive technology already helps human beings, it is my belief that interactive divination is one of the most empowering.

CHAPTER 9
Destiny, Fate and Creativity

The Fool
Innocence, trust, folly.

Rider-Waite Tarot
© US Games Systems, Inc.

Destiny is not a matter of chance; it is a matter of choice. It is not a thing to be waited for; it is a thing to be achieved.

—William Jennings Bryan

Awareness of who we are, together with good timing, gives us power to see clearly and refine the direction of our lives. While we know that we're never completely in control of the way things unfold, divination provides a way to stay in sync with our personal destiny by increasing self-knowledge and helping us make the right moves at the right time. These are essential ingredients for living a creative life.

In ancient Greece, Destiny was personified by the Goddess Tyche.

Creativity is a big topic, far beyond the scope of this book. But a few things should be pointed out that are relevant to using divination to become more creative in how you manage your life. First of all, every one of us is creative, at least in that we shape our lives in concert with Creative Power (or 'God' or whatever we choose to call the divine). How well we co-create our lives depends on our level of self-awareness and the quality of the choices we make.

No matter how well we do, the existential dilemma of the human condition still brings up some basic questions about freedom and power. How do free will and destiny operate? To what extent are we the passive recipients of whatever fate may have in store for us? How is our present situation the result of choices we made in the past? Such questions have been pondered, and debated, since the beginnings of human civilization.

The Goddess Destiny was depicted holding a ship's rudder or steering wheel, indicating her ability to steer our lives, and a cornucopia to represent the abundance she could bestow. The wheel also symbolized the cyclically changing nature of fortune. In the Tarot deck, this goddess is considered the patron of the Wheel of Fortune card. In ancient times, Destiny was such a popular goddess that the Greeks and Romans prayed to her in a variety of situations. The Fates, on the other hand, were the three daughters of the Goddess of Necessity, to whom

The three Fates of Greek mythology (Clotho, Lachesis, and Atropos) are depicted here weaving, measuring, and cutting the fabric of a mortal's life.

all living beings must eventually submit, including our death.

Steven Forrest, author and astrologer, describes the difference between the words destiny and fate, in his article, "Fate and Freedom: A Middle Path," which appeared in *Mountain Astrologer* magazine.

> **In the dictionary the two words are not far apart in meaning, but they certainly carry a different emotional resonance. Destiny sounds much more inspiring. The distinctions run deeper than verbal legerdemain such as calling old age the 'golden years'.... Fate and Destiny are different animals, I think. Destiny is higher; it has more to do with one's potential, or dharma, or divine plan ...Destiny is something for which we must strive; Fate is what happens to us if we don't.**

If Destiny is something we must strive for, the question becomes: How do we achieve our highest Destiny? And how much control can we hope to have in the process?

Today, in spite of religious ideologies, we are no closer to proving whether there is a master plan for our lives, or if we just roll along life's paths. It is largely your attitude—whether you consider your life to be destiny-bound or ruled by fate—that determines how it all plays out. I am an optimist. In addition to believing in reincarnation, I go a step further in choosing to believe that each of us ultimately will fulfill her or his destiny. Oh, we may be slow learners. Our fulfillment could even take more lifetimes. We have the freedom to digress along the way, or even regress for a while, but it is my belief that eventually we are all going to fulfill our deepest desires.

SEEING ALL OF OUR CHOICES

Most people go through life on autopilot, unaware of the opportunities and creative choices they have. They are not even aware of their Heart's Desires, so they let their egos run the show and never know the difference. However, when we are in sync with our destiny, the choices we make take us closer to the manifestation of our Heart's Desires. Should I relocate? Have a child?

Start a new business? Each way we respond to similar questions is like a little adjustment to Destiny's nautical steering wheel.

The steering action of making choices, agreements and commitments determines where we are headed and what kind of journey it will be. There's no reason to think that life should unfold in a straight line. It's going to be more like sailing. Sometimes we sail along with a breeze at our back, but much of the time this voyage requires constant course corrections, including times when we have to tack directly into the wind.

Certainly, our personal stories are not written out anywhere in clear detail. As astrologer Steven Forrest points out, "…we make choices, and our choices have marked power in shaping our lives. We all periodically, and at astrologically predictable times, face existential crossroads. There, actively or passively, we select a path that defines … our biographies." The choices we make hold the key to realizing the potentials that we are wired for in this lifetime.

Critical choice-points sometimes show up as crises, when normal patterns have been disrupted. At times like these, an element of chaos or uncertainty—often accompanied by feelings of fearful apprehension—arises. However, these moments always offer new possibilities, sometimes great ones. As John F. Kennedy reminded us, "When written in Chinese, the word *crisis* is composed of two characters. One represents danger and the other represents opportunity." A crisis is a dramatic turning point—an opportunity to make great strides—if you choose to see it that way. If you approach crises as a victim, however, you can paralyze yourself with anxiety.

The story of my friend Hope illustrates how important one's choice of attitude can be. A few years ago she was negotiating the purchase of her first house and was not certain that the deal would go through. Meanwhile, the house she was renting was filled with the belongings of old friends and former tenants, making the prospect of moving more daunting than exciting. The day she was supposed to hear if the deal closed, her current home caught fire due to an electrical malfunction. While it was burning down she called to check on the status of her

Danger

Opportunity

In Chinese the word "crisis" is composed of two characters, one meaning danger and the other opportunity. To turn a crisis into an opportunity or into a danger is our choice to make.

181

new home—after all, she wanted to know if she would have a place to move into! It turned out that Hope's offer had been accepted just thirty minutes before she called—about the same time the fire started.

Hope lost almost all of her possessions in the fire, but this crisis was also an opportunity. It offered her the choice: to let go of the past and start fresh, with the help of her fire insurance—like a phoenix rising from the ashes—or play the victim over the loss of her favorite possessions and the shock of the fire. If you were in Hope's position, would you have emerged with grace, embracing the opportunity, or would you have fallen victim to self-pity and powerlessness? Reframing a crisis as an opportunity is one of the challenging choices we face in life, but it is our choice.

THE KARMIC CIRCLE

> *Fate has a strange sense of humor.*
> —*The Simpsons*

The Law of Karma is both complex and elegantly simple. The *American Heritage Dictionary* defines karma (Sanskrit for "action") as: "The total effect of a person's actions and conduct during the successive phases of the person's existence, regarded as determining the person's destiny."

Every belief you adopt, every thought you dwell on and every action you take sets resulting events in motion. The consequences will be pleasant or unpleasant depending on the quality of the originating energy and the intention behind it. Even though she handled it well and made the best of her tragedy, Hope's fire may have contained karmic payback for some previous destructive action—either in this life, or a past one.

A common misconception of karma is that it is a predetermined fate—that you will get what you deserve and there is nothing you can do about it. But karma's impact is in constant flux depending upon the choices you make in the present moment. The karmic balance of your life is affected by everything you think and do, how you react to life's circumstances, what your mind dwells upon. It is possible to redeem negative karma through spiritual transformation.

While there is widespread familiarity with the idea of

karma, the word is often associated with only negative consequences—always as a kind of cosmic punishment. But acknowledging the positive flip side of its dues-paying aspect is important. A lifetime of selflessness can make up for previous lifetimes of greed. It is possible to burn off accumulated negative karma by means of loving acts and personal sacrifice. New acts of kindness, generosity, and selfless service will also come back to us at some fortuitous moment. The Law of Karma is the basis for the Golden Rule, which is taught by all the world's religions in one form or another.

Karma is cosmic justice resulting from nature's tendency to keep things in balance. Individuals should never take it upon themselves to act as agents of karma. Attempts to play god, such as repaying the negative actions of others, will only add to your suffering and the suffering of the world, giving rise to more bad karma and more negative consequences. Of course, there is no downside of good deeds, as long as we are not faking them to aggrandize ourselves, or seeking to benefit from anticipated responses to our kindness or generosity.

The Beatles' John Lennon sang of "Instant Karma"— and it seems to work that way sometimes—but karmic returns are generally not immediate. Nor are karmic fruits even obvious. Sometimes consequences will not come back around for years or even lifetimes.

Ignorance of the law is no excuse; karma is impersonal and affects us all. In the article "Karma, Free Will, and Destiny," Chakrapani Ullal describes the fairness of karma: "There is no favoritism in the determination of the law of karma as everyone is treated equally, and equal opportunity for growth is given to everyone as well." The playing out of karma interconnects all sentient beings, as well as organizations, governments, businesses, and the like. The fact that even the thoughts we choose to dwell on produce karma makes it especially important to maintain a positive attitude, even in difficult times.

If you make unskillful choices out of fear, spite, anger, or jealousy, then life will repay you with unpleasant circumstances. That's just the way it works. When this happens it is wise to accept the consequences, and write it off as payment of karmic dues. The exact cause

Karma is what we have created by our actions in the past that will bear result in the future.

—Chakrapani Ullal, Vedic astrologer

XII • The Hanged Man

The Hanged Man Tarot card symbolizes a scape-goat or victim.

usually cannot be determined, so it is a waste of time to belabor the question, "Why did this happen to me?" The value of the concept of karma lies not in being able to trace cause and effect, but in the acceptance of responsibility for our part in whatever happens, so that we attend to the development of virtue within ourselves and avoid just feeling bad and playing the victim.

It can be tempting to resist consequences, and play the victim, but that approach only leads to more suffering. Trusting in karma, or cosmic justice, makes it easier to accept anything that happens, celebrate the passing, and move forward. Too much analysis stemming from the ego's demand to know why, or to defend itself, gets in the way of what needs to be done, to the point of being paralyzing. Your attitude—what you dwell on and how you choose to think about your life—is the primary thing to focus on.

Victim Consciousness

If you are not the coordinated partner of Destiny, you will be the victim of your Fate. This is the ultimate choice we all have to make. Victim consciousness is a form of negative thinking based on a subconscious belief in one's personal powerlessness. Victims tend to react as if they have no control over their circumstances or even their emotional reactions, as if life is something that just happens to them, rather than something they are co-creating. Victimness is a downward spiral, in contrast to the empowerment that results from taking responsibility for what you have created in your life, which is in part determined by how you respond to what happens around you.

Often, victim consciousness is coupled with resentment when things don't go as desired or planned. Such indignation is a form of self-righteousness. While feeling angry may seem justified to the personal ego, indulging in emotional reaction reinforces the victim syndrome. Resistance to reality is futile. As we say in counseling circles, "What you resist is what you are stuck with."

Fortune-tellers routinely appeal to victim consciousness because taking advantage of people is how they make the most money. When a client is open and vulnerable, he or she is easy to scare and manipulate. Some

charlatans are even able to convince relatively normal people that their money is cursed, that it is the root of their problems, and that it must be "spiritually cleansed." Of course, the money never reappears and the victim is left with even more reasons to feel sorry for herself.

If it seems incredible that people can fall for such a con, think back to times of crisis in your life. Did you ever behave in an erratic or desperate manner, or seek advice from a friend or co-worker who was not particularly qualified to give good advice on the subject? Feelings of insecurity encourage unscrupulous readers (or manipulative friends, for that matter) to suggest ideas that may be contrary to your greater good and your true destiny. Not only is the advice poor, the worst cases of a counselor manipulating someone's victim feelings and self-pity end up making that person feel even more powerless.

> Without confidence in your own intuition and creativity, life is more of a guessing game.

Feelings of personal powerlessness take many forms and have many possible origins. They can stem from childhood experiences of neglect or denial. They can be further reinforced by poor decision-making skills, inexperience, or stubborn pride. The manipulators can be institutional, such as the government or a religious group, or personal, such as a spouse or child. Some form of emotional, sexual or physical abuse may be involved.

There are countless ways we learn to give away our personal power. It can be squandered on addictions. It can be sold or traded in exchange for something. The good news is that personal power can also be rediscovered, nurtured, and expanded. First it is necessary to get past victim consciousness and into alignment with your destiny. The choice is yours—to be at the mercy of what happens to you or to participate in creating your experience of life.

The question of how people become victims of violent crimes has been the subject of extensive research. One such study, conducted by Betty Grayson and Morris Stein in 1984, indicated that posture and gaze, stride, fluidity, and other subtle, even unconscious indicators can attract predatory individuals. The researchers concluded that people can minimize their risk of assault by simply moving their body with confidence.

> "Every circumstance—no matter how painful—is a gauntlet thrown down by the universe, challenging us to become who we are capable of being."
> —Marianne Williamson, in *The Gift of Change: Spiritual Guidance for a Radically New Life.*

Spiritual teacher and author Carolyn Myss describes the Victim as a universal archetype. In a recent article called "The Victim Archetype," she put it this way:

> The purpose of the Victim is to lead us in and out of these situations until we have had enough and stand up for ourselves. We are not meant to be victimized in life; rather, we are meant to learn how to handle the challenges of our lives and to outrun our fears so that we can truly understand the meaning of strength.

You can transcend victim consciousness by taking responsibility, exercising your personal power, and making good decisions at the turning points in your life. You have the strength and you have the tools. It's up to you.

If the choices you make at the crossroads of your life are primary in helping your highest destiny to unfold, it is in your best interests to discover when and how to make better choices. The skillful use of divination can help you avoid feeling like a victim by providing a cosmic perspective on any situation or relationship. It can help you see new possibilities for manifesting what your heart desires. Divination can also help you identify the opportunities in those dilemmas that, like waves, are tossed your way. A problem arises and dealing with it results in greater awareness. Although it may have seemed like a sorry fate, it was all to the good. To the extent that they wake us up, our struggles make us stronger. They are blessings in disguise.

In general, an authentic divination practice will help you respond to situations and people more skillfully. It will help you make better choices with regard to important questions and issues that life presents to you, which is the best you can do.

Until you face your bigger challenges and discover the opportunities within them, it's a waste of time to fret over unimportant matters. It would be unwise to invest your psychic energy in deciding what color to paint the apartment you're moving into, when the more essential question is whether or not it's a good idea to move there in the first place. Divination reflects the most profound questions that are on your mind, sometimes even if they're not the ones you're asking.

Creative power resides within each of us, and when we tap that inner resource we are on the path to fulfilling our destiny. It is your choice to live in a world where you actively participate and achieve what you want, or one in which your fate is out of your hands and you are powerless to make your dreams come true. Divination can help you realign yourself at critical moments, make quality decisions and move forward in a coordinated way, like the steps of a dance, toward the fulfillment of your Heart's Desires.

Even if you make poor decisions and often seem to be in the wrong place at the wrong time, it's never a fatal setback. It only postpones your date with destiny. You will get what your heart desires more quickly if you are in step with life's rhythms and make good decisions on how best to follow your Destiny. In the overall scheme of things, it may take lifetimes to get there, but you might be closer than you think ... and you will get there. Keep the faith. The author of *Autobiography of a Yogi,* Parmahansa Yogananda, is reported as saying that once we get to the point where we consciously desire the freedom of enlightenment, we are almost there. Such good news!

Timing is Everything

A crucial part of making better decisions is making them at the right time. Good timing is the result of an enlightened attitude, an open mind, a sense of balance, and the faith that you are being guided.

Of course, our existence is not limited to our desires and choices, but includes our external reality, which usually operates outside of our control, is ever-changing and increasingly complex. Imagine being asked to dance to music you don't know. It is up to you to get in sync, use your instincts to anticipate the changing rhythms, let your body flow along with your partner, stay positive and have fun. In other words, improvise! Don't be your own worst critic—that will affect your rhythm, coordination, and your ability to learn new moves with confidence. Take some chances, stumble a bit. Go easy on yourself; even your missteps serve a purpose.

It is paradoxical, but true, that Change is the only constant in this world—the one thing we can count on.

> In many Asian cultures, auspicious timing is considered critical to success. The form of Chinese Astrology known as the Four Pillars of Destiny is based on the year, month, day and time of birth and advises the best times for all of life's major milestones.

You must be the change you wish to see in the world.

—Gandhi

Keeping up with it in a balanced way is not easy when we are bombarded with terrible news and inaccurate or distracting information. But no matter how accelerated the rate of change is becoming, life's patterns are still cyclical. When we have confidence in our ability to stay balanced no matter what, to ignore the static, and surf the larger cyclical waves of change, we are able to follow Destiny's lead. Then change starts to feel like a friend—and quite an interesting friend at that—one that supports our creativity.

Everybody wants to be happy and successful, and the quality of the choices and decisions we make determines, more than anything, how well we do. In these times of accelerating change, there is no doubt that we face challenging or urgent issues more often than ever before. To make matters worse, when crises or emotional reactions overtake us, our reasoning abilities become impaired, if not totally blocked. We need all the help we can get in order to make the right choices at the right time. Even a short divination ritual can provide guidance by reducing ego interference and removing us from our problem or situation long enough to hear the voice of inner wisdom.

Once you adopt an attitude that translates fear into excitement, you can get what you want more quickly with less effort, and with less stress. When life is a struggle, and times seem hard, remember that it's all part of a cycle, and that good times will return. Stay nimble and coordinated in the flow of the dance—that is the challenge. It behooves us to learn how to manage the impact of change on our lives, to consider change as a friend, and to inform our reality with our Heart's Desires.

Luckily for us, divination is available to help us read the mind of God, as it were, to decipher divine will, practice good timing, get in touch with our deepest desires, and function more effectively within a constantly changing world. As long as you make choices that are in sync with your Heart's Desires and your Destiny, you can feel secure in the knowledge that you are doing the best you can and that you will be provided for. Divination, practiced with sincere intention, will help you manifest your highest destiny with confidence.

Nevertheless, the development of such faith requires a bit of courage and cooperation on your part.

The Art of Co-Creation

No matter how much guidance is available to you, achieving your destiny requires your active participation. Co-creation is a term used to describe working in conjunction with your Higher Power to manifest what you want in life, what your heart desires. Depending on your perspective, this Higher Power could be referred to as God, Spirit, Gaia or Destiny—whatever term or concept you are comfortable with.

> *Following our bliss is something no one can teach us. It is co-creation in action. And it happens when we begin listening to our inner voice and following our spiritual urges.*
>
> —Jacquelyn Small

Co-creation is distinct from prayer, at least the way that most people understand prayer. Commonly prayer is used to beseech God to do something for us, to actualize our dreams for us. We make a sincere request of God, like a charming child. Unfortunately this approach to Creative Power doesn't generally work very well. The Universe requires a bit more from us than childish begging, and so do other people.

First identify your true desires, and then visualize their manifestation—while inviting Higher Power to do its part, working through you and around you. Work with what you've been given, which could be an opportunity or person you've never looked at with an open mind before. Be prepared to accept the opportunities that arise, even if they don't appear the way you expected or thought they should. They rarely do!

Never deny your own role and responsibility when you are involved in co-creating a vision. Giving away your power to influence a situation is always a psychically bankrupt strategy that leads to greater powerlessness. The co-creation process consists of a joint effort between you and Higher Power. Through this kind of active prayer, the direct experience of creative power strengthens your faith in yourself, while making you more aware of how connected you really are with the divine.

When it comes to engaging directly with the source of all wisdom—which is what divination helps us do—perseverance is critical. As any successful visionary will tell you, if you are manifesting a creative destiny, one of your mantras must be 'I will never give up!'. Do not

The Magician:

"The Magus serves as a catalyst and change agent. Be playful, and stay open. Don't limit yourself—the possibilities are endless when your mind is open."

The Queen of Coins:

"When the Queen of Coins is in this position, you have a natural and instinctive ability to manifest good things. You know how to achieve the goals you set for yourself and to satisfy your longing."

The Queen of Swords:

"Make your own decisions. Exercise as much independence as you know you can handle. The Queen of Swords knows what she wants, and she knows how to get it."

forget that, in the final analysis, how well you manage your life, how well you learn to dance with Destiny, is ultimately up to you. Creative Power will help, but only if you align with it and help yourself.

Take the case of Alex, for example. He was employed as a cabinet-maker, earning a good wage, but he was worn out and bored by the work. His true passion was music. Alex was quite a gifted guitarist, but had yet to find a way to make a living at it, despite having assembled a well-received performance group the previous year. On the whole, his life seemed good—he was in a loving relationship of three years; he had ample opportunities to play music to appreciative audiences; and in a climate of high unemployment rates, he had a job. Nevertheless, Alex couldn't shake the nagging feeling that he wanted a change—but what?

Alex thought about his different options, started to put in fewer hours at work, and opened himself to the possibilities. A few months later, he received a call from Sarah, an old friend he used to perform with. She and her current ensemble were booked for a three-month tour of Europe—all expenses paid, plus a healthy salary. But Sarah's guitarist had to cancel at the last minute, and they needed a replacement in a week. Could Alex drop everything and go?

While this may sound like a dream-come-true, imagine having to put your entire life on hold with a week's notice. Feeling insecure in the face of a major decision, Alex wondered if he was good enough, and questioned his own musical abilities. It took him two tortured days to come to his decision, with the help of Tarot readings he gave himself. A Tarot.com reading (the box on the left shows the cards he got) was particularly helpful.

After this reading, it was clear to Alex that he had to seize the opportunity, in spite of his fears. Up to this point in his life, Alex had no regrets, but he knew if he turned down this trip, he would be sorry. He decided to go, wrapped up the loose ends of his life at home, and departed on a great adventure. It turned out to be the first of many—and it was a miracle for Sarah too.

Alex may not have had regrets, but many of us aren't so lucky. But what good is holding on to feelings

of regret? Lingering regret is a form of encrusted guilt, combined with a lack of faith that everything is happening for a perfectly good reason, even if we don't immediately understand or like the way it is unfolding right now. If you were able to take absolutely everything into consideration—including your own complex psychological conditioning—you would know that you have always done the best you could. It does not help to judge yourself, condemn yourself, or care less for yourself for being imperfect. At this stage in your soul's journey, of course you are less than perfect! To indulge in regret is to be negatively stuck in the past.

Stay in tune with your Heart's Desires in the present, because whether you maintain awareness of them or not, they are what propel you forward and drive your behaviors. When you learn to identify your deepest desires, you will develop confidence that they will be fulfilled—through intuitive readiness, good timing, and skillful decision-making. In Alex's case, he knew that his heart's desire was to make a living at what he loved—music. When the opportunity presented itself, he used divination to align himself with his vision, conquer his fears, take a risk, accept a big change, and embrace his destiny.

The skillful use of divination can help you leave behind confusion and fear and move toward greater clarity and creative freedom. Even a short divination ritual can help you more calmly accept conditions you cannot change, and make better decisions regarding the relationships and situations you *can* influence. You can co-create your life into a flow of experience that is balanced by wisdom, confidence and love. And you will begin to know the joy of creatively manifesting your dreams.

Once you are in touch with your deepest desires, you can attain them by making the right choices. To do so without forcing things is to be in the flow. By managing change with good timing, you will create the level of happiness and success that is your birthright. Authentic divination systems, now so readily available, are "spiritual power tools" that will help you create a fulfilling life. A sincere divination practice will help you create meaning in your life, and align your personal good with the greater good.

> Today is a new day; you'll get out of it just what you put into it. If you have made mistakes, even serious mistakes, you can make a new start whenever you choose. For the thing we call failure is not the falling but the staying down.
>
> —Mary Pickford

Chapter 9: Destiny, Fate and Creativity

> *You may not know it, but at the far end of despair, there is a white clearing where one is almost happy.*
>
> —Jean Anouilh

Choose the system of divination that appeals to you. That will be the one that works best. Use it, and be prepared to enter a world in which you have access to more insight and guidance than you ever imagined. Be prepared for some confusion at times—after all you are still human—but do not give up.

One lesson is to go for help when you need it to make better decisions. A divination practice is like a counselor who is available at any time, day or night, to get in tune with your energy. A live, in-person session may be preferable, but you no longer need to depend on the availability of another person for insights and advice. When you do it for yourself—either by learning traditional methods or using a divination web site—the experience is free or costs next to nothing. And *your* intuition is the one that gets developed in the process!

With a working knowledge of the right tools, you can become your own counselor and "go direct" for divine wisdom any time you want to. Learning how to use divination as a form of insight meditation—one that calms you as it calls up wise answers from within you—will empower you. You will discover that your intuition is an amazing channel for most of the wisdom you will ever need.

With a sincere intention to stay in touch with the inner voice of intuition, you will notice a heightened experience and deeper levels of confidence in your ability to make the right moves at the right time. With clear awareness, wisdom when you need it, acceptance of change, an active participation in co-creation, and the patience to achieve your Heart's Desires, you will see your dreams start manifesting right before your eyes.

Fulfillment of your unique destiny is what you were born for, and called upon to co-create. This is the most important challenge of life as a human being. May the sacred power tools of divination, which were given to our wise ancestors, and passed down to us, prove to be helpful and rewarding for you in this quest.

Appendices

APPENDIX A
Archetypes of Divination

A philosopher will not believe what he sees because he is too busy speculating about what he does not see.
—Le Bovier de Fontenelle

Archetypes are the universal forms of human existence that are present in all of us to some degree at some point in our lives. They are expressed in our actions, reactions, and desires. However, no single naming convention for the archetypes exists, and they have been described in any number of different terms. Therefore this summary of the archetypes of the five classical divination techniques is not meant to be an authority on archetype naming, but merely a descriptive comparison of the energies represented in each of the five classical oracles.

NUMEROLOGY

1- Leader, Magician

2- Peacemaker, High Priestess

3- Explorer, Creative

4- Worker, Emperor

5- Student, Adventurer

6- Lovers, Peacemaker

7- Truth Seeker, Eccentric Visionary

8- Wealth, Leadership

9- Philanthropist, Humanitarian

11- Intuitive, Inspiring

22- Master Builder

I-Ching Hexagrams

1. Creative Power
2. The Receptive
3. Difficulty at the Beginning
4. Youthful Folly
5. Patience
6. Conflict
7. Organized Discipline
8. Holding Together
9. Small Influences
10. Treading Carefully
11. Harmony
12. Standstill
13. Fellowship
14. Affluence
15. Humility
16. Enthusiasm
17. Following
18. Repairing the Damage
19. Approach of Spring
20. Overview
21. Cutting Through
22. Grace and Beauty
23. Disintegration
24. Returning
25. Innocence
26. Containment of Potential
27. Nourishment
28. Excessive Pressure
29. Dangerous Depths
30. Clinging like Fire
31. Mutual Attraction
32. Endurance

33. Retreat
34. Great Vigor
35. Easy Progress
36. Darkening of the Light
37. Community
38. Diverging Interests
39. Temporary Obstacles
40. Deliverance
41. Decrease
42. Increase
43. Determination
44. Liaison
45. Gathering Together
46. Pushing Upward
47. Oppression
48. The Well
49. Revolution
50. The Cauldron
51. Shock
52. Keeping Still
53. A Steady Pace
54. Careful Affection
55. Great Abundance
56. The Wanderer
57. Gentle Penetration
58. Joy
59. Dispersing
60. Limits and Connections
61. Centering in Truth
62. Attention to Detail
63. After Completion
64. Nearing Completion

TAROT

Major Arcana (the trump cards)

0. Fool - Folly	10. Wheel of Fortune - Change
1. Magician - Will	11. Justice - Assessment
2. High Priestess - Mystery	12. Hanged Man - Sacrifice
3. Empress - Nurturance	13. Death - Transformation
4. Emperor - Rule	14. Temperance - Combination
5. Hierophant - Belief	15. Devil - Materialism
6. Lovers - Choice	16. Tower - Destruction
7. Chariot - Triumph	17. Star - Hope
8. Strength - Courage	18. Moon - Illusion
9. Hermit - Wisdom	19. Sun - Joy
	20. Judgment - Liberation
	21. World - Wholeness

Minor Arcana (the 4 suits)

Ace of Cups - Feelings	9 of Cups - Satisfaction
2 of Cups - Attraction	10 of Cups - Happiness
3 of Cups - Friendship	Page of Cups - Dreamy
4 of Cups - Lethargy	Knight of Cups - Seductive
5 of Cups - Loss	Queen of Cups - Sentimental
6 of Cups - Memories	King of Cups - Moody
7 of Cups - Desires	
8 of Cups - Discontent	

Ace of Wands - Ideas

2 of Wands - Self-determination

3 of Wands - Enterprise

4 of Wands - Harvest

5 of Wands - Striving

6 of Wands - Leadership

7 of Wands - Boldness

8 of Wands - Progress

9 of Wands - Vigilance

10 of Wands - Burdens

Page of Wands - Inspired

Knight of Wands - Adventurous

Queen of Wands - Passionate

King of Wands - Proud

Ace of Swords - Intellect

2 of Swords - Indecision

3 of Swords - Sorrow

4 of Swords - Recuperation

5 of Swords - Division

6 of Swords - Objectivity

7 of Swords - Strategy

8 of Swords - Constraint

9 of Swords - Depression

10 of Swords - Endings

Page of Swords - Agile

Knight of Swords - Aggressive

Queen of Swords - Frank

King of Swords - Analytic

Ace of Coins - Value

2 of Coins - Fluctuation

3 of Coins - Cooperation

4 of Coins - Consolidation

5 of Coins - Hardship

6 of Coins - Compensation

7 of Coins - Appraisal

8 of Coins - Proficient

9 of Coins - Prosperity

10 of Coins - Tradition

Page of Coins - Studious

Knight of Coins - Persistent

Queen of Coins - Contented

King of Coins - Affluent

ASTROLOGY (SUN SIGNS)

Aries—The Pioneer

Taurus—The Builder

Gemini—The Communicator

Cancer—The Nurturer

Leo—The Leader

Virgo—The Server

Libra—The Diplomat

Scorpio—The Controller

Sagittarius—The Philosopher

Capricorn—The Practical Idealist

Aquarius—The Individualist

Pisces—The Mystic

RUNES

Fehu (Wealth)

Uruz (Vitality)

Thurisa (Protection)

Ansuz (Communication)

Raido (New Beginnings)

Kenaz (Creativity)

Gebo (Balance)

Wunjo (Perfection)

Hagalaz (Changing Forces)

Nauthiz (Need)

Isa (Challenge, Stagnation)

Jera (Cyclical Change)

Eihwaz (Other Planes)

Pertho (Transformation)

Algiz (Protection)

Sowilo (Inner Growth)

Tiwaz (Justice)

Berkana (Fertility)

Ehwaz (Partnership)

Mannaz (Cooperation)

Laguz (Emotion)

Inguz (Initiation)

Othila (The Earth)

Dagaz (Paradox)

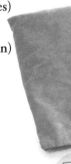

APPENDIX B
How to Give Yourself a Reading

Education sows not seeds in you, but makes your seeds grow.

–Kahlil Gibran

We strive to know ourselves better. Those of us with a strong independent streak would like to find this information on our own, without the help of a therapist, reader, guide, or practitioner. Although they can be computed by hand, it makes the most sense these days to generate Astrology charts using Astrology software. Well-designed divination software or an authentic web site provide the easiest way to do the other forms of divination also, but it is not that difficult for an individual to perform a Tarot, I Ching or Runes reading manually.

Numerology; Key to Your Inner Self by Hans Decoz.

This appendix includes a brief description of the classical divinatory rituals in order to help readers decide which form might work best for them. This information is a springboard to further inquiry, as none of the meanings for the divinatory outcomes are provided here. (However, recommended resources are included.)

Learning to read Numerology and Astrology charts is a long-term project—for many, a life's work. Most practitioners of these arts use computer programs or print resources to generate charts or reports. Unlike Runes, Tarot, and the I Ching—manual divination rituals involving the creation of new synchronicities—these two divinatory forms derive information from your personal history such as your date and time of birth, given name, and birth location. As mentioned previously, finding a good personal reader can be difficult. I recommend using the Numerology and Astrology sections of Tarot.com (www.tarot.com/numerology and www.tarot.com/astrology, respectively) for an objective, easy to use, and affordable way to generate charts, reports and their interpretations. Many Tarot.com members use Tarot.com readings as a starting point for a discussion with their

It is advisable to keep a journal or record of your readings and experiences with oracles.

personal reader, or in conjunction with other sources of information.

Books can also be a valuable resource when it comes to creating your own numerological or astrological charts. Often simple calculations (Numerology) or generalized sun sign and moon sign interpretations (Astrology) can be found in this manner. In the Numerology area, one of the best available resources is by world-renowned numerologer Hans Decoz—*Numerology; Key to Your Inner Self.* It is an easy-to-read guide to understanding the philosophical basis of Numerology, its history, how to calculate your key numbers (easy enough for a math-phobic to use), numeric meanings, and chart interpretations. Some of Hans' best Numerology reports are found on Tarot.com, and he distributes his Numerology software from www.decoz.com.

When it comes to the intricacies of experiential divination rituals—like Tarot, I Ching, and Runes—it's important to remember that your attitude and state of mind heading into the ritual will affect the outcome of divination, as well as your ability to interpret the meaning it offers. I recommend creating a centering ritual of some kind (see chapter 7) to prepare yourself and open your mind to the potential of an interactive divination experience. Also, it is advisable to keep a journal or record of your readings and experiences with oracles. Very few of us have encyclopedic memories, yet it is very helpful to have a resource for re-examining a body of readings over time. New insights can emerge after we have had some distance from the dilemma or situation.

TAROT

For most do-it-yourself Tarot readers, the process begins with getting a deck of Tarot cards and a book of meanings. (Some people insist that you cannot buy your own cards—that they must be given to you—but I do not believe that.) How people go about Tarot divination is varied, however. There are many different ways to do a Tarot reading—so many in fact that volumes have been written on the subject. (Note: Do-it-yourself readings on Tarot.com require neither cards nor a book—just an Internet connection!)

Generally, seekers will first identify a situation or question to frame the reading. Next they shuffle the Tarot deck while focusing on that subject. Frequently the cards are then fanned out, face down, before the seeker begins to

There are no right or wrong positions or spreads in Tarot.

pick cards (though in some cases, cards are dealt into a spread from the top of the deck). Each position in a spread has a unique meaning. The positions in a three-card spread might be Past, Present, and Future. A six-card spread might include six of the positions from a standard eleven-card Celtic Cross spread: Situation, Challenges/Opportunities, Advice, Daily Lesson, and Near Future. There are literally thousands of spreads that people have invented, and you can invent your own too (just make sure you don't change what the position in a spread was supposed to mean after you pick your cards!). There are no right or wrong positions or spreads in Tarot, which makes it an ideal instrument for tightly focused readings.

Some readers interpret a reversed meaning for cards that appear upside down in the spread. For instance, The Lovers card facing upright might mean attraction, making a choice and commitment. The reversal could be interpreted as meaning unstable relationships, infidelity, and conflict. Whether or not to interpret cards as reversals is a personal choice that will come with practice and use of the Tarot. Mary K. Greer's *The Complete Book of Tarot Reversals* is an indispensable guide to seeing reversals as more than the dark side of Tarot, and includes the upright as well as reversed meanings for the cards.

Another common variation that new Tarot users will encounter is the order, naming, and structure of the cards in Tarot decks. Over the last 35 years, as Tarot has become more popular, artists and creators of new decks

The *I Ching*—which translates as Book of Changes—is all about change, and its entire structure reflects this orientation. The Chinese philosophy of the opposing forces of yin and yang, and the recognition of change as a cycle, are the foundation of the I Ching. Each of the four types of lines that create the hexagram is either young or old, and yin or yang—and they may be in a state of "changing" as well. When a force becomes 'old,' it turns into its opposite and begins the cycle again, becoming young. Likewise, the young become old and the cycle repeats infinitely.

have taken certain liberties with the naming and positions of cards. For example, the "King of Swords" is also known as the "Father of Wands," "Master of Swords," "Man of Law," and "Father Wind," depending on the deck. "The World" (also known as "The Universe") is often numbered 21, although in the Esoterico deck it's numbered 22. While these variations may seem confusing to the novice, familiarity with the cards and their meanings will increase with experience and practice.

When interpreting the meanings of the cards, it is best to take a moment and reflect on the imagery, connecting themes, and contrasts in your spread before reading a book's interpretations. Often colors, thematic elements, concentrations in a certain suit, or sequences of numbers can be stimulating to your intuition. Look at the way the cards relate to one another in addition to their individual meanings. Trust your intuition to help you in the process of deciphering the meaning in the cards. A particularly powerful way to gain skills in Tarot interpretation is to use a program like the *Tarot Magic* CD-ROM, which has a feature that allows you to record readings, card by card, that you turn up for yourself from a physical deck. Not only can you print out the spread in color, but it will also give you the position-specific interpretations of Christine Payne-Towler, one of the world's foremost authorities on Tarot. Using this feature at Tarot.com, you can compare your interpretation with that of a Tarot expert.

I CHING

The ancient method for I Ching casting involves a relatively laborious process of sorting fifty yarrow stalks. A more modern method uses a series of coin tosses using three identical coins (I Ching coin tossers prefer Chinese bronze coins with the square hole in the middle). For the sake of historical accuracy, both techniques will be presented here, as well as our modern software-based method. In each case, the process is done six times, with each outcome producing one line of the hexagram. Like a building, the hexagram is assembled from the ground up.

If you wish to use the yarrow stalk method, you can

harvest your own stalks, purchase them at a craft store, or substitute bamboo stalks, barbeque skewers (with sharp points removed), or thin wooden dowels. In any case they should be of uniform size (approximately one-eighth inch diameter), clean, and roughly ten inches long. Be prepared to spend an hour on the yarrow stalk method of I Ching casting.

1. Center yourself. Focus on the question at hand. Place the *I Ching* book in front of you. Remove the bundle of stalks from their container. Put one back—it will not be used. You are left with 49 stalks in your hands.

2. Divide the bundle into two similar-sized bundles (do this randomly, no counting) and put each on one side of the book.

3. From the bundle on the right, remove one stalk and place it above the book.

4. Pick up the bunch on the left and divide it into bundles of four stalks. The bundle that is left over will have 1, 2, 3, or 4 stalks—place them with the single stalk above the *I Ching*.

5. Repeat step four with the bunch on the right. After adding the final bundle to the pile above the I Ching, there should be either 5 or 9 stalks.

6. Collect the bundles on the right and left of the *I Ching* into one bundle. Repeat step 2 (divide roughly in half and put the bundles back on either side of the book).

7. Repeat step 3.

8. Repeat steps 4 and 5. Now there should be 9, 13, or 17 stalks above the book.

9. Collect the bundles on the right and left of the *I Ching* into one bundle. Repeat step 2 (divide roughly in half and put the bundles back on either side of the book).

10. Repeat step 3.

11. Repeat steps 4 and 5. Now there should be a total of 13, 17, 21, or 25 stalks in the top pile.

NUMBER OF STALKS	COIN COMBOS	NUMBER	LINE
36	3 Heads	9	—○—
32	2 Heads, 1 Tail	8	—✕—
28	1 Head, 2 Tails	7	————
24	3 Tails	6	—— ——

12. Collect the bundles on the right and left of the *I Ching* into one bundle in your hands. (With 36 stalks in hand, there should be 13 stalks left above the book; with 32 stalks in hand there should be 17 stalks left above the book; with 28 stalks in hand there should be 21 stalks left above the book; with 25 stalks in hand there should be 24 stalks left above the book. If you didn't end up with one of these combinations, you made a mistake and must begin again.)

13. Count the stalks in hand; divide by four (36/4=9; 32/4=8; 28/4=7; 24/4=6). This number corresponds to the bottom line of the hexagram (see chart below). Repeat all 13 steps five more times, adding a line on top of the previous ones each time to get your hexagram.

The coin toss method is much faster and more commonly used than the yarrow stalk ritual. However, the statistical probabilities do vary between the two styles, and certain "future hexagrams" are more likely to appear with the coin method than with yarrow stalks. (The programming behind the I Ching section of Tarot.com is based on the probabilities of using yarrow stalks.) Three identical coins are used to cast your hexagram. If you are using Chinese coins where there are no obvious heads or tails (at least not obvious to you!), simply choose for yourself which is which before beginning, and stick with your decision.

As with all other oracles, remember to stay focused on your question when casting. Hold all three coins loosely in your hands, shake them briefly, and then toss them. The line is determined by assigning numerical values to heads and tails, then adding the total. Each heads is a 3, and each tails is a 2. (See chart.) So, if you cast one heads and two tails (3+2+2), your starting line

COIN TOSS RESULTS	LINE	NUMBER	NAME
36	—○—	9	Old Yang
32	— —	8	Young Yin
28	———	7	Young Yang
24	—✕—	6	Old Yin

would be a 7. Collect the coins and toss again (a total of six times), recording the numerical values and the corresponding line each time, building your six-line hexagram from the bottom up.

The hexagram you create from the yarrow stalk method or with coins is considered the "present hexagram." Changing lines, marked with an 'x' or an 'o,' into their opposite, is how you produce the "future hexagram," which derives in that way from the present. Any broken lines marked with an 'x' (Old Yin) become the opposite—a solid line (Young Yang)—and solid lines marked with an 'o' (Old Yang) become opposing broken lines (Young Yin). If there are no changing lines in your hexagram, it represents both your present and future outlook—in other words, things are not in flux that much at this time.

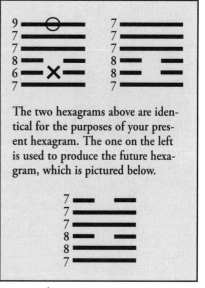

The two hexagrams above are identical for the purposes of your present hexagram. The one on the left is used to produce the future hexagram, which is pictured below.

Once you have identified your present and future hexagrams, use the Hexagram Identification Chart in your *I Ching* book to locate the hexagram numbers, and their corresponding statements. These typically include a translation of the original text, changing line descriptions, and an explanation of the imagery and symbolism. Like any other ancient text, *I Ching* books on the market today offer an assortment of translations to choose from. Some translators have modernized the text, removing gender bias and archaic language. Others have elaborated on the explanations, and only roughly paraphrase the original text. There is a range of quality in translations. Although the Wilhelm/Baynes version by Princeton Press, with its forward by Carl Jung, is certainly the most popular, it is tainted by the politics of the 19th century and tends to be stilted in a slightly Germanic way (it was translated into English from German, which was the original language of translation from the ancient Chinese). It has faithfully preserved the militarism and sexism of patriarchal China going back to the time of Confucius and before. Another version that is also faithful to the original Chinese, but far easier to digest, is *The Complete I-Ching* by Alfred Huang, a modern I Ching scholar from Shanghai.

By far the easiest way to cast the I Ching is to use our www.I-Ching.com web site. As mentioned earlier, it utilizes the math of the yarrow stalk method, and it is programmed so that you actually do determine the lines that you get in your hexagram by the way that you use your mouse. The interpretation, which I wrote in 1988, is a faithful but modernized rendition of the Wilhelm/Baynes version. I took great pains to meditate on every hexagram sufficiently in order to eliminate sexism (we have no "superior man" here) and militarism (there is no "army marching to the southwest") and, in general, to make the text more Taoist than Confucian, and more poetic throughout. This I Ching is not available in book version at this time, but only on I-Ching.com. Aside from the usefulness of the text, a great feature of using a computer to cast a hexagram is the fact that there is no "busy work" to interrupt your meditative focus on your question. Once you have entered the subject of your reading (if you want to), the computer takes care of figuring out and recording what kind of line you got. The quality of such a computer-assisted ritual has to be experienced to be appreciated!

'Wyrd' is the Nordic mythological word for the cosmic web of destiny woven by the three goddesses of fate—the Norns. Wyrd was essentially another word for destiny, and the Norse believed that all human actions in the past, present, and future contributed to each person's individual 'wyrd'—a kind of universal karma. The Norns Spread in Rune divination represents Urd, or Wyrd, the goddess of "that-which-has-become" (the past), Verdandi, the goddess of "that-which-is-becoming" (the present), and Skuld, the goddess of "that-which-should-become" (the future).

RUNES

Like the Tarot, there are many different ways to cast the Runes. There is little historical evidence of how casting was done in the days when the Runes were created, so there is quite a bit of flexibility when it comes to the spreads and techniques for casting Runes. Below are three different suggestions for casting.

The most basic of spreads is the drawing of a single Rune. Just focus on a question or situation you want more information about. Gently mix the Runes in their bag or container until you feel it is time to draw. This single Rune is a representation of your present situation. If drawn early in the day, it can be used as a meditation on the day ahead. If drawn at the end of the day, it can be a new lens through which to view your actions, reactions, and interactions of the day.

Perhaps the most common layout for reading Runes is the Norns Spread, which consists of three Runes—the first for past, the second for present, and the third for

the future, or the likely outcome if one stays on the current path. To use this spread, draw one Rune at a time, laying them in a row.

A more complex spread uses nine Runes (nine was a sacred number in Norse mythology). One method is to pick nine Runes stones; focus on the question, then toss them onto the table or cloth. First read any that are face up—they relate to the present and how past actions have influenced the present. Turn the rest of the Runes face up. Stones toward the center are more specific influences while the ones on the perimeter are more general forces in your life. Runes that are touching can be considered especially important, or part of the same concept.

A slightly more complicated nine Rune cast is based on the Norse 'map' of the Nine Worlds of Creation on the Web of Wyrd. Like the other methods of casting, meditate on your question and draw one Rune at a time. Place them in the positions of the picture below.

Interpreting the Runes in this spread becomes more complicated, but the rules for the other nine Rune cast apply—those at the center have the most influence, while the outer circle has less of an impact.

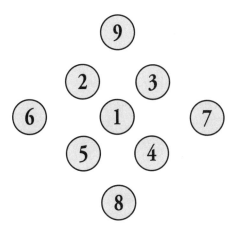

APPENDIX C
Divination in the Bible

It ain't those parts of the Bible that I can't understand that bother me, it is the parts that I do understand.

—Mark Twain

To save the reader considerable effort, I have provided below many of the New King James Version Bible passages relevant to divination. I have not included passages referring to dream interpretation, channeling, or prophecy, and have only included the references to divination that are most closely tied to the topics of this book.

VERSES CONDEMNING DIVINATION

Exodus 22:18 You shall not permit a sorceress to live.

Leviticus 19:26 You shall not eat *anything* with the blood, nor shall you practice divination or soothsaying.

Leviticus 19:31 Give no regard to mediums and familiar spirits; do not seek after them, to be defiled by them: I *am* the LORD your God.

Leviticus 20:27 A man or a woman who is a medium, or who has familiar spirits, shall surely be put to death; they shall stone them with stones. Their blood *shall be* upon them.

Deuteronomy 18:10-11 [10]There shall not be found among you anyone who makes his son or his daughter pass through the fire, or one who practices witchcraft, or a soothsayer, or one who interprets omens, or a sorcerer, [11]or one who conjures spells, or a medium, or a spiritist, or one who calls up the dead.

Deuteronomy 18:14 For these nations which you will dispossess listened to soothsayers and diviners; but as for you, the LORD your God has not appointed such for you.

Joshua 13:22 The children of Israel also killed with the sword Balaam the son of Beor, the soothsayer, among those who were killed by them.

1 Samuel 6:2 And the Philistines called for the priests and the diviners, saying, "What shall we do with the ark of the LORD? Tell us how we should send it to its place."

1 Samuel 28:8 So Saul disguised himself and put on other clothes, and he went, and two men with him; and they came to the woman by night. And he said, "Please conduct a seance for me, and bring up for me the one I shall name to you."

2 Kings 21:6 Also he made his son pass through the fire, practiced soothsaying, used witchcraft, and consulted spiritists and mediums. He did much evil in the sight of the LORD, to provoke *Him* to anger.

2 Chronicles 33:6 Also he caused his sons to pass through the fire in the Valley of the Son of Hinnom; he practiced soothsaying, used witchcraft and sorcery, and consulted mediums and spiritists. He did much evil in the sight of the LORD, to provoke Him to anger.

Isaiah 2:6 For You have forsaken Your people, the house of Jacob, Because they are filled with eastern ways; They *are* soothsayers like the Philistines, And they are pleased with the children of foreigners.

Isaiah 8:19 And when they say to you, "Seek those who are mediums and wizards, who whisper and mutter," should not a people seek their God? *Should they seek* the dead on behalf of the living?

Ezekiel 21:21 For the king of Babylon stands at the parting of the road, at the fork of the two roads, to use divination: he shakes the arrows, he consults the images, he looks at the liver.

> A thorough knowledge of the Bible is worth more than a college education.
>
> —Theodore Roosevelt

Micah 3:6 Therefore you shall have night without vision, And you shall have darkness without divination; The sun shall go down on the prophets, And the day shall be dark for them.

Micah 3:7 So the seers shall be ashamed, And the diviners abashed; Indeed they shall all cover their lips; For *there is* no answer from God.

Micah 3:11 Her heads judge for a bribe, Her priests teach for pay, And her prophets divine for money. Yet they lean on the LORD, and say, "Is not the LORD among us? No harm can come upon us."

Acts 19:13 Then some of the itinerant Jewish exorcists took it upon themselves to call the name of the LORD Jesus over those who had evil spirits, saying, "We exorcise you by the Jesus whom Paul preaches."

Acts 8:9 But there was a certain man called Simon, who previously practiced sorcery in the city and astonished the people of Samaria, claiming that he was someone great.

Acts 13:6 Now when they had gone through the island to Paphos, they found a certain sorcerer, a false prophet, a Jew whose name *was* Bar-Jesus.

Acts 13:8 But Elymas the sorcerer (for so his name is translated) withstood them, seeking to turn the proconsul away from the faith.

Acts 19:9 Also, many of those who had practiced magic brought their books together and burned *them* in the sight of all. And they counted up the value of them, and *it* totaled fifty thousand *pieces* of silver.

VERSES SUPPORTING DIVINATION

Genesis 44:4-5 [4]When they had gone out of the city, *and* were not *yet* far off, Joseph said to his steward, "Get up, follow the men; and when you overtake them, say to them, 'Why have you repaid evil for good? [5]Is not this *the one* from which my lord drinks, and with which he indeed practices divination? You have done evil in so doing.'"

Exodus 28:30 And you shall put in the breastplate of judgment the Urim and the Thummim, and they shall be over Aaron's heart when he goes in before the LORD. So Aaron shall bear the judgment of the children of Israel over his heart before the LORD continually.

Leviticus 16:8-10 ⁸Then Aaron shall cast lots for the two goats: one lot for the Lord and the other lot for the scapegoat. ⁹And Aaron shall bring the goat on which the LORD's lot fell, and offer it *as* a sin offering. ¹⁰But the goat on which the lot fell to be the scapegoat shall be presented alive before the LORD, to make atonement upon it, *and* to let it go as the scapegoat into the wilderness.

Numbers 26:55 But the land shall be divided by lot; they shall inherit according to the names of the tribes of their fathers.

Numbers 26:56 According to the lot their inheritance shall be divided between the larger and the smaller.

Numbers 27:21 He shall stand before Eleazar the priest, who shall inquire before the LORD for him by the judgment of the Urim. At his word they shall go out, and at his word they shall come in, he and all the children of Israel with him--all the congregation.

Deuteronomy 33:8 And of Levi he said: "Let Your Thummim and Your Urim *be* with Your holy one, Whom You tested at Massah, And with whom You contended at the waters of Meribah."

Joshua 7:13 Get up, sanctify the people, and say, 'Sanctify yourselves for tomorrow, because thus says the LORD God of Israel: "*There is* an accursed thing in your midst, O Israel; you cannot stand before your enemies until you take away the accursed thing from among you." '

Joshua 7:16-19 ¹⁶So Joshua rose early in the morning and brought Israel by their tribes, and the tribe of Judah was taken. ¹⁷He brought the clan of Judah, and he took the family of the Zarhites; and he brought the

family of the Zarhites man by man, and Zabdi was taken. [18]Then he brought his household man by man, and Achan the son of Carmi, the son of Zabdi, the son of Zerah, of the tribe of Judah, was taken. [19]Now Joshua said to Achan, "My son, I beg you, give glory to the Lord God of Israel, and make confession to Him, and tell me now what you have done; do not hide *it* from me."

Joshua 14:2 Their inheritance *was* by lot, as the LORD had commanded by the hand of Moses, for the nine tribes and the half-tribe.

Joshua 18:6 You shall therefore survey the land in seven parts and bring *the survey* here to me, that I may cast lots for you here before the LORD our God.

Joshua 18:8 Then the men arose to go away; and Joshua charged those who went to survey the land, saying, "Go, walk through the land, survey it, and come back to me, that I may cast lots for you here before the LORD in Shiloh."

Joshua 18:10 Then Joshua cast lots for them in Shiloh before the LORD, and there Joshua divided the land to the children of Israel according to their divisions.

Judges 6:36-40 [36]So Gideon said to God, "If You will save Israel by my hand as You have said—[37]look, I shall put a fleece of wool on the threshing floor; if there is dew on the fleece only, and *it is* dry on all the ground, then I shall know that You will save Israel by my hand, as You have said." [38]And it was so. When he rose early the next morning and squeezed the fleece together, he wrung the dew out of the fleece, a bowlful of water. [39]Then Gideon said to God, "Do not be angry with me, but let me speak just once more: Let me test, I pray, just once more with the fleece; let it now be dry only on the fleece, but on all the ground let there be dew." [40]And God did so that night. It was dry on the fleece only, but there was dew on all the ground.

1 Samuel 10:20 And when Samuel had caused all the tribes of Israel to come near, the tribe of Benjamin was chosen.

1 Samuel 10:21 When he had caused the tribe of Benjamin to come near by their families, the family of Matri was chosen. And Saul the son of Kish was chosen. But when they sought him, he could not be found.

1 Samuel 14:8-10 8Then Jonathan said, "Very well, let us cross over to *these* men, and we will show ourselves to them. 9If they say thus to us, 'Wait until we come to you,' then we will stand still in our place and not go up to them. 10But if they say thus, 'Come up to us,' then we will go up. For the Lord has delivered them into our hand, and this *will be* a sign to us."

1 Samuel 14: 42 And Saul said, "Cast *lots* between my son Jonathan and me." So Jonathan was taken.

1 Chronicles 24:31 These also cast lots just as their brothers the sons of Aaron did, in the presence of King David, Zadok, Ahimelech, and the heads of the fathers' *houses* of the priests and Levites. The chief fathers *did* just as their younger brethren.

1 Chronicles 25:8 And they cast lots for their duty, the small as well as the great, the teacher with the student.

1 Chronicles 26:13-14 13And they cast lots for each gate, the small as well as the great, according to their father's house. 14The lot for the East *Gate* fell to Shelemiah. Then they cast lots *for* his son Zechariah, a wise counselor, and his lot came out for the North Gate.

Nehemiah 10:34 We cast lots among the priests, the Levites, and the people, for *bringing* the wood offering into the house of our God, according to our fathers' houses, at the appointed times year by year, to burn on the altar of the LORD our God as *it is* written in the Law.

Nehemiah 11:1 Now the leaders of the people dwelt at Jerusalem; the rest of the people cast lots to bring one out of ten to dwell in Jerusalem, the holy city, and nine-tenths *were to dwell* in *other* cities.

Psalms 22:18 They divide My garments among them, And for My clothing they cast lots.

Proverbs 16:33 The lot is cast into the lap, But its every decision *is* from the LORD

Proverbs 18:18 Casting lots causes contentions to cease, And keeps the mighty apart.

Obadiah 1:11 In the day that you stood on the other side—In the day that strangers carried captive his forces, When foreigners entered his gates And cast lots for Jerusalem—Even you *were* as one of them.

Jonah 1:7 And they said to one another, "Come, let us cast lots, that we may know for whose cause this trouble *has come* upon us." So they cast lots, and the lot fell on Jonah.

Matthew 27:35 Then they crucified Him, and divided His garments, casting lots, that it might be fulfilled which was spoken by the prophet: "They divided My garments among them, And for My clothing they cast lots."

Mark 15:24 And when they crucified Him, they divided His garments, casting lots for them to determine what every man should take.

Luke 23:34 Then Jesus said, "Father, forgive them, for they do not know what they do." And they divided His garments and cast lots.

John 19:24 They said therefore among themselves, "Let us not tear it, but cast lots for it, whose it shall be," that the Scripture might be fulfilled which says: "They divided My garments among them, And for My clothing they cast lots." Therefore the soldiers did these things.

Acts 1:26 And they cast their lots, and the lot fell on Matthias. And he was numbered with the eleven apostles.

APPENDIX D
Tarot: The Shrink-in-the-Box

The following article was copied with permission from the "Hot Trends to Watch" column in the *Trends Journal**, a financial investor newsletter*.

 large public, strapped for cash, starved for psycho-spiritual advice and disillusioned with conventional professional guidance, is turning to the Tarot deck. Despite its fringe-and-flake image, the resurgence of the Tarot is not a fad, but part of a widespread new-millennium trend.

Once available only in several traditional designs and found only in specialty mail-order catalogs and little back-alley occult emporiums, Tarot has exploded into dozens of varieties and is now found prominently displayed at the checkout counters of the major bookstore chains. Tarot web sites and chat rooms proliferate on the Internet.

The Tarot deck, an early victim of rational science, has been derided for several centuries by a skeptical public as pure superstition; the province of Gypsy fortune-tellers and sidewalk psychics. But as the millennium approaches, increasing numbers of devotees are rediscovering the deck for themselves.

In this capacity, Tarot has been invested with a legitimacy found among influential and respected leaders in the arts and letters. William Butler Yeats, the great poet and playwright of the Irish literary renaissance, knew the Tarot well and incorporated its symbolism into his critically acclaimed poem "The Tower." The English poet T.S. Eliot, the Italian novelist Italo Calvino and the most influential German artist of the last Renaissance, Albrecht Durer, have all created works based on Tarot imagery.

Tarot's popularity today goes beyond the tabloids; its audience is primarily the extensive New Age book-buying public and a broad stream of Generation Xers. They look to it, not as a fortune-telling tool, but rather

The West (thus) developed a new disease: the conflict between science and religion. The critical philosophy of science became as it were negatively metaphysical—in other words, materialistic—on the basis of an error of judgement(sic); matter was assumed to be a tangible and recognizable reality. Yet this is a thoroughly metaphysical concept hypostasised by uncritical minds. Matter is an hypothesis. When you say "matter" you are creating a symbol for something unknown, which may just as well be a spirit or anything else; it may even be God.

—Carl Jung

Some say that the Tarot images were derived from the symbolic reliefs of ancient Egypt.

The Chariot card from the *Palladini* Tarot deck

© U.S. Games Systems, Inc.

as a form of do-it-yourself therapy; a way of unlocking secrets of the self and providing directions toward specific life goals.

HELP!

Institutionalized sources once relied upon for guidance and counseling have lost their appeal or become less accessible or too expensive. People looking for help have been obliged to find ways to help themselves. Among the reasons for Tarot's resurgence:

* The loss of faith in traditional religion has left a spiritual vacuum among large numbers of a disenfranchised congregation.
* The decline of the nuclear family, the increase of single family households and an absence of other traditional/community social units has removed the emotional support system that could once be relied upon (for better or for worse).
* Renewed interest in ancient wisdom and the New Age conviction that a sophisticated spiritual science existed in deep antiquity in which Tarot played a role.

Tarot, seen by practitioners as a form of spiritual solitaire, will become increasingly popular as people integrate its ideas and activities into their daily lives.

Note: Beyond the mystical attraction that Tarot has always exercised, it has in recent years acquired some support from a core of leading-edge astronomers, mathematicians and physicists. They claim that the most recent advances in cosmology find direct parallels to the illustrations of the Marseilles Tarot, the oldest deck known, which some say is derived from the symbolic reliefs of ancient Egypt. (See Paul LaViolette, *Beyond the Big Bang: Ancient Cosmology and the Science of Continuous Creation*, Inner Traditions International, 1995.)

*The *Trends Journal* is a quarterly publication of the Trends Research Institute of Rhinebeck, NY. For information on the institute's work and the journal, click on www.TrendsResearch.com or call 1-800-258-7363.

APPENDIX E

The Use of I-Ching, Tarot and Other Divination Tools for Everyday Life

By Deepak Chopra, M.D.

The world consists of physical, quantum and virtual realms of existence. The physical realm includes the material world and our physical bodies. The quantum realm includes the forces and subatomic particles that underlie the material world, as well as our thoughts, feelings, emotions and beliefs. The virtual realm contains personal, archetypal (mythical), and universal domains. Our soul is in the personal domain, which uses the seeds of memory and desire in shaping how we perceive and interpret our current reality.

> *Synchronicity is God sending us messages anonymously.*
>
> —Deepak Chopra

Our personal soul is the manifestation of archetypal themes. It is through our attention and intention that we determine which theme, which story, which interpretation to manifest. Moment by moment the virtual realm actualizes through our thoughts. Every thought is either a memory or desire. Unconsciously, we weave stories around our memories and desires and act out these stories in what we experience as our everyday life. The same phenomenon is at work in our dreams, only during dreams we are not engaging with the outer world.

Oracles, such as Tarot and I-Ching, allow us to become consciously aware of what is going on in the virtual realm. Depending on our own spiritual awareness, we may access the personal, collective or universal domain. An oracle is not a substitute for spiritual evolution or spiritual disciplines. It is however, an excellent tool, particularly when we are practicing a meditation discipline. With meditation we find the appropriate interpretation that will enable us to be conscious of how our soul is acting out its stories, recognizing that every interpretation is unique.

Spiritual disciplines and oracles reinforce each other. If we meditate we are better able to prophesize, and we have greater access to the virtual realm. Through spiritual

219

Appendix E: Deepak Chopra article

> *Where no one asks, no one needs to answer.*
> —Carl Jung

disciplines we can go beyond the personal to the archetypal and ultimately get in touch with God.

The virtual realm is beyond space, time, and causality. Depending upon the depth we reach, we can know it as the immeasurable potential of all that was, is and will be. All time lines, all event lines coexist as possibilities. There is no linear time. This is the domain of awareness that is available in meditation and that can be also accessed through the oracles.

Oracles like the I-Ching and Tarot Cards help us access our intuitive response. Intuition is a form of intelligence that is contextual, relational, holistic, nurturing. It doesn't have a win/lose orientation. It goes beyond linear cause/effect relationships. It is your mind eavesdropping on the mind of the cosmos. The essence of the intuitive response is revealed in the New Testament in the words of Christ when he says, "Seek and you shall find. Ask and you shall receive. Knock and it shall be opened unto you." The great Sufi poet Rumi says, "The whole universe exists inside you. Ask all from yourself." The self that you ask from is not your ego self but your soul, which is part universal consciousness. I-Ching and Tarot cards are tools that allow you to access this deeper domain of universal consciousness. You and I may get the same reading, but will have different interpretations because the interpretations are a result of the meanings, contexts, relationships and archetypal themes of our individual lives. In other words, they are derived from our karmic software.

Whenever you approach an oracle, sit for a few moments with your eyes closed and allow your awareness to settle. Bring your attention into your heart and ask Spirit to provide you the guidance you are seeking. Cultivate an attitude of curiosity, innocence and openness, and you will be able to interpret the information that emerges in a way that is most evolutionary for you. The more open you are to hearing the clues provided through the oracle, the more likely they will guide you toward greater meaning, creativity and fulfillment in your life.

For further information on Deepak Chopra, MD and The Chopra Center for Well Being, please visit www.chopra.com. To keep up with Deepak, visit www.choprablog.com.

220

APPENDIX F
Tarot and I-Ching for Relationships
By John Gray

ncient divination systems like Tarot cards and the Chinese I-Ching are becoming more and more popular, at the same time that their psychological usefulness is being recognized. For thousands of years these classical systems have been used to help humanity make better decisions around questions and issues that logic alone cannot handle—like most relationship issues. Now modern psychology is explaining how and why they work.

The father of depth psychology, Carl Jung, studied classical oracles for over 30 years. He used the term "archetypes" to describe internal energy sources available to every human being from the "collective unconscious." Each one of the 78 cards of a Tarot deck, each one of the 64 hexagrams of the I-Ching, is such an archetype. In this sense, Tarot cards can be looked at as symbolic flash cards for one's inner life, because each of the 78 archetypes represented are within each and every human being.

According to my friend, Paul O'Brien—the founder of Tarot.com and I-Ching.com—most of the queries that people bring to these "intuitive decision-making" tools are about relationships and love.

This makes sense, because relationship questions often do not lend themselves to strictly logical analysis. A well-informed intuition is an important relationship skill. Counselors and coaches rely on this. Tarot and the I-Ching are tools we all can use.

> Because relationship questions often do not lend themselves to strictly logical analysis, I Ching and Tarot which are "intuitive decision-making" tools can aid in receiving answers.

Unfortunately, we are usually taught to push logic beyond its limits when confronted with personal issues. Too often that push takes us down some path of rigid expectations of how things "should be."

The alternative is to take time to reflect, and to gain perspective. But how do we step outside the "rational" realm to activate intuition and gain perspective? Meditation is good. I have used classical divination

221

> Relationships are like Rome. Difficult to start out, incredible during the prosperity of the 'Golden Age,' and unbearable during the fall. Then, a new kingdom will come along and the whole process will repeat itself until you come across a kingdom like Egypt, that thrives, and continues to flourish. This kingdom will become your best friend, your soulmate, and your love.
>
> —Helen Adams Keller

tools, including the Tarot and the I-Ching, which are forms of meditation when understood rightly, for over twenty years to do just that.

TAROT AS A CREATIVE RELATIONSHIP TOOL

I don't rely on Tarot cards to tell me what to do, but I have found that they help one think outside the box, to view situations and relationships with more creativity and wisdom.

The simple act of using Tarot cards (whether physically or via the tarot.com website) can be liberating. The very act of turning to such a tool to stimulate insights and activate intuition gives you a bit of distance from whatever might be on your mind. The exercise also gives rise to curiosity and anticipation—you are about to engage the power of your intuition! For many people, to do so consciously is a somewhat new and satisfying experience. As Jung said, "Intuition does not denote something contrary to reason, but something outside the province of reason."

How Tarot Works

The spread, or layout of the cards, represents a situation or relationship in the present moment. (True Tarot or I-Ching is NOT fortune-telling!) A Tarot reader, or someone using Tarot.com to give themselves a reading, will interpret the cards based on the classical meaning of each card and the particular slant derived from its position in the spread.

Once the cards are in place, we are able to see the archetypes which came up for us in context, which stimulates our natural intuitive abilities to look more deeply into the situation. We can identify discrete forces and understand better how we are reacting to them. Tarot provides a way to look at relationships and situations in a global, more objective way—in the NOW—not as chaotic forces that may someday make sense. With the Tarot, one can use symbolism to paint any number of "possible pictures" thinking outside the box of normal, more self-limiting modes of thinking.

Use Authentic Tarot, Like Tarot.com

There are two keys to getting the most out of the Tarot, 1) timely access to the deep wisdom, and 2) enlightened interpretations of each card and its positional meaning.

The Tarot.com website provides convenient access to a deep and helpful experience. The fact that one can pick one's own cards and access profound interpretations without needing the help of a "psychic friend" is empowering. I recommend Tarot.com to anyone who wants to bring new creativity and wisdom to their relationships and their daily life.

The Lovers card from the *Palladini* Tarot deck
© U.S. Games Systems, Inc.

John Gray writes about relationships and personal growth and is best known as the author of several books offering relationship advice. The most prominent of these is the 1992 book, *Men Are from Mars, Women Are from Venus.*

Bibliography

Bibliography

Preface

Devi, Indra. 2005. *Renew Your Life Through Yoga*. Vila, Mont.: Kessinger Publishing.

Khema, Ayya. 2001. *Being Nobody, Going Nowhere: Meditations on the Buddhist Path*. Somerville, Mass.: Wisdom Publications.

Ray, Paul H. and Sherry Ruth Anderson. 2000. *The Cultural Creatives: How 50 Million People Are Changing the World*. New York: Harmony Books.

Watts, Alan. 1968. *The Wisdom of Insecurity*. New York: Vintage Books.

Introduction

Heenan, Jan Ferris. "Divination = Divine Sales," *Publishers Weekly*. Issue 21. 21 May 2001. 19 April 2005 http://www.publishersweekly.com/article/CA83275.html.

Hunter, James Davison. 1991. *The Culture Wars: The Struggle to Define America*. New York: Basic Books.

Zimmerman, Rachel. "Chronically ill turning more to spiritual healing." *Houston Chronicle* (Apr 10, 2005): section A, page 18.

Chapter 1

Bolles, Richard Nelson. 1981. *What Color is Your Parachute?* Berkeley, Calif.: Ten Speed Press.

Choquette, Sonia. 1997. *Your Heart's Desire: Instructions for Creating the Life You Really Want*. New York: Three Rivers.

Hesse, Hermann. 1982. *Siddhartha*. Translated by Hilda Rosner. Reprint, New York: Bantam Classics.

Hillman, James. 1996. *The Soul's Code: In Search of Character and Calling*. New York: Random House.

Keyes, Ken. 1984. *Handbook to Higher Consciousness*. Coos Bay, Ore.: Love Line Books.

Rand, Ayn. 1964. *Virtue of Selfishness: A New Concept of Egoism*. New York: Signet Books.

Wapnick, Kenneth. 1998 *Forgiveness and Jesus: The Meeting Place of "A Course in Miracles" and Christianity*. 6th Roscoe, New York: Foundation for "A Course in Miracles."

Chapter 2

Currot, Phyllis. 2004. *Witch Crafting: A Spiritual Guide to Making Magic*. New York: Broadway Books.

Dalai Lama. 2004. *Practicing Wisdom*. Translated by Geshe Thupten Jinpa. Somerville, Mass.: Wisdom Publications.

Ehrman, Bart D. 2005. *Lost Christianities: The Battles for Scripture and the Faiths We Never Knew*. New York: Oxford University Press.

Smoley, Richard. "The Religion of No Religion." *Gnosis* (Spring 1995).

Talib, Gurbachan Singh. 1995. *Sri Guru Granth Sahib*. Columbia, Misso: South Asia Books.

Toffler, Alvin. 1970. *Future Shock*. New York: Random House.

Chapter 3

Chopra, Deepak. 2003. *The Spontaneous Fulfilment of Desire: Harnessing the Infinite Power of Coincidence*. Easton, Pa: Harmony.

James, Michael S. "Tarot Novice?" *ABC News*. 15 May 2004 http://www.abcnews.go.com/sections/us/DailyNews/shootings_tarot021009.html.

Jung, Carl Gustav. 1964. *Man and His Symbols*. London, England: Aldus Books.

Jung, C. G. 1970. "The Archetypes and the Collective Unconscious." *The Collected Works of C. G. Jung*. Vol. 18. Edited and translated by G. Adler and R.F.C. Hull. Princeton, N.J.: Princeton University Press.

Jung, C. G. 1970. *Psychological Reflections*. Princeton, N.J.: Princeton University Press.

Jung, C. G. 1973. "Synchronicity: An Acausal Connecting Principle." *The Collected Works of C. G. Jung*. Vol. 8. Edited and translated by R.F.C. Hull. Princeton, N.J.: Princeton University Press.

Jung, C. G. 1976. *The Portable Jung*. Edited by Joseph Campbell. Translated by R.F.C. Hull. New York: Penguin.

Lundstrom, Meg. "A Wink from the Cosmos." *Intuition Magazine*. (May 1996)

McFarlane, Thomas. 2002. *Einstein and Buddha: The Parallel Sayings*. Berkeley, Calif.: Ulysses Press.

McFarlane, Thomas. 2000. "Quantum Physics, Depth Psychology, and Beyond." 13 June 2003 http://www.integralscience.org/psyche-physis.html.

Bibliography

More, L.T. 1962. *Isaac Newton: A Biography*. 1934 Reprint, New York: Dover Publications Inc.

North, Carolyn. 1994. *Synchronicity: The Anatomy of Coincidence*. Berkeley, Calif.: Regent Press.

Osborne, Stephen. "The Coincidence Problem." Geist (Winter 2002).

Rosengarten, Arthur. 2001. *Tarot and Psychology: Spectrums of Possibility*. New York: Paragon House Publishers.

Schoenholtz, Larry. 1975. *New Directions in the I Ching: The Yellow River Legacy*. Seacaucus, N.J.: University Books.

Smoley, Richard. "The Stars We Are." *Gnosis* (Winter 1996).

Van der Post, Laurens. 1976. *Jung and the Story of Our Time*. New York: Vintage Books.

Wilhelm, Richard. Translated by Cary F. Baynes. 1967. *The I ching; or, Book of Changes*. 3rd Ed. Bollingen Series 19. 1950 Reprint. Princeton N.J.: Princeton University Press.

Chapter 4

Bluestone, Sarvananda. 2001. *How to Read Signs and Omens in Everyday Life*. New York: Destiny Books.

Blum, Ralph. 1993. *The Book of Runes: A Handbook for the Use of an Ancient Oracle*. 10th Ed. New York, NY: St. Martin's Press.

Confucius. 1998. *The Analects*. Translated by D. C. Lau. London: Penguin Books.

Crowley, Aleister. 1969. *Book of Thoth*. York Beach: Weiser Books.

Hand, Robert. 2002. *Planets in Transits: Life Cycles for Living*. 2nd expanded edition, Atglen, Pa.: Schiffer Books.

Matthews, John, ed. 1992. *The World Atlas of Divination: The Systems, Where They Originate, How They Work*. Boston, Mass.: Bullfinch Press.

O'Brien, Paul. 1997. *Oracle of Changes*. CD-ROM. Portland, Ore.: Visionary Networks.

O'Neill, Robert. 1994. *Tarot Symbolism*. Berkshire, England: Fairway Press.

Ptolemy, Claudius. 2002. *Tetrabiblos*. Translated by J. M. Ashmand. Bel Air, Maryland: Astrology Classics.

Riseman, Tom. 1995. *Understanding the I Ching: The History and Use of the World's Most Ancient System of Divination*. Reprint, Wellingborough, England:

Thorsons Publishers.

Tacitus, Cornelius. 1999. *Germania*. Clarendon Ancient History Series. Translated by James Rives. London, England: Oxford University Press.

Tzu, Lao. 1988. *Tao Te Ching: The Book of Meaning and Life*. Translated by Richard Wilhelm & D.C. Lau. New York: Penguin.

Chapter 5

The American Heritage Dictionary of the English Language. 2000. 4th ed. Boston, Mass.: Houghton Mifflin.

Kramer, Heinrich and James Sprenger. 2003. *Malleus Maleficarum*. Whitefish, Mont.: Kessinger Publishing.

Nightingale, Juliet. "Psychic Hotlines: An Insider's Story." 4 August 2004 http://www.towardthelight.org/psychichotlines.html.

Smoley, Richard. "The Stars We Are." *Gnosis*. (Winter 1996).

"Tarot: The Shrink-in-the-Box." *Trends Journal* (1998). See Appendix D for text.

Chapter 6

Kim, Margaret. *Banned From the Bible*. History Channel, 10 November 2005. Television Boradcast.

Pike, Albert. 1942. *Morals and Dogma*. 1871 Reprint, Richmond, Virg.: L.H. Jenkins, Inc.

Shlain, Leonard. 1999. *The Alphabet Versus the Goddess: The Conflict Between Word and Image*. New York: Penguin.

Chapter 7

Decoz, Hans. 1993. *Numerology: The Key to Your Inner Self*. New York: Perigee Books.

Gray, John. "Relationships and Divination." 1 September 2004 http://www.tarot.com/about-us/articles/gray.

O'Brien, Paul. 1989. *Synchronicity*. CD-ROM. Version 1.0. Visionary Software.

Payne-Towler, Christine. 1999. *The Underground Stream: Esoteric Tarot Revealed*. Eugene, Ore: Noreah Press.

Chapter 8

Alcorn, Al. 1972. Atari. *Pong*. Version 1.0.

Bibliography

Cinematronics. 1978. *Space War*. Version 1.0.

Douglas, Mark and Marcia Moore. 1971. *Astrology the Divine Science*. York Harbor, Me.: Arcane Publications .

Madden, Mary. 2006. "Internet Penetration and Impact." Pew Internet & American Life Project. 24 July 2006 http://www.pewinternet.org/PPF/r/182/report_display.asp.

Negroponte, Nicholas. 1995. *Being Digital*. New York: Alfred A. Knopf.

Rainie, Lee, Stewart Hoover and Lynn Schofield Clark. 2004. "Faith Online: 64% of wired Americans have used the Internet for spiritual or religious purposes." Pew Internet & American Life Project. 24 June 2004 http://www.pewinternet.org/report_display.asp?r=126.

Chapter 9

The American Heritage Dictionary of the English Language. 2000. 4th ed. Boston, Mass.: Houghton Mifflin.

Forrest, Steven. "Fate and Freedom: A Middle Path." *The Mountain Astrologer*. (Feb. 1997)

Myss, Carolyn, Ph.D. "The Victim Archetype." Beliefnet.com. 28 May 2003 http://www.beliefnet.com/story/84/story_8452_1.html.

Ullal, Chakrapani. "Karma, Free Will, and Jyotisha." (Pts. 1-4) *Hinduism Today*, March-June, 1996. 22 May 2003 http://www.hinduismtoday.com/archives/1996/3/1996-3-09.shtml

Williamson, Marianne. 2004. *The Gift of Change: Spiritual Guidance for a Radically New Life*. San Francisco, Calif.: Harper.

Yogananda, Paramhansa. 2003. *Autobiography of a Yogi*. 1946 Reprint ed., Nevada City, Calif.: Crystal Clarity Publishers.

Appendices

Greer, Mary K. (2002. *The Complete Book of Tarot Reversals*. Woodbury, Minn.: Llewellyn Worldwide.

Huang, Alfred. 1998. *Complete I Ching: The Definitive Translation*. Rochester, Verm.: Inner Traditions.

LaViolette, Paul. 1995. *Beyond the Big Bang: Ancient Myth and the Science of Continuous Creation*. Rochester, Verm.: Park Street Press.

After fifteen years in the field of software marketing, Paul O'Brien took a leap from an executive position in high-tech and founded Visionary Networks to create and publish the world's first divination software. He called his interactive version of the I Ching "Synchronicity," and as the first to publish such a program he became known as the "father of modern divination."

With the help of fellow Taoist Charles Jennings, Paul composed an accurate, modernized version of the I Ching for the *Synchronicity* program in 1988. By 1995 the company had developed the *Tarot Magic* and *Oracle of Changes* CD-ROMs and websites. Tarot.com has since spread to the worldwide web, providing millions of people with authentic do-it-yourself Tarot, I Ching, Astrology, Numerology and Feng Shui.

Paul is an ordained minister, a Buddhist meditation teacher and a spiritual counselor. His training includes two years of residency in monasteries and spiritual communities around the world. He sees authentic divination as a spiritual ritual that is perfectly suited to the Aquarian Age. Eliminating the need for priests or any kind of religioius middlemen, the ability to use a divination system by and for oneself gives every individual direct and equal access to profound wisdom that can help guide choices and actions and stimulate creativity.

For twenty-two years, Paul has been the host of "Pathways," an interview program on KBOO FM radio in Portland, Oregon, which focuses on personal and cultural transformation (broadcast via www.kboo.fm on Sundays at 8:30 am Pacific time, or 90.7 FM in Portland). Paul also speaks on a variety of subjects—including the skillful use of divination, the Law of Attraction, the process of creative manifestation, purpose-driven entrepreneurism, and intuitive decision-making. As co-founder of the Divination Foundation (divination.com), Paul continues to exercise his passion for helping people to clarify and fulfill their life purpose.

To request interviews or speaking engagements, or for more information, please visit the foundation's website at www.divination.com or send an email to info@divination.com.